CONTROVERSIAL CINEMA

The Films That Outraged America

Kendall R. Phillips

 PRAEGER

Westport, Connecticut
London

Library of Congress Cataloging-in-Publication Data

Phillips, Kendall R.
    Controversial cinema : the films that outraged America / Kendall R. Phillips.
        p. cm.
    Includes bibliographical references and index.
    ISBN: 978-0-275-99464-8 (alk. paper)
    1. Sensationalism in motion pictures. 2. Motion pictures—Censorship—United States.
I. Title.
PN1995.9.S284P45 2008
791.43′653—dc22   2007045056

British Library Cataloguing in Publication Data is available.

Library of Congress Catalog Card Number: 2007045056
ISBN: 978-0-275-99464-8

First published in 2008

Praeger Publishers, 88 Post Road West, Westport, CT 06881
An imprint of Greenwood Publishing Group, Inc.
www.praeger.com

Printed in the United States of America

∞™

The paper used in this book complies with the
Permanent Paper Standard issued by the National
Information Standards Organization (Z39.48–1984).

10 9 8 7 6 5 4 3 2 1

The author and publisher gratefully acknowledge permission to quote passages from the
following source:

Phillips, K. R. (1998). "Interpretive Controversy and *The Silence of the Lambs*." *Rhetoric Society Quarterly*, 28, 33–47. Taylor & Francis Group. www.informaworld.com.
Reprinted with permission.

This book is dedicated to a man who took a chance on me many years ago, and that has made all the difference. To Dr. Bob Derryberry—teacher, mentor, and friend.

Contents

Acknowledgments

The work on this book has taken several years and has been greatly supported by a vast number of people—many of whom I'll undoubtedly forget. Some of those who have provided vital help have been Jill Sachs and Greg Baker, student research assistants who helped dig up great piles of fascinating information; the students in CRS 483: Rhetoric of Film in Spring 2007, who endured my first tentative attempt at talking through these ideas and provided invaluable feedback and engagement; Dan Harmon, of Praeger, without whom this book would never have moved beyond the "idea" phase; my colleague Diane Grimes, who kindly read several of these chapters and provided invaluable comments; and, as always, my best editor, interlocutor, partner, and friend—my wife, Catherine Thomas.

I would also like to acknowledge the kind support of Syracuse University, especially for a sabbatical granted by the Dean of the College of Visual and Performing Arts, which provided that most precious commodity, time. As well, I am pleased to acknowledge the editors of *Rhetoric Society Quarterly*. Portions of Chapter One are derived from an essay— "Unmasking Buffalo Bill: Interpretive Controversy and *The Silence of the Lambs*"—which was originally published in that fine journal.

Introduction

When I was beginning work on this project, I ran across a promotional button with a picture of President George W. Bush's face encircled by the words: "Controversy ... What Controversy?" Across the bottom was the name of the film the button was designed to promote, Michael Moore's *Fahrenheit 9/11*. Released in June 2004, Moore's film unleashed a firestorm of controversy because of its explicit indictment of President Bush, his administration, and their handling of the post-9/11 "war on terror." In Moore's version of events, not only was Bush's presidency illegitimate—Moore insinuates that Vice President Al Gore rightfully won the 2000 election—but its central policy of fighting the war on terror was based largely on fabricated evidence that ultimately served the goal of creating profits for the military-industrial complex. Weaving together poignant personal stories, news footage, humorous staged events—like Moore encouraging members of Congress to have their children enlist—and Moore's own incisive commentary, *Fahrenheit 9/11* was a cinematic assault on the Bush administration, designed with the explicit purpose of influencing the upcoming November election.

In a technical sense, Moore's documentary is a polemic, an argument designed to divide and exacerbate differences in the service of creating an even more intense opposition. But in all fairness, Moore's film is not the first film to cause controversy because of its overt political intentions. The 1976 Alan Pakula film *All the President's Men*, for example, which recounted the Woodward and Bernstein investigation into Watergate, was perceived by many as directly influencing the election in which Governor Jimmy Carter defeated President Gerald Ford.[1] Nor was the reaction to Moore's 2004 cinematic polemic without precedent. As early as 1922, Dr. Ellis Paxon Oberholtzer, a former censor for Pennsylvania, warned, "If the press is a large factor in politics the screen may be a yet greater one. The pen is mightier than the sword," he reasoned, "but here is the moving picture which has become a good deal mightier, one must conclude, than the pen."[2] Moore took the political potential of film to its natural end by attempting to make a film that, by his own admission, was designed to influence the 2004 presidential election.[3]

Fahrenheit 9/11 was not, of course, Moore's first effort at polemic. The documentary filmmaker has consistently courted controversy since his very first film, *Roger & Me*. Released in 1989, *Roger & Me* focused on the economic and social consequences of corporate downsizing through a deeply personal case study of Moore's hometown of Flint, Michigan, which was devastated by layoffs at General Motors. That film was also the target of much criticism, including accusations that Moore's film distorted facts, staged events for effect, and failed to account for opposing viewpoints.[4] His Academy Award–winning 2002 documentary *Bowling for Columbine* was a more diffused critique of America's violent gun culture, but Moore still provoked intense controversy when, during his Oscar acceptance speech, he declared that America was being led by a "fictitious president" into a "war for fictitious reasons." Reactions to the speech were widely divided, and with that, Moore had set the stage for the 2004 documentary that would become the most financially successful documentary in history, earning more than $100 million at the domestic box office.[5]

Ultimately, however, Moore's efforts backfired. As much as his *Fahrenheit 9/11* provided a provocative and in many ways insightful critique of the war in Iraq, the controversy it provoked may have done more to motivate conservative support for President Bush than to activate a mass opposition, and Bush won reelection by a narrow margin in 2004. But more directly relevant was the reaction of much of the public to Moore's effort. Dan Bartlett, the White House communications director, called it "outrageously false," and other conservative groups declared it "nothing more than a two-hour political commercial."[6] Objections arose not only from officials. A columnist in a Birmingham, Alabama, newspaper labeled Moore a "muckraking blowhard," and a letter-writer in Utah called him "a propagandist hatchet man."[7] In his insightful analysis of Moore's film and the ensuing controversy, film historian Robert Brent Toplin observed:

> Millions of viewers greatly appreciated the film and recommended it to others, but a steady stream of negative comments about *Fahrenheit 9/11* made an impact. Many newspaper readers, radio listeners, television viewers, and Internet users began to get the impression that Moore's production was problematic.... They sensed that the controversial motion picture had been discredited in public discussions and should not be praised with enthusiasm in sophisticated company.[8]

"Controversy ... what controversy?" If there was one overarching misstep in Moore's plan to produce a provocative and influential documentary aimed at unseating a president, it was his belief that he could control a controversy, even directing it at the targets of his choosing. However, that is not the nature of controversy; it is not what controversies *are* in their essence. While there are numerous instances when a controversy seems manufactured for the sake of creating a smokescreen to divert attention from something else—a notion brilliantly captured in Barry Levinson's *Wag the Dog* (1996)—once provoked, a controversy may wind its way from courtrooms to pulpits and from newspaper headlines to the halls of government. The controversy surrounding Moore's 2004 documentary extended to college campuses—where some administrators feared the legal implications of having Moore deliver a lecture—and to charges that the film violated the McCain–Feingold bill's restrictions on political "issue ads." There were also numerous polemical rebuttals, ranging from the book *Michael Moore Is a Big Fat Stupid White Man* to the film *Michael Moore Hates America*.

At first glance, the intensity and impact of the controversy provoked by Moore's 2004 documentary may seem like some anomaly—driven, perhaps, by the already intense emotions surrounding the 2004 presidential campaigns. But, in many ways, *Fahrenheit 9/11* is one in a long line of films that have become the center of intense and spectacular controversies. Indeed, the history of American cinema is rife with instances in which a film was deemed so shocking, provocative, and dangerous that some felt compelled to express their disapproval in loud and at times quite dramatic ways.

There are numerous examples within recent memory: I recall attending a screening of *The Last Temptation of Christ* during its initial release in 1988. It was a few weeks after the first showings, and I was practically alone. The large throngs of picketers and pamphleteers handing out biblical literature and haranguing those entering the theater had dwindled to a few devoted protestors who called out to the handful of us entering the theater. I recall a woman calling me a sinner and a man shouting out that he would be praying for me. At the time, as a young college student, I dismissed these individuals as religious zealots, hard-core Christian fundamentalists who needed to "get a life." Looking back on it, however, I realize that in many ways my youthful bravado had missed a larger point entirely. Whatever their cause—and I'll confess to still not fully understanding the venomous objections to Martin Scorsese's adaptation of the Nikos Kazantzakis novel—these individuals had chosen to leave their homes and their regular routines to stand in front of a downtown movie theater because, to them, this film was so offensive as to represent a threat that could not go unchallenged. They had mustered whatever courage and capacity was at their disposal to meet this threat. They had chosen to dive headlong into a controversy that was deeply meaningful and vitally important to them.

This book is about the kinds of dangerous films that seem, at least to some, to threaten to leave the confines of the theater and run rampant, eroding some moral pillar of our society. In particular, it is about those films that appear to present such a danger that there are those in society who feel the need, perhaps even obligation, to voice their concerns, to sound the alarm to others. My central focus is on the controversies themselves—the arguments issued in response to a particular film, the political alliances that arose in opposition to or in defense of a particular film, the ways that various communities expressed their outrage, concern, or revulsion at a particular idea or image in a film. This focus leads me to consider not only the sorts of films that provoked these reactions and the means by which these reactions were resolved or satisfied but, most important, the reactions themselves—the ways they were presented, articulated, and transformed by the dynamic environment of a "live" and ongoing controversy. In this way, my focus is very much on the "rhetoric" of controversy, by which I mean precisely on the kinds of persuasive arguments issued during protracted disputes about particular films or trends within American cinema.

Often, negative responses to films are framed in terms of censorship, and for much of the history of film, and in some regard even today, censorship is one useful and indispensable frame for studying these disputes. When some theater chains refused to exhibit Moore's controversial *Fahrenheit 9/11*, for instance, critics charged that they were infringing on people's First Amendment rights.[9] American cinema's past is deeply marked by the forces of film censorship, to which I turn in the first chapter. But it is erroneous to characterize every negative reaction to a film—even a very vocal negative reaction, as in, for instance, boycotting or picketing—as solely or even mainly an issue of censorship. One of the main problems with thinking about film controversies in this way is that it equates all objections to film with calls for censorship, thus placing them squarely in opposition to the protections of the First Amendment. Certainly, however, the First Amendment rights that we now conceive of as extending to the free expression of ideas within a film also extends to those outside the theater who seek to voice their opposition to it.

In this way, the frame of censorship is too limiting for a broad discussion of films that have provoked vocal and critical responses from various segments of society. While some, perhaps many, of these negative responses in fact may have called for a form of film censorship—whether the traditional governmental intrusion or a looser communal or corporate restriction on a given film—framing these responses *exclusively* in terms of censorship overlooks much of the dynamism and potency of the reactions themselves. Yet, whenever we talk about films that provoked vocal opposition to their exhibition, our initial tendency is to consider the legality of censorship and the sanctity of the First Amendment. This tendency is certainly visible in film studies and histories of film, which are replete with numerous treatments of censorship, ranging from histories of the Production Code to discussions of the Catholic Legion of Decency to the legal battles over state boards of censorship or ratings codes.

Another way of thinking about provocative films is to focus on the notion of obscenity or offensiveness. Here we might seek out films that were designed with the express purpose of challenging norms of morality and decency. Some pornography fits into this category, but so too do "exploitation" films, like those featured in grindhouse cinemas, as well as any number of independent niche films whose notoriety is based mainly on their power to repel. These kinds of films are interesting and useful, but a focus solely on the movies that were meant to offend once again misses the vital point where that revulsion is stated publicly. While some level of offense is clearly at play when people choose to vocalize their opposition to a film, what is missing in this approach is any sense of that vocalization. To be offended, in other words, is a deeply subjective sentiment. I might be horribly offended by something—a film or some offhand comment—but that does not necessarily mean I will voice my feelings.[10] Focusing on the controversies surrounding films can be more objective because the evidence of a controversy will be part of the public record, and the debates, protests, and responses will become visible to others through various modes of public address.

The central conceit of this book is that there is a vital stage that falls in between the feeling of offense and the legal machinations of censorship—a stage in which those who are offended first articulate that offense to others. This stage is marked by performances of offense and opposition—letters to editors, calls for boycotts, picketing, and so forth—and is often both vociferous and poignant. It is my contention that controversial films are important: They are important in that they serve as a kind of barometer for the deeper cultural pressures surrounding issues of, for instance, sex or race or violence. Moore's *Fahrenheit 9/11*, for instance, did not create the perceived division between conservative "red states" and liberal "blue states," but the controversy surrounding it revealed something about how deeply that division was felt. Such films are important in that it is often these provocative and controversial films that push the creative and political envelope for future generations of both producers and consumers.[11]

The notion of controversy is a useful way of thinking about that vital middle stage between the first feelings of offense and the subsequent efforts at resolving these objections—which at times might involve the mechanisms of censorship. When individuals choose to voice their objections to the world around them, these objections pose the possibility of controversy, the possibility that they will enter into a prolonged dispute with others that will raise sometimes difficult questions and challenges. Once in a while, these protestations draw out others with similar concerns, and soon a community or communities of people begin raising concerns. But interestingly, while controversies seem remarkably pervasive in our society—over topics ranging from military actions to off-the-cuff remarks by politicians to football rankings to the style choices of celebrities—we rarely talk about what controversies *are*, how they operate, and what they mean to our broader society.

This general neglect for the concept of controversy, in spite of the prevalence of the term in contemporary parlance, may be one of the reasons that, when we seek to understand controversial films, we are prone to jump immediately from offense to censorship while only skimming the middle phase of the controversies themselves.[12] Given the historical consistency and potency of controversial films, however, they cannot be dismissed as merely peculiarly provocative, isolated instances, nor as being only indicative of general cultural trends. Rather, attention to the history of contentious films should reveal the complex interplay between cultural politics, aesthetic tastes, the forces of film production (especially Hollywood), and the unique artistic vision constructed in a given film.

In a similar vein, film historian Francis Couvares argues, "Works that evoke a strong response from a variety of audiences, that trigger contentious interactions among producers, reformers, politicians, protestors, and boycotters cannot be taken for granted, as either isolated objects of formal analysis, or as generic products of a system, or mere reflections of popular impulses." Appreciating the complexity of these controversial films and their concomitant debates requires exploring both the films that provoke controversy and the voices that articulate it. This, in turn, calls for an important pause in that cultural moment between offense and regulation, a pause in the moment of controversy itself.

What I hope to do across the chapters of this volume is to linger in that middle phase, to explore the controversies surrounding certain types of films. I have chosen to approach this exploration by considering controversial films grouped into different categories that seem to offer a reasonably coherent breakdown. My concern here is not to engage every possible controversy or even, for that matter, every possible category of controversial film. *Fahrenheit 9/11*, the example I began this introduction with, is one example of a controversial film, but in the long history of film it is a fairly rare instance of a film designed with the specific purpose of *provoking* a controversy. As such, Moore's film is a useful if atypical example of a film that was designed to instigate a reaction. More common are those films that provoke controversy by stepping, at times inadvertently, too firmly upon some existing cultural fault line—and these are the films that will occupy the majority of my attention here. In this book, I attend to the four categories of films that have most consistently provoked public outcry and debate: films depicting sex, sexuality, and issues of gender; films that depict acts of violence and criminality; films that represent racial and ethnic communities; and finally, films that engage religion or religious topics.

There are, of course, numerous films and film themes that have provoked different types of objections. Movies such as Clint Eastwood's *Million Dollar Baby* raised serious debate related to the representation and rights of people living with disabilities, and Oliver Stone's *JFK* provoked public debate about the historical accuracy of its narrative. While these and many other types of controversial films are worthy of further consideration, my purpose here is to begin an exploration of film controversies, and as such, I have chosen to focus on the four categories that have provoked opposition most consistently throughout the history of American cinema. Thus, while my categories are not comprehensive of all film controversies, I feel confident in asserting that they are among the most consistently contentious.

The other problem with categorization is that inevitably there will be some films that fall across multiple categories. For example, Mel Gibson's *The Passion of the Christ* was enormously controversial, and at first glance that controversy would fall squarely into the "religious films" category—indeed, that is the chapter in which I will consider Gibson's passion play. Nevertheless, a good portion of the vocal criticism of the film was aimed at the unrelenting violence in the film. The same concern can be raised for any number of films that incorporate sex and violence, or sex and race, or other combinations. In the pages that follow, there are numerous examples of films that cross the boundaries of my neat categories, and in those instances, I have tried to both make the most reasonable categorization and acknowledge the various complicating intersections.

This seems like a good place to lay out in more detail the approach to controversial films I will use throughout this book. To be clear, my purpose here is not to offer a comprehensive, encyclopedic listing of films that have provoked controversy.[13] Beyond the difficulty in tracking down every film debate, such a treatment of controversial films might lead to a superficial collection of titles and issues. On the other hand, neither is my purpose to focus solely on a series of representative case studies. While I will spend some time on individual films, I hope to connect these films to the longer history of unrest surrounding similar films.

The four categories of controversial films outlined above are defined by major cultural fault lines—sex, violence, race, and religion—and my intent is to trace those fault lines and sketch out the ways these controversial topics have consistently provoked vocal eruptions from parts of the population. In each chapter, I combine a broad historical overview of the arguments provoked by a given topic as a way of establishing the historical context. Subsequently in each chapter, I also focus in greater detail on the specific controversy that embroiled a particular film—for example, the controversy surrounding race in Spike Lee's *Do the Right Thing*. At the heart of this approach is an attempt to understand the dynamic interactions between the film itself and the historical conditions surrounding it that drew it into the center of cultural firestorms of controversy.[14]

Before beginning this extended survey of the various controversies that have erupted around particular films, it is worth pausing briefly over a question that has been begged throughout this introduction, namely, "What is a controversy?" At first glance this might seem a pointless question—the nature of controversies seems obvious. And yet, the term has become so ubiquitous as to make the concept itself close to meaningless. Often the aura of conflict seems to be consciously designed to publicize a film. There can be little doubt that the early controversy over who would distribute *Fahrenheit 9/11*—after Miramax's parent company Disney refused to be part of its distribution—helped generate buzz about the film, and indeed some critics charged that it was a publicity stunt from the beginning.[15] Filmmakers, or more precisely film promoters, have certainly added to the extensive use of the notion of controversy, and in my research for this book, I have been led down many a dead end and false turn by the promotional claims for "the most controversial film of the year!" On these occasions, the claims to controversy and the seemingly provocative subject matter belied the reality that no one, or virtually no one, had ever raised their voice in protest against the film in question. Thus, as suggested earlier, the central feature for the notion of controversy is both that people were offended and, more importantly, that they *articulated* this offense in front of others in such a way as to create a kind of political or cultural spectacle.

What then are the broad parameters for a controversy? While I am loath to define "genuine" controversies versus "artificial" ones, I will suggest some qualities that make something a controversy, qualities that have guided my research into controversial films.[16]

First, controversies occur when people are provoked to leave their usual routines—at least the kind of people who do not make a regular practice of picketing, writing letters to editors, or pamphleteering outside theaters. While it is possible to manufacture an uproar through systematic provocation of groups of people, a genuine controversy requires that people engage it in some meaningful way. For the vast majority of us, of course, picketing a movie theater or writing letters to our local paper's editor to either condemn or defend some film is not on our regular to-do list. So, in looking for examples of controversial cinema, we must search for those instances in which individuals have actively engaged in the process of arguing about and contesting some film.

This sense of controversy as drawing people into the irregular situation of conflict and contestation raises a second issue: What is it that makes people choose to leave their regular routines and engage in public debate? Obviously, the concrete answer to this question is dependent upon the specific situation, but we can posit a general idea that controversies emerge when our basic assumptions about the world—those taken-for-granted assumptions that allow us to move through the world with a sense that things will be regular, understandable, and predictable—are violated. This may explain why there is often so much energy and anger in the early stages of a controversy. It is not just that some subject, say, child sexuality or graphic violence, is represented in a film, but that for many people there was a deeply held, if unvoiced, assumption that, in the world they live in, such a subject could not possibly be depicted in a film. In the midst of controversy, our orientation to the world is violated, and we are in a very real sense disoriented.[17]

Of course, there are genres and subgenres within film that serve a kind of fetishistic purpose with regard to the kinds of taboo subjects that may provoke controversy. Pornography is an easy example of this, as are "splatter films" within the horror genre. While there are certainly moments of controversy surrounding these graphic depictions of, respectively, sex and violence, as long as these genres remain within their cloistered and generally hidden enclaves, there is a kind of social tolerance. For my purposes, I will generally exclude these kinds of films, which may be exceptionally offensive—indeed, far more offensive than anything I'll consider in these pages—and focus instead on those films that emerged within mainstream cinema and in so doing provoked the kind of reactions that mark controversy. In other words, graphic depictions of sexual acts are not particularly controversial if they are contained within the social spaces designated for pornography; it is only when these acts are represented in mainstream theaters as part of mainstream movies that some people may find their sense of the world and of decorum radically disoriented.

Often, the disorienting moments of controversy are resolved fairly quickly, as people turn to some set of authorities to resolve the situation. In terms of film, this was particularly true during periods of extensive external and self-regulation—for instance, the period of the more stringent Production Code Administration (1934–1966) or during the height of local and state censorship boards. Prior to the 1952 *Burstyn v. Wilson* decision—discussed more fully in the first chapter—which effectively began the process of eliminating governmental film censorship, those who were offended, shocked, or discomfited by a given film—or even the mere prospect that such a film might be shown in their neighborhood—had recourse to at least petition some official agency for relief.

In contemporary America, however, there are no such singular authorities through which we can hope to block the exhibition of an offensive film in our area, and citizens are left in a position of having to seek other means to express their outrage and respond to films they perceive as objectionable. Of course, even during the period of "official" censorship through state and local boards as well as through the Production Code Administration, there were still film controversies. But it is certainly clear that with the dissolution of the official network of film censorship and control, virtually the only recourse left open to those who find a certain film objectionable and wish to block its showing is to engage in public opposition.

A final aspect of controversy that is especially important in my present exploration is that those engaged in a controversy must *perform* their objections. It is not enough to simply be offended by a film nor even to refuse to see it. To be a controversial film, there must be some individuals who choose to go beyond their inner feelings of outrage or even their own decisions about seeing or not seeing a film and instead choose to vocalize their concerns. This vocalization, of course, can take many forms: petitions to authorities, picketing, letters to editors, boycotts of commercial venues, letters to producers, and so on.

These vocalizations are central to the chapters that follow. Thus, it is not only the issues raised that are important, but in a very real sense it is the rhetoric of the controversy that is of interest. How do people raise objections? How do they respond to others' objections? What is said or written? Examining these questions should provide insight into the parameters of the controversies, and if the notion of controversy sketched above has any validity, then these articulations of objection will suggest the deeper cultural rifts that both motivated and shaped their dynamics. In seeking to understand controversial cinema, we are in effect asking a series of important questions about our cultural sense of the boundaries of normalcy, morality, and decorum. Throughout much of what follows, I attend to the interesting intersections between these vocalized objections and the films that provoked them.

As noted earlier, one of most notable historical effects of objections to particular films was the extensive system of legal censorship that existed in the United States from roughly 1907 to 1968. The apex of this era was the voluntary system employed by Hollywood studios between 1930 and 1968 as a means to mitigate censorship concerns and guide filmmakers in avoiding controversies—the Production Code Administration. Often, perhaps too often, the understanding of controversial cinema has been rendered exclusively within the broader terms of these legal structures that served to police the boundaries of the acceptable within film. My purpose here is to examine the controversies surrounding films without relying too heavily on the question of censorship.

One way I hope to tease out the distinctions and interrelationships between controversial films and film censorship is to focus some attention on controversial films that were produced before the onset of the uniform Production Code or after the end of official legal censorship in 1968. This is not to say that those films appearing within the era of the Production Code were not controversial—or that I will neglect this period—but, rather, what I hope to demonstrate is the interesting parallels and disjunctures between the very early controversies surrounding films and those of our most current era.

Another way to help differentiate between the extensive mechanisms of film censorship and the public outcries that define controversies is by laying out an initial history of formal censorship that will provide a useful backdrop for the later consideration of the controversies that intermingled with it. Thus, in chapter 1, I offer a brief history of film censorship that should serve as a general primer. Following this brief detour, I return in the next four chapters to considering in greater detail the controversies surrounding films related to sex, violence, race, and religion with the hopes of shedding light on the complex interconnections among film, cultural history, and politics.

CHAPTER 1

Censorship, Culture, and Controversy

The origin of cinema is marked with a fascinating, if likely apocryphal, anecdote. It was December 28, 1895, in Paris when the Lumière brothers famously invited Parisians to view a publicly projected series of short films. This moment of public projection can be rightly said to mark the emergence of film into an age of cinema. There had, of course, been films shown in public for decades—in apparatuses like Edison's peephole Kinetoscope—and, if we stretched the notion of film we could even contend that such inventions as Father Athanasius Kircher's magic lanterns of the seventeenth century with their use of light and animated cells constitute a very early and rudimentary sense of film. But, cinema, as the public display of such images, represents a deep and fundamental shift in the cultural understanding of film. No longer were individuals hunkered over their individual machines in arcades, cranking the handles to affect the illusion of motion. When the Lumière brothers developed the means to project these short films out onto a screen that would be immediately shared by all in the audience, the notion of cinema was born and with it a vastly more complex set of cultural and political relations that would grow to encompass the notion of film.

Some of these cultural and political implications are suggested in the mythic story that accompanies the birth of cinema. The short films were scenes from everyday life and one of them, *L'Arrivée d'un train en gare de la Ciotat*, depicted, as its name suggests, the arrival of a train at a station. By most accounts the reaction to this film bordered on a panicked riot. Audience members were filled with terror as the onrushing train threatened to run them over. Somehow the illusion of film, that magic of shadow and light that makes still images jump to life, had, at least for these initial patrons, threatened to cross over into their three-dimensional world and crush them under the force of its apparent reality.

What could it have been about the projected film that created such reported concern and confusion among its viewers? Was it the size of the images projected onto the wall of Grand Café? Was it the promise of a new projection device that opened the door for imagining that the train projected before them would manifest itself in the physical world? Or was it the unique moment of sharing this experience in the newly inaugurated cinematic setting—a setting that must have been in some ways familiar as it borrowed so heavily from the common experience of live theater but also strange in its presentation of projected images that moved with such apparent life and material reality?

In spite of the remarkable lack of evidence for this mythic story of panic at the Grand Café in 1895, it has remained a strikingly consistent element in film history. And, in a way, it is the endurance and power of the story of a panicked audience that is more interesting than the historical question of its actual occurrence because this single anecdote of the audience's fear of the onrushing train is at the kernel of another consistent element in the history of film, fear.[1] The fear of the projected image extends well beyond any moment of pure confusion and, in many ways, this fear has been one of the dynamics that has deeply marked the development of contemporary cinema. Consider, for instance, the early nickelodeon theaters of the early twentieth century, which Charles Musser suggests constituted the beginning of the modern cinema.[2] The rapid growth of these storefront moving picture theaters in major urban areas like New York, Chicago, and Pittsburgh in 1905 has been called the "Nickelodeon Boom," and this boom set off one of the earliest moral panics surrounding film exhibition. The increasing availability of films at the cost of a mere nickel attracted Americans from a variety of walks of life, especially children, into these early movie theaters. Joseph Meddill Patterson wrote in a 1907 issue of *The Saturday Evening Post* that approximately one-third of the typical nickelodeon audience was made up of children, and it was the presence, or at least perceived presence, of these impressionable minds that gave particular impetus to early protests against the nickelodeon theaters. John Collier, for instance, called the nickelodeon parlor a "carnival of vulgarity, suggestiveness, and violence" as early as 1908.[3] The *Chicago Tribune* ran an extended campaign against the early nickelodeons in 1907 and recounted numerous stories of young boys incited to violence and "a number of little girls who should have been playing with dolls who were ruined through going to the nickel theatre."[4]

In many ways, while the articulation of these fears has changed, their deeper roots have not. The early years of the twenty-first century have produced similar concerns to those of the early twentieth century that representations in film may cause or at least contribute to some erosion of our moral core. Just as in the early 1900s, these concerns often arise around issues of children and, yet while concern for the impressionable minds of children remains constant, our fear of film seems to have a broader and more encompassing foundation. Many of our concerns about particular films, both now and in the past, relate to a more general objection that some images are simply too dangerous, offensive, or suggestive to be shown in public. We fear that violent images might exacerbate our already-violent society. We are, at times, frightened that graphic depictions of sexual depravity may erode whatever sense of normal morality we retain. We worry that films derived from our sacred stories may systematically distort our faith. We object to images that represent us, or those we care for, in ways that are demeaning or damning. Over one hundred years after the beginnings of the modern cinema and in spite of its immense popularity we continue to retain a certain fear of film.

For much of the history of cinema, one of the effects of this fear has been the creation and maintenance of various systems of regulation. Some of these systems have been formal, governmental structures for restricting certain types of films and certain kinds of images. Other systems have been more or less voluntary systems of self-regulation by the film industry itself. Still other systems of regulation have arisen from informal agreements between industry figures and other, external pressure groups whose threats of censure and boycott were sufficient to cause films to be reedited or even scrapped altogether.

As noted in the introduction, the focus of this book is the films that have provoked controversies, and in the long history of film these films have often faced censorship pressure or, at times, have been the cause of renewed calls for censorship. Given this, it is not surprising that most treatments of these kinds of films have been framed in terms of censorship. My purpose in this chapter is to begin the work of teasing out the distinction between censorship and controversy by focusing attention here on the history of censorship. By laying out a broad sketch of the history of censorship in this first chapter, I hope to be able to attend more closely in later chapters to the dynamics of specific controversies without needing to recount in detail their relationship to systems of censorship.

The history of film censorship is a fascinating and twisted story filled with dramatic legal battles, bombastic politicians and social reformers, wily and stubborn film directors, and a fickle population of filmgoers who often seem to simultaneously shout out their offense at a film while filling the seats at its showings. Fortunately, many of these tales have been well told in numerous earlier volumes, and the reader interested in film censorship can pursue their various strands, including legal history, religion, film production, and cultural values.[5] For our purposes, however, only a gloss of this convoluted history is necessary, and toward that end I have divided the history of film censorship into four periods.

1905–1914

As noted in the introduction, the diffusion of projection technology in the early years of the twentieth century led to the "Nickelodeon Boom" of 1905. Nickelodeons popped up in large numbers in urban settings, often in lower socioeconomic-status neighborhoods. This sudden proliferation of "five-cent theaters" created what can best be characterized as a moral panic among American elites in this period, and this quickly turned into calls for governmental regulation. In his excellent history of these early years of cinema censorship, Lee Grieveson argues that this "policing of the social functioning of cinema was linked to broader concerns about morality, public order, and governance."[6] The rhetoric of these early calls for regulation was filled with precisely this language of moral panic, fear of public disorder, and disintegration. Progressive social reformers and conservative religious leaders alike feared that because of their vividness, films would directly impact behavior, especially that of children, through a kind of mimicry effect. Of this period, film historian Gregory Black observes:

> These "moral guardians"—a loose-knit confederation of reformers who range from thoughtful and sometimes perceptive critics like Jane Addams to religious reactionaries like New York's Canon William Shaefe Chase—claimed that movies were changing traditional values, not reflecting them, and demanded that government use its licensing and regulatory powers to censor this new form of entertainment.[7]

There were, of course, numerous reasons for this cacophony of voices calling for the regulation and censorship of nickelodeons. On the one hand, there was a deep concern about the attendance of moving pictures by lower-class and immigrant populations. The inexpensiveness of this form of entertainment, along with its visual nature, allowed those with limited education and/or English language skills to enjoy the pictures as much as anyone else. But, for reformers worried about the susceptibility of these audiences—a concern derived from both classist and racist assumptions— there was a distinct danger in allowing such audiences to consume films filled with crime, sexual suggestion, and other acts of immorality. Religion also played a considerable role in these early reform calls. Among the earliest advocates of regulation of moving picture theaters were clergy members who wanted film exhibitions banned on Sundays, in line with the numerous bans on live theater performances and other "blue laws" in many jurisdictions.[8] These calls for keeping the Sabbath sacred were exacerbated by the broader concern that films, with their depictions of kissing and prizefighting and violence, were degrading the morals of audience members. Some called the nickelodeons "moral sinkholes" in which the future citizens of the nation were being led into a "new form of degeneracy."[9]

The most poignant appeals for regulation came with regard to children, and among the early proponents of censorship were various organizations designed to protect the young. The Children's Aid Society, for instance, sued a number of film exhibitors for degrading children by exhibiting such films as 1907's *The Unwritten Law*. This film was a depiction of the real-life Stanford White–Harry Thaw murder case from 1906 in which prominent architect White was shot in public by Thaw, the angry husband of Evelyn Nesbit Thaw with whom White was having an affair. The eventual criminal trial revealed a number of salacious details about the illicit relationship and various implements, including a red velvet swing, used by the couple. Dubbed the "Trial of the Century," the court case was covered heavily by the sensationalizing papers of William Randolph Hearst. *The Unwritten Law* sparked an enormous amount of controversy and helped to consolidate the various public concerns about what was on the screens of these early movie theaters and what kinds of activities they were promoting.[10] As Grieveson contends, it was "the first film in the United States to be widely constructed as 'scandalous,' singled out as a specific focus for the 'moral panic' about dangerous representations and spaces that emerged in early 1907."[11]

Perhaps not surprisingly, 1907 is also the year when the first city censorship ordinance directed at film was established, in Chicago. Soon censorship boards were being established in cities across the country, including Seattle, San Francisco, St. Louis, Dallas, Detroit, and New York City. Several of these boards became extensions of the already-existing theatrical licensing bureaus. The state of New York, for instance, had passed a comprehensive theatrical licensing law in 1839, and early efforts in New York City to regulate the operations of nickelodeons were derived from those laws. One of the key components of the original statutes was that theatrical shows could not be conducted on Sundays. Nickelodeons, however, slipped through the language of these laws as they did not actually use "performers" or "stages." When it became clear that the laws governing vaudeville performances were insufficient to regulate this new form of mass entertainment, Mayor George B. McClellan Jr. revoked the operating licenses of all the city's movie theaters on Christmas Eve 1908 and ordered an inspection of every theater before new licenses would be issued. He justified his action by stating:

> I have decided that licenses for moving picture shows shall only be issued hereafter on the written agreement that the licensee will not operate the same on Sunday. And I do further declare that I will revoke any of these moving picture show licenses on evidence that pictures have been exhibited by the licensees which tend to degrade or injure the morals of the community.[12]

The move from moral panic to calls for regulation having been made, the development of censorship mechanisms moved forward quickly. By

1911, the first state board of censorship was established in Pennsylvania, followed quickly by similar boards in Kansas and Ohio in 1913. The proliferation of state boards would have an important impact on films because a strict state board in, for example, Kansas would affect distribution of a film in not only that state but the entire region within which a particular cut of the film was distributed. Faced with such specific cuts from a particular state, the distributor, as Ira Carmen describes it, "will simply alter the particular movie as ordered and send it along to the exhibitors within the total exchange area in its expurgated condition."[13]

The growing movement in local and state censorship boards inevitably raised the prospect of federal legislation and the possibility of a federal board of censorship. Indeed, in 1912, Congress enacted the first major legislation to govern the exhibition of film, known as the Sims Act. This Act was aimed generally at the emerging genre of boxing films in which real boxing matches were filmed and later screened. Of course, the real motivation for this law was the racist furor caused by the preeminence of African American heavyweight champion Jack Johnson. The film version of the Johnson–Jeffries fight, in which Johnson had pummeled white challenger James Jeffries in 1910, sparked an enormous controversy based largely on the fear that wide exhibition of an African American man fighting with and even beating a white man might stir racial tensions and trouble the heavily guarded system of white privilege.[14] While this is an important element of the film controversy, to which I'll return in chapter 3, the broader legal effect of the Act was its definition of film as commerce and the expansion of the Interstate Commerce Clause to include regulating the distribution of films. This logically opened the door for all film distribution, or at least distribution across state lines, to be regulated by the federal government, and because the Sims Act had focused on the *content* of the films—in this case, fight films—it created a clear legislative precedent for a federal system of censorship.[15]

Producers, distributors, and exhibitors of film were considerably anxious not only about the growing local and state mechanisms of censorship but also about the emerging prospect of federal regulation of their industry. The strategy they developed as early as 1909 was to promote the notion of self-regulation. The Moving Picture Exhibitors Association (MPEA) was formed in 1907, and in 1909 it first proposed the development of an industry-based, rather than legally mandated, board of review. Working with the cultural reform group the People's Institute, the MPEA developed an Executive Committee on Censorship, which held its first meeting in March 1909. By June of that year, the group had changed its name to the National Board of Censorship of Motion Pictures. Within five years, the New York–based voluntary censorship board claimed to be reviewing up to 95 percent of the films being produced in the United States.[16]

However, this early effort at self-regulation was not without its problems or its critics. For many reformers, the MPEA's efforts seemed evasive and defensive rather than regulatory. Continued calls for legal regulation abounded, as did the continued expansion of state censorship boards. These calls and efforts, in turn, were resisted by the rapidly growing film industry. The escalating struggle reached a crucial turning point in 1915.

1915–1933

Two momentous events occurred in 1915 that would change the course of film history, one legal, the other cultural. The legal event was the Supreme Court's decision in the case that became the foundation for thirty-seven years of court rulings on issues of film censorship. The case had begun in 1913, when the Mutual Film Corporation filed suit against the new state censorship board that had been established by Ohio only months before. Mutual Film argued that the state board's power of censorship infringed on the rights of both private property and free speech.[17]

When the case arrived before the U.S. Supreme Court, William B. Saunders, the lawyer for Mutual, argued that film ought to be considered protected by free speech rights, particularly as film was increasingly used as a means of "spreading knowledge and the molding of public opinion."[18] However, the Court unanimously rejected this and other arguments, and in its decision in *Mutual Film Corporation v. Ohio Industrial Commission*, it denied any free speech protection for film. In an oft-quoted passage of Justice Joseph McKenna's decision, he argues:

> That the exhibition of moving pictures is a business, pure and simple, originated and conducted for profit, like other spectacles, not to be regarded, nor intended to be regarded by the Ohio Constitution, we think, as part of the press of the country, or as organs of public opinion. They are mere representations of events, of ideas and sentiments published and known; vivid, useful, and entertaining, no doubt, but, as we have said, capable of evil, having power for it, the greater because of their attractiveness and manner of exhibition.[19]

Three crucial concepts expounded here would guide most of the legal decisions about film censorship for the next four decades. First, the decision explained, film was not to be considered political expression, but rather was "a business pure and simple." The rendering of film as a purely commercial enterprise, a notion already established in legislation by the Sims Act of 1912, removed it from the possible protection of the First Amendment. Second, film was not even considered *expression* in any sense of creating or crafting public opinion or knowledge but was "mere representation." These two initial thoughts diminish the cultural and political importance of film by arguing that it is only a for-profit facsimile of free expression. However, the third argument creates a degree of tension with the previous two. In the Court's third argument, in which it lays the foundation for future censorship mechanisms, Justice McKenna argues that film is not only "capable of evil" but is uniquely dangerous through its attractive manner of exhibition. Here again is the cultural fear of film as a representation that is so seductive in its visual power and so capable of overwhelming the reason of its audience that it must be subject to careful scrutiny and rigid legal structures of control.

As if to validate the Court's concern, in early 1915 a film emerged that would fundamentally change the nature of filmmaking and provoke a nationwide cultural controversy. D. W. Griffith's *The Birth of a Nation* has been called "the film that started it all," and in many ways this is true.[20] Never before had a film exploited the numerous and complex narrative possibilities of film—cutting between scenes with a uniquely visual pacing that serves to establish tone and mood, moving between spatially separated events to craft a narrative connection, and so forth—and rarely had a film so expansively and explicitly crafted an underlying apologia for American racism.[21] These competing elements—a wildly progressive cinematic aesthetic and viciously conservative racist depiction of the Reconstruction era—made the film profoundly influential, incredibly popular, and intensely controversial.[22]

In cities as culturally diverse and geographically separate as Boston and Lexington, Kentucky, police and Pinkerton agents were interspersed among *Birth of a Nation*'s audience members to head off any racial violence. The film was banned in numerous cities and states and was condemned by the still fairly young National Association for the Advancement of Colored People and by progressive reformers such as Jane Addams. At the same time, President Woodrow Wilson made it the first film ever screened in the White House and is famously quoted as saying of Griffith's film, "It is like writing history with lightning; my only regret is that it is all so terribly true." Griffith himself mounted a vigorous campaign in defense of his film, arguing that it was historically accurate and condemning the social reformers who sought to censor his film. Indeed, his follow-up to *Birth*, the film *Intolerance*, was an allegory about the intolerance of those who would censor his film. Griffith also sought to invoke rights of free expression for himself and his film (all the while ironically arguing that African Americans should be excluded from the political process).[23]

While I will return to the turmoil created by Griffith's film in more detail in a later chapter, it is an instructive example of the increasing realization of the political potency of film during this period. These fears, in turn, were exacerbated by the prominence of film in the propaganda efforts of World War I and the emergence of Hollywood as the global center of filmmaking in the 1920s. The growth of Hollywood also led to the birth of the movie star, and the 1920s saw not only the growing prominence of movie stars—Douglas Fairbanks, Mary Pickford, and Charlie Chaplin, among others—but also a series of star scandals, most famously the Fatty Arbuckle murder trial of 1921, which also fueled calls for Hollywood to be regulated.

The film industry's response came largely through the Motion Picture Producers and Distributors of America (MPPDA), an organization begun in 1922. The previous efforts at self-regulation through the Motion Picture Exhibitors Association, which later renamed itself the National Association of the Motion Picture Industry (NAMPI), had been undermined by two problems. First, the NAMPI remained largely centered around New York City, and its National Board of Censorship lost its potency as the industry moved west to California. Second, the creation of an official New York State board of censorship rendered it largely irrelevant. The renewed effort centered in Hollywood took a more savvy political tack by recruiting a Midwestern conservative Republican named William Hays to be its new head. Under Hays, the MPPDA worked on numerous fronts to promote and protect the preeminence of the U.S. film industry. The organization worked to standardize exhibition contracts and to ward off regulatory infringements, promoted American films in foreign markets, and, of course, sought to assuage the growing furor over film controversies.[24]

Hays's first two efforts to develop a satisfactory system of self-regulation were unsuccessful. The first, begun in 1924, was known as "the Formula." Under this system, producers voluntarily submitted proposals for scripts or adaptations of plays or novels to Hays's office, which would then judge their acceptability. However, as film historian Black notes, "Even though 125 proposals were rejected, 'The Formula' did little to quiet protests."[25] The second effort, through the newly established Studio Relations Department, promoted a new code for acceptable film representations. This second code became known as the "Don'ts and Be Carefuls." The Don'ts included such things as profanity, nudity, and drugs. The Be Carefuls consisted of topics like criminal behavior and adultery. However, this early attempt at a film code failed because it was largely left to the studios to interpret as they saw fit.

The eventual, if temporary, solution to the question of how Hollywood could self-regulate—as this was the only way of staving off the looming threat of federal regulation—came from an unlikely place. In 1929, a group of ardent Catholic critics of American film began meeting to formulate their own code for film behavior. Among this group were Martin Quigley, Father Fitz-George Dinneen, Father Daniel Lord, and Joseph Breen. What they developed would become known as the Lord–Quigley Code. The Code was based on the assumption that "the moral importance of entertainment is something which has been universally recognized" and that Hollywood must strive to "improve the race" rather than "degrade human beings." Further, the Code included such dicta as "The courts of the land should not be presented as unjust," "The presentation [of a crime] must not throw sympathy with the crime," and "Impure love must not be presented as attractive and beautiful."[26]

The stock market crash of 1929 convinced Hollywood studio heads to approve whatever measures were needed to stave off both a massive Catholic boycott of films and the continuing threat of federal regulation. There were very real concerns about both. In 1933, the same group that developed the Catholic Code for films would establish the Catholic Church's Legion of Decency, an organization that would put continuing pressure on Hollywood to produce more moral films for the next forty-two years. On the federal front, the concerns were about both imposed censorship and antitrust actions. As Black notes, Hays used both these arguments to gain acquiescence from the studios, arguing that the new code would "quiet demands for federal censorship and undercut the campaign to eliminate block booking."[27] "Block booking" was the practice of selling motion pictures to exhibitors in large bundles, thus preventing them from refusing particular films they did not want to show. This practice, along with studio ownership of theaters, had been raising concerns at the Federal Trade Commission since 1921, and Hays effectively used the specter of federal regulation in selling his new, stricter motion picture code.[28]

The adoption of the Code came in 1930, but it did not have the immediate effect that Hays, Quigley, and the others had anticipated. Indeed, it was partially in response to Hollywood's lax attitude toward the newly adopted Code that the Catholic Legion of Decency was officially formed in 1933. That year also saw another damning blow against the "corrupting" and "lurid" nature of contemporary motion pictures with the publication of Henry James Forman's *Our Movie Made Children*. Forman's book was a summary of studies done under the auspices of the Payne Foundation. These studies sought to explore the impact of film on society, especially youth, and the reports—particularly in Forman's sensationalizing summary of them—condemned American films for corrupting America's children. Seemingly scientific evidence could now be laid at the feet of Hollywood, and reformers wasted no time in doing so.[29]

The formulation of the Production Code shared many of the assumptions about film that have become obvious to this point in our historical narrative, namely, that films are particularly dangerous in their ability to influence, even seduce, audiences. As John Nichols describes it:

> In the Code's formulation film's vibrant approximation of reality, which stems partly from its visual impact and partly from its novelty as a new medium made it more powerful than other arts and therefore deserving of stricter regulation than other media such as literature.[30]

Thus, the Code was formulated to contain this danger and protect audiences from the deleterious moral impact some films might have.

By the end of 1933, it became clear to Hays, and to the motion picture industry as a whole, that survival in this new age—an age changed not only by the Depression and the newly conservative cultural climate but also by the advent of the "talkies" in 1929—would require a more stringent application of the Code. As an editorial quoted in the *Oakland Tribune* in October 1933 observed, the existing Hays Code "has been disregarded, possibly because it could not survive in the face of cutthroat competition."[31] In December 1933, William Hays announced a new chief censor, and in 1934 the Studio Relations Committee was transformed into the Production Code Administration.

1934–1951

Lea Jacobs expresses the general sentiment of most film historians when she notes that 1934 was "a turning point" in the way Hollywood approached self-regulation.[32] This year has become the defining point for most film histories, with earlier films referred to as "pre-Code" and later films often labeled "post-Code." Technically, of course, this is inaccurate, as the Code itself was begun in 1930. But it was the ascension of Joseph I. Breen to the leadership of the Production Code Administration (PCA) that heralded a sea change in self-regulation for Hollywood.

A deeply conservative Catholic, Breen, as noted earlier, was among the small group who first articulated the need for a religious response to Hollywood films, and his background included stints as a reporter, as a civil servant, and in public relations. The appointment of Breen was meant at least in part as a conciliatory gesture toward the Legion of Decency. Soon the PCA was engaged in increasingly heavy-handed reviews of scripts and films. As one contemporary editorial in the *Lincoln* (Nebraska) *Star* put it: "The laundry for Hollywood's motion picture productions, demanded by church organizations throughout the country for the past month, will open here July 15th. Plans for insuring 'clean' pictures were disclosed by Joseph I. Breen."[33] Within a year, there was a general feeling of satisfaction among opponents of Hollywood's loose morals with, as Black puts it, "Breen's success in purging overt sexuality from most films and infusing a sense of moral compensation, however shallow."[34]

Under Breen's watch, the Code system had a more specific mechanism for enforcement than did the earlier iterations under Hays. Essentially, no film could be exhibited without a Production Code Seal of Approval, and those films that received the seal had to conform, or be brought into conformity, with the dictates of the adapted Lord–Quigley Code. The Code expanded beyond explicit issues of sex, violence, religion, and crime and began to utilize a vague standard that prohibited films whose content might be dangerous to the industry's health. The Code also encompassed issues ranging from the explicitness of a depiction—nudity was strictly forbidden, as was any suggestion of actual sex—the intention and motivation of characters, and the ultimate moral message. Crime, for instance, was acceptable so long as the film ultimately served to represent the demise and failure of the criminal.

Armed with an incredible amount of power to deny scripts, cut films, or even take films out of circulation, the Production Code Administration had a profound impact on American film. This is not, of course, to suggest that film directors and producers simply surrendered and accepted the rule of Breen and the PCA. On the contrary, the history of the PCA is replete with resistance, revolutions, and challenges. Additionally, as numerous film critics have observed, far from being shackled by the moral strictures of the Code, many directors found subtle ways to outmaneuver its prohibitions. In this way, the Code was not so much a clear prohibition as it was an intricate and difficult process of negotiation between various components of the same industry—it is worth underscoring here that the PCA was an arm of the MPPDA and, thus, a system of self-regulation.

A considerable amount of attention has been paid to the various machinations, personalities, and effects of the Production Code, and for this reason, the details can be omitted from this account. For our purposes, it is also worth noting that the emergence of the PCA did not end condemnation of the film industry as whole or prevent controversies over individual films. Quite to the contrary, the PCA simply became a conduit and focal point for such critical voices—voices like those of the Legion of Decency, which at times felt the PCA's standards were applied too laxly.[35] Thus, while the Code had a profound impact on American filmmaking during its reign, the controversies surrounding cinema did not really end but were channeled into the official mechanisms of resolution. The PCA, for example, received an enormous number of complaints from individuals and groups regarding various films that had received the official Production Code Seal of Approval.

The demise of the Production Code was the result of many of the same forces that would eventually lead to the demise of the Hollywood studio system itself. At least two of these broad forces had relatively little to do with the explicit system of self-censorship defined by the Production Code. The first was the legal challenge to the monopoly that had been established through both block booking and studio ownership of theaters. The one thing Hollywood had feared most, and that had been a major reason for studio heads to acquiesce to the Production Code, came to pass—antitrust regulation.

The process of breaking up the Hollywood monopoly took a decade. In 1938, the Department of Justice began legal proceedings against Paramount Studios, but after only two weeks the trial was suspended and a negotiated settlement between President Franklin D. Roosevelt's Justice Department and the studio heads was reached. The settlement, generally known as the Consent Decree of 1940, provided some loose regulation of block booking but allowed the studios to retain their theaters. The negotiated settlement, however, did not include the smaller studios—Universal, Columbia, and United Artists—or the independent producers, and soon the big studios were back in court with the federal government.

In 1945, the court battle over Hollywood's monopoly on booking and theaters was engaged again, and this time the case made it all the way to the Supreme Court. At stake was the very nature of the U.S. film industry. The eight litigants represented the majority of films produced in the United States—around 70 percent, and close to 90 percent of the feature, or "A," pictures. This time the three smaller studios were lumped in with the five major corporations—Paramount, Loew's, RKO, Twentieth Century Fox, and Warner Bros. In 1948, the Court finally ruled in the case of *United States v. Paramount Pictures, Inc.*, and the decision was against the studios. This legal blow effectively ended the studio system that had been developing since the 1920s. The court ruled that the studios must "divorce" their theaters and prohibited block booking, and these shifts in the practices of filmmaking, distribution, and exhibition undermined the power of the Production Code Administration, which relied on the studio monopoly to enforce its will.[36]

Where the Supreme Court undermined the structure that allowed for censorship, another major cultural trend was also weakening the Code, namely, the decline in box office receipts. In 1946, Hollywood dominated not only the movies but even the very idea of entertainment across most of the globe, with box office revenues exceeding $1.5 billion. A decade later, in 1956, revenues had dropped to $1.2 billion—and this in spite of a hefty increase in ticket prices. Numerous reasons have been cited for the implosion of Hollywood in the postwar years.[37] Gerald Mast, for instance, attributes this decline to the emergence of television and suggests that the lure of TV led film producers to challenge the Code more directly.[38] Even the strictures of the Breen Code were less stringent than the production codes applied to television, and therefore filmmakers sought to differentiate themselves from their cathode cousins by pushing the boundaries of acceptability. This drive to differentiate film from other forms of entertainment available to the increasingly suburban American consumer also led to a fairly dramatic rise in foreign and "art house" films, and it was from this arena that the lethal blow to the system of state and self-imposed censorship came.

1952–1968

On December 12, 1950, a small film entitled *The Way of Love* opened in New York City's Paris Theater. The film was a trilogy of short foreign films, including a second segment titled *The Miracle*, directed by Robert Rossellini and written by Federico Fellini. Rossellini's segment depicts a young simple peasant woman who is seduced by a visitor she believes to be Saint Joseph. She comes to believe that her eventual pregnancy is divine, and though she is mocked by many in her village, she maintains the belief until, in the end, she gives birth alone in a small church. Twelve days after it opened, protests reached the city commissioner of licenses, who found the film "officially and personally blasphemous" and rejected the theater's license.[39]

The controversy over *The Miracle* indicates precisely how the broader regulatory mechanisms, which were most fully in place after 1934, failed to eliminate controversy or even quiet protests. *The Miracle* had been approved by U.S. Customs and the Motion Picture Division of the New York State Education Department. But the ensuing controversy, driven largely by religious interest groups who found the film offensive, soon led to the revocation of the license. What made this particular incident different is that the distributor of the film, Joseph Burstyn, initiated legal action against the revocation. The case went first to the New York State Supreme Court, which ruled in favor of the film on the relatively narrow grounds that a city commissioner could not revoke a license of a film already approved by the state. After the film resumed showings in New York City, pressure from various groups, including the head of the New York Catholic archdiocese, Cardinal Spellman, the New York Board of Regents revoked the film's license on the ground that it was "sacrilegious."[40] When the state supreme court upheld the regents' revocation, the stage was set for what would be a crucial legal battle over censorship in the nation's highest court.

In the four decades since the Court's declaration in *Mutual v. Ohio* that film was "business pure and simple" and therefore not afforded First Amendment protection, the legal groundwork had been laid for reconsidering the status not only of film but also of the notion of free expression. For instance, in *Gitlow v. New York*, the Court established a link between First Amendment rights to free expression and Fourteenth Amendment rights to due process, and in *Near v. Minnesota*, the Court established that prior restraint on free expression could occur in only the rarest of circumstances. Perhaps the most important legal precedent for the Court's eventual decision came from the reasoning in one of Hollywood's biggest legal losses. In the same *Paramount* decision that restructured the studio system, Justice William O. Douglas, writing for the majority, reasoned, "We have no doubt that moving pictures, like newspapers and radio, are included in the press whose freedom is guaranteed by the First Amendment." Thus, the Court's ruling that New York was not justified in revoking the license of *The Miracle* follows a certain preceding logic of an expanded First Amendment. Of course, in terms of the legal notion of film censorship, the decision in

Burstyn v. Wilson fundamentally undermined the structure of state-sponsored censorship.[41]

At the root of the decision in *Burstyn v. Wilson* was the vagueness of the censorship standards themselves. The Court did not, at least at this point, revoke any right of censorship over film held by the state, but rather insisted that the basis for such censorship decisions be fair, clear, and explicit. The New York regents' decision had been based on *The Miracle*'s violation of the "sacrilegious standard," which the Court found to be hopelessly vague and to run the risk of a potentially endless expansion of state censorship powers. While not explicitly ending the state's right to censor, the *Burstyn v. Wilson* decision did lay the fundamental groundwork for the dismantling of all forms of state censorship over the next sixteen years. As Dawn Sova writes in her account this episode:

> After its decision in the *Miracle* case, the Supreme Court issued five court opinions to reverse rulings in state supreme court cases that had supported decisions made by censorship boards to ban given films. Citing their decision in *Burstyn v Wilson* ... the justices changed the basis for movie censorship by striking down all but one of the censorship criteria ("obscenity") that had been used for nearly five decades by city and state censorship boards.[42]

Indeed, just four years later, the Pennsylvania Supreme Court ruled against the state's censorship law, thus closing the nation's oldest state censorship board.[43]

The legal win for Hollywood, however, was at least partially tempered by the increasingly hysterical conservative climate in the postwar era. The House Un-American Activities Committee (HUAC) began investigating Hollywood in 1947. Seeking to root out Communists and Communist sympathizers within the entertainment elite, the HUAC hearings sent a shockwave through the film studios. The House committee supplied the studios with lists of writers who were members of unions or other "dangerous" organizations and provided the basis for their dismissal without cause. The Hollywood blacklist and the concomitant McCarthy hysteria about Communism helped to generate a great deal of trepidation about the "political nature" of the entertainment industry, leading several studios to explicitly back away from politically progressive or "edgy" films.[44]

By 1954, however, the McCarthy-inspired hysteria had imploded—due in large part to the junior senator from Wisconsin's own hysterical performance on live television during the Army–McCarthy hearings—and the American film industry was undergoing considerable change. In addition to facing increasing competition from television, the dismantling of the studio system also led to a dramatic rise in independent, often B-movie producers such as Roger Corman and Herschell Gordon Lewis, who increasingly pushed the previous boundaries of film decorum with gimmicks and gore.[45] Foreign films like *The Miracle* were also becoming increasingly common, and Hollywood directors such as Elia Kazan and Otto Preminger, both of whom released controversial films in 1956, began pushing for more artistic license. Kazan's *Baby Doll*, which deals provocatively with a young female's awakened sexuality, was called by *Time* magazine "the dirtiest American-made motion picture that has ever been legally exhibited."[46] When Preminger's film, *The Man with the Golden Arm*, starring Frank Sinatra as a heroin addict struggling to get clean, was denied a seal of approval by the Motion Picture Association of America (MPAA), United Artists chose to withdraw from the organization and released the film without a seal—something that would have been virtually impossible prior to the 1948 court-ordered break up of the studio monopolies.[47]

As the system of self-regulation began to unravel, so too did the legal basis for state regulation of movies. In 1959, the Supreme Court rejected New York State's right to order cuts from Marc Allégret's *Lady Chatterley's Lover*. The state had argued, in a vein similar to many censorship arguments, that the film dealt with adultery in a sympathetic manner and insisted upon cuts of specific scenes and dialogue from the film. The Court, however, found that in trying to stop the representation of an idea, here regarding sex and adultery, the state had violated the very essence of free speech protection. In 1965 the Court invalidated a Maryland censorship board decision and ordered that decisions about "obscenity" and the like would require judicial process, therefore greatly curtailing the freedom of state boards to make decisions about the acceptability of a given film.[48] A similar decision came in the 1968 case *Interstate Circuit v. Dallas*, in which the Court rejected the city of Dallas's right to classify films as, in this instance, "not suitable for young people" based on the notion of "sexual promiscuity." The *Interstate* decision was also based on the vagueness of the standard being used to prevent a film from being circulated among potential audiences.[49]

With the demise of state and local censorship boards, the last vestige of the official structure of film censorship remained with the Production Code Administration and the Motion Picture Association of America. However, in the late 1960s it became increasingly clear that this system no longer functioned. Considerable controversy surrounded Sidney Lumet's 1965 *The Pawnbroker*, a heart-wrenching film about a Holocaust survivor and his memories of those horrific events, starring Rod Steiger. The film was harshly opposed by the Legion of Decency—who would give it a "Condemned" rating—because of scenes of nudity. The MPAA, however, approved it.

The final blow to the MPAA's system of self-censorship came in the form of Mike Nichols's 1966 film *Who's Afraid of Virginia Woolf?* Adapted by Warner Bros. from the popular stage play by Edward Albee, director Nichols and screenwriter Ernest Lehman sought to keep the play's sexual content and graphic language. In spite of opposition from some quarters, it was clear from the beginning of this process that *Woolf* would be approved, in part because of Warner Bros. desperate need for a hit, and that this approval would become official validation of what most saw as a fundamental change in the cultural mood. Gregory Black makes the observation that "when Elizabeth Taylor and Richard Burton hit the screen screaming and tearing at each other with a hateful vengeance it was obvious that the movies had been changed forever. No longer were they going to be reigned in by codes."[50] The MPAA's approval of the film, in the words of Leonard Leff, "opened the floodgates. Motion picture classification was implemented within two years of the premiere of *Virginia Woolf*, and films became increasingly more outspoken in theme, content, and language."[51]

Approving *Woolf* was one of the first actions of the new president of the MPAA, a Texan named Jack Valenti who had worked in the Johnson White House. And, it was Valenti who two years later introduced an idea that had been floating around the MPAA for some time: a ratings system. In 1968 the Production Code Administration was retired and replaced by the Code and Rating Administration (CARA), and soon moviegoers were confronted with the same mysterious letters attached to films as contemporary audiences are: G, PG, R, and X. A few decades later, PG-13 was added, and in 1990, X was replaced with the "less pornographic"–sounding NC-17 (no child under 17).

The end of official censorship and the adoption of the rating system, of course, did not mean an end to calls for films to be suppressed. As Marjorie Heins, director of the Free Expression Policy Project, observes, "Movie censorship today has . . . shifted almost completely to the realm of private industry 'self-regulation' and to indirect but still potent venues for suppression like schools and libraries."[52] The ratings system, while not censorship in the strictest sense of that word, continues to have enormous economic repercussions, especially for films threatened with an NC-17 rating. Further, there are still court cases emerging around objections to films—in 1997, for example, the Oklahoma City district attorney filed charges of "child pornography" against Blockbuster for renting copies of the Academy Award–winning German film *The Tin Drum*.[53] While the charges were later dismissed, the legal atmosphere around issues of children and sexuality remains tense.

Contemporary efforts to regulate film have taken on a more diffused, almost populist tone. Sova sums this condition up nicely when observing, "Censorship today now rests less with federal, state, or local ordinances that dictate appropriate film content than with force of opinion by smaller groups with more specialized agenda."[54] The 1988 release of Martin Scorsese's *The Last Temptation of Christ*, for example, brought enormous protests and calls for boycotting all Universal Studios films from religious leaders such as the Reverend Jerry Falwell and political conservatives like Pat Buchanan.[55]

CONCLUSION

This brief review of the history of American film censorship should provide a useful historical background against which to consider the various
controversies that have embroiled particular films. At the very least, this
survey suggests that some familiar topics have consistently emerged as
provocations for protest and censure: sex, violence and crime, race, religion, politics, and the like. Additionally, this brief history should allow us
to move beyond the particulars of legal precedents, production codes, and
other machinations of regulation as we turn, instead, to the voices of protest that raised objections, and the films that became embroiled in these
controversies.

In the end, the system of censorship, in all its varied forms, is not the
same as the processes of controversy. Certainly in many ways the two
ideas—protests over films and the regulatory mechanisms invoked, at
times, in the name of these protests—are interconnected. But, as I contended in this book's introduction, reading the history of controversial cinema primarily in terms of systems of censorship effectively erases the
rhetoric of protest being issued by various interested parties, and it is precisely this rhetoric of protest that provides the underlying justification for
the system of censorship in the first place. In other words, focusing on censorship rather than controversy puts the theoretical cart before the horse. It
is the protest that fuels calls for regulation. If the history of film censorship
in America tells us nothing more, it surely tells us that the systems of regulation were and are in constant flux as they negotiate between various competing interests, and the points at which these various competing interests
come into vocal conflict with each other are the points of controversy that
are of interest in the present study.

CHAPTER 2

Sex, Gender, and Sexuality: Jonathan Demme's *The Silence of the Lambs*

T he gala ceremony for the sixty-fourth Academy Awards was, in many ways, fairly typical. Filled with stars, red carpets, and the inevitable comedian emcee and clocking in at more than three hours, the event was everything the world had come to expect from Hollywood's annual moment of self-recognition. There were, however, two elements that made this particular ceremony—held on the evening of March 30, 1992, in the Dorothy Chandler Pavilion in Los Angeles—unusual.

The first happened inside the auditorium when Jonathan Demme's film adaptation of Thomas Harris's *The Silence of the Lambs* swept the top five awards. While numerous films in Oscar's long history have taken more awards, only two previous films had swept the five "major" awards—the 1934 Frank Capra film *It Happened One Night* and Milos Forman's 1975 *One Flew Over the Cuckoo's Nest*. The story of a young female FBI agent's pursuit of a sadistic serial killer and her strange relationship with an incarcerated cannibalistic psychiatrist became an unlikely hit in 1991, and the Oscar for Best Picture added even more validation to this stark and thrilling police procedural. Jodie Foster won her second Best Actress award for her portrayal of the vulnerable but defiant FBI trainee, Clarice Starling, and veteran Welsh actor Anthony Hopkins won his first Oscar for his lead role as the charismatic monster, Dr. Hannibal Lecter. Jonathan Demme took the award for Best Director, and screenwriter Ted Tally's win for Best Adapted Screenplay rounded out the film's remarkable night.

The second unusual aspect to this Academy Awards ceremony occurred outside the pavilion and, in part, as a reaction to the overwhelming accolades heaped upon Demme's thriller. Hundreds of protestors from various gay rights and advocacy groups such as Queer Nation disrupted the entrance to the gala event by chanting, picketing, defacing the giant golden Oscar statues with stickers reading "Fag," and even throwing objects at those on the vaunted red carpet. At least eleven protestors were reportedly arrested as "police in riot gear and on horseback interposed themselves between the demonstrators and the pavilion."[1] The events surrounding the ceremony, as a *New York Times* reporter put it, "resembled a barricaded war zone in which the police, the paparazzi, and demonstrators engaged in running skirmishes."[2]

The protest, which had begun hours before the ceremony and continued until after the awards show was finished, had been threatened for weeks. At the root of this controversy was what Judy Sisneros, a leader of Queer Nation, called "Hollywood homophobia." The AIDS crisis, which had come to national prominence in the mid-1980s, had provoked a dramatic rise in gay, lesbian, and transgender activism, and by the early 1990s, numerous groups such as ACT-UP, the Gay Lesbian Alliance against Defamation (GLAAD), and Queer Nation were taking increasingly vocal stands against legal and cultural forms of discrimination—and Hollywood had become one of the targets. A few weeks before the Academy Awards, for instance, a group of Queer Nation activists led by Michelangelo Signorile had disrupted a Directors Guild screening of documentaries to protest the Academy's snub of the documentary *Paris Is Burning*, a film about New York City's drag queen culture.[3]

The real provocation for the action against the Academy Awards, however, came from two Oscar-nominated films: Oliver Stone's *JFK*, for its negative portrayal of gay characters, and Demme's *Silence of the Lambs*. The harsh condemnations of *Silence* were largely due to the suggestion that the vicious serial killer, Buffalo Bill, was a homosexual and, in part, to the shock over the involvement of artists like Demme, a favorite of the independent film crowd for years, and Foster, long rumored to be a lesbian. How could such progressively minded liberals, some of the protestors asked, be involved in such a viciously homophobic film? Of course, Hollywood has a tragically long history of negative depictions of gays and lesbians. As Vito Russo puts it in *The Celluloid Closet*, his landmark study of gays and lesbians in American film:

> As expressed on screen, America was a dream that had no room for the existence of homosexuals. Laws were made against depicting such things onscreen. And when the fact of our existence became unavoidable, we were reflected, onscreen and off, as dirty secrets.[4]

Demme's *Silence* is a particularly interesting example of the kinds of controversies surrounding depictions of sexuality, not only because of its critical and popular success but also because—as much as the film became the focal point for vilification from some gay and lesbian critics—it was also hailed by some feminist critics as an importantly empowering film. The prominence of its female protagonist as well as its explicit and critical depiction of the demeaning sexual politics surrounding women in contemporary America led many to hail it as a landmark feminist film. Additionally, some reviewers also praised Demme's film for refusing to sexualize or glamorize violence and instead separating sex from violence in an effective and insightful manner. In this way, the example of *Silence* points to one of the broader tendencies in controversies over sex and film, namely, the interconnection of sex, identity, and morality. The tension among various communities over the underlying meaning of Demme's film arose, in part, because these two communities—feminist and homosexual—responded to the film along lines of what it was saying about their identity, whether validating or vilifying.

Sex has been the subject of the restrictions of morality for so long that it seems almost impossible to imagine sexual behavior without invoking some sense of moral value—whether in praise or condemnation. Because of this, representations of sex on-screen have also provoked reactions related to questions of the broader public morality. Interestingly, the historical controversies over sex and film—as I elaborate in the next section of this chapter—have typically focused on some sense of the culture's moral health. These issues, in turn, have not always been about the fear that behaviors depicted on-screen would be mimicked by those watching—a concern that does arise but also becomes more prominent in the next chapter's discussion of violence. Rather, the concerns about sex on-screen often have been that the simple representation of certain sexual images, ideas, or behaviors would somehow in and of themselves be damaging. In the example of *Silence*, some in the gay and lesbian community feared that the image of the homosexual-as-killer would further the broader cultural bias against their community by supplying symbolic evidence of some alleged moral depravity. On the other hand, some among the feminist community praised the film for portraying what they felt was an important lesson in sexual morality, namely, a liberated female protagonist.

Not surprisingly, the controversy over *The Silence of the Lambs* began more than a year before the spectacular protests outside the Dorothy Chandler Pavilion, and it is to this extended controversy that I return at the end of this chapter in order to consider in more detail the internal dynamics that occur in a controversy related to sex, gender, and sexuality. To be clear, here I understand *sex* to be both the biological quality that delineates male from female and a term that captures the physical aspects of the sexual act. *Gender*, on the other hand, is a cultural conception of the kinds of roles appropriate and inappropriate for those who are biologically male or female. *Sexuality*, as the third term of significance here, denotes the personal and cultural orientation of one's sexual desires. In this way, *Silence* is an especially interesting case study of the controversies over issues surrounding sex because it embroils all three of these broad concepts as well as pitting various communities against Hollywood and, at times, against each other in the lengthy struggle to make sense of the film's sexual politics.

Before turning to the intriguing particulars of the protracted controversy over *The Silence of the Lambs*, however, it is worth acknowledging that sex and cinema have a long and contentious relationship. Indeed, not long after the introduction of cinema's predecessor, the kinetoscope, the "indecent" peep show appeared, popping up as early as 1894. In 1897 the first court case involving a film focused on a one-reeler depicting a bride's wedding night, which was called "an outrage to public decency" by the presiding judge.[5] With the diffusion of projection technology, pornographic stag films began to appear. In her study of the history of pornography, titled *Hard Core*, Linda Williams discusses early stag films, such as the German *Am Abend* from 1910, and notes that their structures parallel those of contemporary pornography videos with similar close-ups on genitalia and medium shots of sexual activity.[6] Yet, while the proliferation of pornographic films is an important element of the relationships among sex, film, and American culture, so too is the representation of sex in mainstream, or public, film. As Tanya Krzywinska observes, "Precisely because cinema is in the public arena, the representation of sex accrues an added transgressive edge."[7] In part because sex—particularly in American culture with its lingering Puritan roots—is conceived as such a cloistered and private act, the depiction of sexual activities on the enormous and publicly visible screen of the cinema has held an especially provocative position. Indeed, Guy Phelps observes that throughout the history of film, "American censorship has generally led to more restriction on sexual matters than on violence, while obscenity laws are invariably more applicable to sex."[8]

Given this long history, before turning to the tangled web of sex, gender politics, and sexuality that ensnared Jonathan Demme's *Silence of the Lambs*, it is worthwhile to explore various historical controversies over sex, gender, and sexuality in film. By tracing the way these disparate elements provoked controversy in the past, the controversy over *Silence* should be rendered both more understandable and more important as a representative of the long line of provocative films and the reactions they provoked.

A HISTORY OF CONTROVERSIES OVER SEX IN FILM

As noted above, sex and cinema have made enduring and, at times, contentious bedfellows. Among the earliest films produced by Thomas Edison is a pair of films from 1896, both of which sparked considerable controversy. *Fatima's Coochee-Coochee Dance* was one of the more provocative of a series of short films whose subject was some form of indigenous dance, a series that also included films like *Sioux Ghost Dance* and *Buffalo Dance*. But it was Fatima's provocative and sensual Middle Eastern belly dance that sparked outrage. Fatima's performance at the 1893 Columbia's World Exposition in Chicago was one of the fair's most popular attractions, and the short film of her performance brought young men to the nickelodeons in droves and sparked calls for censorship in numerous locales.[9] Edison's other 1896 scandalous "sex picture" was derived from the contemporary Broadway smash *The Widow Jones*, especially its daring final scene in which May Irwin and John C. Rice, the female and male leads, engage in a, for the time, lengthy and salacious kiss. The fifty-foot reel, titled *The May Irwin–John C. Rice Kiss*, was, as a 1926 edition of the *New York Times* recalls, "regarded as a tidal wave of carnality." One contemporary critic is quoted as condemning the film by declaring, "Magnified to Gargantuan proportions and repeated three times over, it was absolutely disgusting."[10] Early film historian Terry Ramsaye, author of the 1926 history of film *A Million and One Nights*, claimed that the furor over *The Kiss* was the beginning of the movement for American film censorship.[11]

Films in the early years of the twentieth century also engaged sex and sexuality in increasingly provocative and controversial ways. One of the most contentious subgenres within these early years of American cinema was the "white slavery" film, movies that were presented as cautionary tales about young, naïve women who arrive in the big city only to be duped into prostitution. Films in this vein included such titles as *Traffic in Souls* (1913), *The Inside of the White Slave Traffic* (1913), and *Little Lost Sister* (1917). *Traffic in Souls*, which premiered in November 1913, told the tale of a young, innocent candy store worker tricked into a vast, almost corporate, network of "white slavery" before being rescued by her ingenious and determined older sister. Directed by George Loan Tucker under the auspices of Carl Laemmle's Independent Motion Pictures Company, *Traffic in Souls* was immensely popular. According to Christopher Diffee, its release "was greeted with such fanfare that on its opening night ... a thousand people were turned away from Joe Weber's Theater in New York City."[12] The picture, which cost approximately $5,700 to produce, would go on to gross approximately $450,000 but would also encounter considerable legal difficulties.[13] Police raids and injunctions plagued the film, making its eventual box office success all the more impressive.[14]

The controversies over white slavery films were, however, more than merely reactions against salacious details, as had been the case with *The Kiss* and other early sexual films. Films like *The Inside of the White Slave Traffic* had supporters in various quarters who felt they were legitimate cautionary tales helping to educate, and therefore protect, a generation of young women from the dangers of prostitution. Supporters of such films include early feminists such as Carrie Chapman Catt and Charlotte Perkins Gilman.[15] Suffragist and female attorney Inez Millholland Boissevain argued in a letter to the *New York Times* on February 9, 1914, that such films were valuable in two ways. First, because "only by frank, scientific, matter-of-fact and above-board discussion and presentation of all subject pertaining to sex ... can we clear the atmosphere and remove from it the murky, unclean, timid and defiled mental attitudes where are generally current." And second, these films needed to be screened because of the underlying value of free speech—it is worth recalling that Millholland Boissevain was writing a year before the *Mutual v. Ohio* case would see the Supreme Court explicitly deny film the protections of the First Amendment.

However, in spite of these supporters, raids and arrests continued, largely because authorities did not believe in the purported educational value of the films. As Deputy Commissioner Newburger in New York claimed after one of these raids on *The Inside of the White Slave Traffic*, "The pictures are vicious and are intended to cater to morbid imaginations."[16] Justice Gavegon of the New York Supreme Court declared in 1913 that such films ought not to be considered "moral lessons" because they were "not for the uplift of public morals but for private gain."[17]

These "moral lesson" films, however, continued to push the boundaries of sexual mores on the screen. Sexual education films, many of them produced out of concern for venereal diseases among soldiers heading to the front in World War I, began to circulate in theaters following the war, sparking more controversies over, in essence, whether films were reflecting shifts in cultural norms or were transgressing these norms for the base purpose of gaining profits from titillating subjects. In addition to films about venereal disease and the dangers of prostitution, there were films focusing on the perils of abortion, the biological processes of birth, and even cautionary tales about masturbation.[18]

One interesting example of the kind of reaction these early scandalous films received is the book *Morals of the Movie* by Dr. Ellis Paxon Oberholtzer, a member of the Pennsylvania state censorship board, written in 1922.[19] In his polemic, Oberholtzer condemns these films and their distributor, who "often comes to me with the statement that it is educational." For Oberholtzer, as with Justice Gavegon, the claims to moral education are belied by the overwhelming capitalist interest in exploiting the public's desire for forbidden features. In a fascinating line of reasoning—especially from a man writing in 1922—he argues:

> The public, sated by much looking at film, night after night, must be aroused from the apathy which comes from having long ago seen all that is proper to be shown, and we have been plunged into an abysmal morass of fornication, adultery, pandering and prostitution.[20]

The satisfaction of this carnal curiosity, however, the good doctor argued, leads to a slippery slope: "To peep into curious and prohibited fields whets the appetite for a clearer and a fuller view, and we have been taken so far that now, surely, there is but little which any of us has not seen in filmdom."[21]

The persistent controversies surrounding white slavery films and "sex pictures" would eventually lead to specific restrictions on films like *Traffic in Souls* because, as Ben Brewster observes, its

> sensational subject matter linked it and a number of other more or less contemporaneous films with a moral panic that eventually resulted in the inclusion of the "white slave trade" (the entrapment of young women into prostitution) in the list of topics explicitly barred under the Hays Office's Production Code.[22]

The Code was filled with admonitions against salacious sexual details, for instance: "Excessive and lustful kissing, lustful embraces, suggestive postures and gestures are not to be shown" and "In general passion should so be treated that scenes do not stimulate the lower and baser element."[23] The Production Code that would come to dominate Hollywood for more than three decades was, in many ways, explicitly written to address the controversies over film morality that arose during these early decades of film's existence.

As noted in the previous chapter, the development of the Production Code in 1930 had only a limited initial effect, due in large part to the resistance of the studios to submitting to its strictures. In the early 1930s, films were filled with "bad girls" and "fallen women"—so much so that Warner Bros. made their inclusion an explicit policy by requiring screenwriters to find ways to "spice up" films by including vice and allusions whenever possible.[24]

Pressure to take the Code more seriously reached a crisis point in 1933 and was driven, to a large degree, by the continued proliferation and popularity of films filled with sexual images and innuendo. One of the principals at the center of these controversies was a female writer and Broadway star whose stage career had been founded on the plainly titled show *Sex*: Mae West.[25] The impact of West's wisecracking and overt, even celebrated, sexuality can hardly be overstated. Lea Jacobs, for instance, observes that in most histories of film, "West is said to have generated negative publicity for Hollywood and contributed to the institution of stricter mechanisms of film censorship in the mid-thirties."[26] One of the effects of West's sudden rise to film prominence with her first major film role in *She Done Him Wrong* (1933) was to spur various groups into more concrete action. As Gerald Gardner contends:

> Hollywood historians have propounded the theory that the Legion of Decency was established primarily to remove Mae West from the screen. It was scarcely six months after the release of her salacious *She Done Him Wrong* that the most virulent form of censorship took hold in the movie colony.[27]

The reaction to West's first major film, however, was not exclusively negative. Made for a mere $200,000, the film would rake in a healthy $2 million in the United States and an additional million in overseas markets. West became an overnight sensation for film audiences, but West's rise to global prominence only fueled the controversy further.[28] Malcolm D. Phillips contended in a contemporary editorial in the popular magazine *Picturegoer*:

> She should never have been invested with the glamour of a goddess or the importance of a prophet. She should never have been boosted to an eminence that sets a film character that is little more than a common courtesan up as an example and a model for the girlhood of the world.[29]

Mae West, of course, was not alone. The Austrian-Czech import *Ecstasy*, featuring an early performance by Hedy Lamarr, caused a furor with its depiction of sexual pleasure and a scene in which a nude Lamarr is seen walking in the woods. While newspapers and critics railed against this film as an example of European degeneracy invading America's theaters, the film's distributors seized upon its notorious reputation and its lengthy struggle with censors and U.S. Customs agents to promote the film with taglines like "Suppressed Until Now! US Customs has finally released the most amazing motion picture ever produced!"[30] Domestic films also continued pushing boundaries. At the same time *She Done Him Wrong* was going into production, Paramount purchased the rights to William Faulkner's novel *Sanctuary*, the story of a willful young Southern belle who ends up violated and forced into prostitution by a bootlegger. The film adaptation, *The Story of Temple Drake*, received mixed reviews but helped to further enflame the controversy over sex in film and the supposed functions of the new Hays Production Code. As the critic for the *Chicago Tribune* exclaimed: "I've been investigating a sewer. Where's all the clean talk of Hays to women's clubs?"[31] The controversy generated by "degeneracy" in films continued to prove useful in promotion. Ads for *Temple Drake* included taglines like "She tried to be respectable ... but the unconquerable wild streak couldn't be controlled," and in theaters such as the Colonial in Lincoln, Nebraska, additional interest was generated with the declaration "The management suggests that children do not see this picture as it is strictly adult entertainment."[32]

It should not be surprising that when Joseph Breen took over the Production Code Administration (PCA) and Hollywood was forced to take the Code seriously, one of the first targets was the lurid nature of contemporary films. As one clear indication of the changes, Mae West's 1933 follow-up to *She Done Him Wrong* was a film titled *I'm No Angel*. In this romantic comedy, West plays a lion tamer in a small circus who makes it to New York, where she seeks to both take advantage of her various suitors and find her one true love. Teamed again with Cary Grant, this comedic gem is rife with sexual innuendo and double entendres. The cultural shift effected by the Code becomes clear when examining some of West's later films, including *Klondike Annie*, which was released in 1936, two years into the Code era. In *Klondike Annie*, West plays a San Francisco entertainer who has murdered her Chinese lover and seeks to escape the police by, after a series of mishaps, taking on the identity of a Salvation Army missionary worker. In spite of the fact that this film removed a vast majority of the sexual humor that had made her earlier films so successful, newspaper tycoon William Randolph Hearst still railed against it, asking if society had to continue to endure "motion pictures that exalt disreputable living and glorify vice?"[33] One can only imagine what Hearst would have written had he seen the original screenplay before Breen and his PCA cohorts forced the removal of lines like "Men are at their best when women are at their worst" and "Give a man a free hand and he puts it all over you."[34]

Of course, not all filmmakers were willing to quietly accept the strictures of the Code, and the occasional moments of open defiance caused additional controversy. Perhaps one of the most notorious and spectacular such controversies surrounded a mediocre B cowboy movie made by an eccentric millionaire. Howard Hughes's *The Outlaw* tells the story of a love triangle between Billy the Kid, Doc Holliday, and a woman named Rio, played by Jane Russell. The film's plot caused considerable consternation at the PCA. Responding to the final draft of the screenplay, Breen leveled various charges against the film's Code violations. "Billy is characterized as a major criminal who is allowed to go free and unpunished.... There are also two sequences suggestive of illicit sex between Billy and Rio." There was also the admonition "There must be no exposure of Rio's person in the scene where her dress is torn."[35] The final film version was even more audacious, featuring, among other offending elements, numerous scenes with a scantily clad Russell. The day after screening the film, Breen fired off an angry memo to his boss William Hays, part of which read:

> In recent months we have noted a marked tendency on the part of the studios to more and more undrape women's breasts.... Yesterday, we had the exhibition of breast shots in Howard Hughes's picture *The Outlaw*, which outdoes anything we have ever seen on the motion picture screen.[36]

Careful negotiations ensued, and after a number of strategic cuts, Hughes's film received a Seal of Approval from the PCA in 1941.

Inexplicably, though perhaps due to his involvement in the manufacture of aircraft for the war in Europe, Hughes shelved *The Outlaw* until 1943. The film was then released with a torrent of suggestive advertisements and billboard featuring pinup-style photos of Russell and taglines like "Sex has not been rationed" and "Would you like to tussle with Russell?" Critics largely panned the film both for its poor quality and disjointed editing and for its clear affront to established Hollywood moral standards. The Catholic Legion of Decency also condemned the film. Yet in spite, or perhaps because, of these condemnations, *The Outlaw* became an enormous success.[37]

Code controversies were generally a good predictor of success for a film, especially when the controversy was over matters of sex. Hollywood increasingly learned ways to skirt the letter of the censorship law while providing maximum provocation. One of the sources for some of the more lurid tales was the live theater. It is interesting in this regard that live theater had more freedom to depict subjects on the moral boundaries—subjects like infidelity, homosexuality, rape, and so forth—than did the motion picture theater, reaffirming the suggestion made earlier that film somehow has been culturally positioned as uniquely dangerous.

The Tennessee Williams play *A Streetcar Named Desire* debuted on Broadway in 1947 and enjoyed a long and successful run, as well as winning the Pulitzer Prize. Charles Feldman optioned the rights to the play and, with a distribution agreement with Warner Bros., brought playwright Williams along with the play's director, Elia Kazan, and much of the cast, including Marlon Brando, Kim Hunter, and Karl Malden, to re-create their dramatic action for the movies. Not surprisingly, the PCA had considerable objections to the play, especially as it broached numerous subjects—rape, sex with a minor, and another story line in which Blanche's first husband is revealed to be a homosexual—that were strictly forbidden in the Production Code. Joseph Breen recommended a number of changes to the film, including cutting dialogue about Blanche's first husband and crafting the "rape scene" as if it were purely a delusion in Blanche's mind.[38] In their negotiations with the PCA, the trio of Warner Bros., Kazan, and Williams was generally successful. The dialogue about homosexuality was masked with words like "sensitive," and while the rape was allowed to remain in the film, there was a moral consequence, as the ending of the film implies, at least for some viewers, that Stella will leave Stanley as a result of his violent attack on her sister.

The battles over *Streetcar*, however, were not finished. When the film was screened for members of the Catholic Church's Legion of Decency, the film was immediately regarded as worthy of the dreaded Condemned rating, meaning Catholics were essentially forbidden from seeing it. Fearful of the public controversy and losing a vast swath of its potential audience, Warner Bros. hired one of the leaders of the Legion, a man named Martin Quigley, to reedit the film. Kazan and Williams were furious, but their objections were rebuffed by both the Church leaders and by Warner Bros., which held contractual rights to a final edit. The controversy spilled over into the public arena when Kazan wrote an op-ed piece for the *New York*

Times recounting his ordeal and the external forces conspiring to rework his film. In Kazan's words, the studio

> at once assumed that no Catholic would buy a ticket. They feared further that theatres showing the picture would be picketed, might be threatened with boycotts of as long as a year's duration if they dared to show it, that priests would be stationed in the lobbies to take down the names of parishioners who attended. I was told that all these things had happened in Philadelphia when a picture with a "C" rating was shown there, and, further, that the rating was an invitation for every local censor board in the country to snipe at a picture, to require cuts or to ban it altogether.[39]

Kazan objected to the cuts by this external agency, arguing, "My picture had been cut to fit the specifications of a code which is not my code, is not the recognized code of the picture industry, and is not the code of the great majority of the audience." Such cuts, Kazan contended, damaged the integrity of the film and the authority of the creative artist.

Reactions to Kazan's polemic were, not surprisingly, mixed. One letter writer declared, "I protest most vehemently against such an arbitrary and unjustified suppression of a worthwhile motion picture, even in part." Other writers, however, argued that, as one put it, "The Legion of Decency also has a great concern for the public" and that Kazan cannot claim immunity from criticism.[40] A few months after this exchange, Kazan would be thrown back into the public spotlight when he was called to testify about his membership in a Communist group by the House Committee on Un-American Activities.

Streetcar was, of course, not the only Broadway play whose adaptation to the silver screen caused controversy. Another was Robert Anderson's 1953 play *Tea and Sympathy*, which was a smash hit in New York and coincidentally was directed for the stage by Elia Kazan. The play centers on a boys' private boarding school and one particular young man named Tom Lee, a "sensitive" and shy boy who finds himself bullied and, eventually, accused of being a homosexual. After his attempt to prove his "manhood" with a local prostitute fails, Lee shares his problems with Laura, the attractive wife of the school's headmaster. Laura eventually chooses to help the boy establish his manhood by engaging in an illicit sexual affair with him.

Numerous studios expressed interest in the play but were consistently discouraged by the Production Code Administration. The play's central conceits were dangerous areas under the Code. The accusation of homosexuality was strictly forbidden, and the affair between the headmaster's wife and the young boy would have to be depicted in such a way as to condemn it unequivocally. Censors also cautioned the interested studios that the boy's visit to a prostitute was also a potential Code violation.[41] MGM decided to take the gamble on this hot Broadway property and hired

Anderson to adapt his play for the screen. The issue of homosexuality was heavily masked, and the word "homosexual" and all of its more negative euphemisms were absent. Additionally, the relationship between Laura and Tom was addressed in an epilogue set years later when the now grown-up Tom has written a novel dramatizing his time in school and Laura writes Tom a final letter expressing her regrets over the affair.

These changes satisfied the PCA, and the film was granted a Seal of Approval, but once again, the Legion of Decency raised serious objections. As with the earlier episode over *Streetcar*, the studio worked closely with the Legion's Martin Quigley to bring the film into line with the Legion's values. This time Quigley played the role of screenwriter as he rewrote the final letter from Laura to Tom, adding lines like "You have romanticized the wrong we did, you have evaded the unpleasant reality."[42] The altered version of *Tea and Sympathy*, directed by Vincente Minnelli, was a box office success, and due in large part to its alterations at the hands of various censors, it did not cause any substantial controversies. Although not raising the kind of public outrage that occurred over *Streetcar*, writer Anderson was quoted as bitterly vowing, "I will never give in again. You become convinced you're saving the story, but you're not."[43]

Portrayals of homosexuals had, of course, long been part of Hollywood's repertoire. These were generally not positive depictions, though they were often regarded by religious and other moral conservatives as dangerous and subversive. As Thomas Doherty observed, "The imputation of homosexuality, played usually for laughs, sometimes as threat, and most subversively as alternative, was the most scandalous vice element."[44] But the prohibition against any suggestion of homosexuality would gradually be eroded.

Following his box office success with *Ben-Hur* in 1959, director William Wyler announced that his follow-up would be an adaptation of Lillian Hellman's 1934 play *The Children's Hour*, a story in which a young schoolgirl accuses two of her headmistresses of being lesbians, leading one of them to commit suicide. Wyler had directed a heavily altered adaptation of the play in 1936 titled *These Three* but now wanted to bring a closer adaptation to the screen with a screenplay by Hellman herself. When the PCA balked at the plan, citing the prohibition against homosexuality in films, United Artists, which planned to distribute Wyler's film, stepped in and threatened to distribute the film without a seal—a viable option in 1959 since the system of block booking that had maintained studio solidarity with the PCA had been dismantled in 1948. Due in part to this pressure, on October 3, 1961, the Code was amended with the following: "In keeping with the culture, the mores and the values of our time, homosexuality and other sexual aberrations may now be treated with care, discretion and restraint."[45]

Wyler's film, which starred Audrey Hepburn and Shirley MacLaine, received some criticism from both sides of the increasingly visible cultural tension over sexual orientation. Critics such as Bosley Crowther criticized the film for portraying an old-fashioned view of homosexuality, writing, "It is incredible that educated people living in an urban American community today would react as violently and cruelly to a questionable innuendo."[46] On the other side, the conservative magazine *Films in Review* accused the film of "condoning lesbianism, albeit surreptitiously," and further asserted that lesbianism drove women to insanity and suicide.[47] Wyler's film, while in many ways unsuccessful in terms of its adaptation of Hellman's play, did open an important door, and within a year other films touching on the subject appeared, including Otto Preminger's *Advice and Consent* (1962), Edward Dmytryk's *Walk on the Wild Side* (1962), and Jean Genet's *The Balcony* (1963).

As noted in chapter 1, the influence of the Production Code waned dramatically in the 1960s, and by the time the Motion Picture Association of America (MPAA) approved *Who's Afraid of Virginia Woolf* in 1966, the restrictions of the Code had essentially been eliminated. In many ways, the history of the Code era—that period between 1934 and roughly 1966—is a history of contained controversies over sex, gender, and sexuality. Throughout this period, disputes erupted between the PCA and other moral guardians, most notably the Catholic Legion of Decency, and between these censors and filmmakers. The controversies were "contained" in that the emotional and political energy of the objections to a given film were typically channeled into existing institutions.

After the Code came the rating system, in essentially the same form we have today. In this era, the first and most dramatic series of sexual controversies revolved around the dreaded rating of X. The X rating publicly validated "adult films" and in so doing opened a door, at least briefly, for explicitly sexual films to become part of mainstream American cinema. Changes in American cultural mores surrounding sex during the "sexual revolution" of the late 1960s and early 1970s created an atmosphere in which open and explicit discussions of sex, gender, and sexuality were becoming part of mainstream culture. As William Masters, coauthor of the popular Masters and Johnson sexual study and the 1966 book *The Human Sexual Response*, put it, "The '60s will be called the decade of orgasmic preoccupation."[48] From a corporate point of view, the X rating allowed independent producers the opportunity to engage in this new and initially lucrative market, a market in which mainstream studios would be reluctant to engage directly. As Justin Wyatt observes:

> During a period when increasingly explicit content became more prevalent in response to shifts in the country's demographics and its culture, the category of X served, in part, to configure a market segment of adult viewers ignored by the major studios.[49]

Perhaps the most dramatic and controversial film in this regard was the 1972 film *Deep Throat*. This now-legendary film starred Linda Lovelace as a sexually frustrated woman seeking satisfaction and began the brief cultural moment in which hard-core adult films seemed on the verge of becoming part of the American mainstream. *Deep Throat* was received generally well by the critics, many of whom saw it as a lighthearted send-up of earlier private stag films, but it was not greeted warmly by governmental authorities. Without the strictures of the Production Code, *Deep Throat* represented one of the first of many battles in which government officials sought to hold the line against the dangerous content of film. If the industry could no longer provide self-regulation, then it appeared the state and federal government would.

The legal controversies of *Deep Throat* went on for years. In 1972, a New York judge fined New York's World Theatre $3 million for showing the film and had the film itself impounded. The theater owners famously changed their marquee to read: "Judge Cuts Throat—World Mourns."[50] Frank Miller observes, "As attempts to censor *Deep Throat* grew, however, so did its audience."[51] The popularity of the film brought federal prosecutors in on the act, and federal charges were filed against many of the film's backers and one of its actors—Harry Reems, who had been paid the handsome sum of $100 for his one day of work—in a federal court in Memphis. The prosecution of the film by federal authorities, and in particular the targeting of one of the actors, opened an avalanche of controversy, as numerous groups became involved in the struggle between the First Amendment and notions of "decency." The Memphis trial ended with convictions for all involved, including Reems. While these convictions would be overturned on appeal, the opening battle over pornography was joined.

The popularity of *Deep Throat* and a series of subsequent adult films like *The Devil in Miss Jones* opened a brief window in which mainstream studios would dabble in X-rated films. Perhaps the most well-regarded of these was Bernardo Bertolucci's 1973 film *Last Tango in Paris*, starring Marlon Brando and Maria Schneider as two anonymous lovers who engage in a series of sexual encounters in a Paris apartment. The film's combination of filmic artistry and great acting with explicit and at times disturbingly brutal sexual images brought it both praise and condemnation. The growing women's liberation movement in particular targeted Bertolucci's film, and protestors carried signs reading "Porno Kills" and "Repeal the First Amendment" outside theaters screening *Last Tango*. As with *Deep Throat*, *Last Tango* also faced various legal challenges, although these challenges played out differently as *Last Tango* enjoyed the full legal and financial backing of United Artists, which aggressively defended its product. As Jon Lewis notes:

> The controversy contributed significantly to the film's box office success. *Last Tango* is a ponderous and pretentious film; slow moving even by foreign art film standards in 1972. But the legal battles chronicled in newspapers

nationwide allowed UA to exploit the film's controversial content while at the same time insisting in its own print ads that *Last Tango* was first and foremost just an art film.[52]

The end of this "adult/art house" marriage came in 1974 with the release of the French soft-core film *Emmanuelle*. A travelogue of sorts, the film follows the exploits of the title character as she explores her sexual horizons. Distributed by Columbia Pictures, the film enjoyed the backing of a major studio (and their lawyers) as well as strong production values and luscious locations. Yet, in spite of the success of *Emmanuelle* and its predecessors, the film represented the final major excursion of mainstream studios into the arena "adult entertainment." The MPAA and the studios became increasingly aware that the open sexual politics begun in the 1960s were beginning to take a very different shape toward the end of the 1970s.

Increasingly, feminist and women's groups took up the battle against pornographic films. One turning point, according to activist Beverly LaBelle, came with a small independent film entitled *Snuff*. Released in 1975 in order to capitalize on the growing interest in pornographic films, *Snuff* was rumored to contain footage of the actual murder of a young woman, along with scenes of graphic sex. In LaBelle's recollection, the film "finally made the misogyny of pornography a major feminist concern."[53] Various groups such as Women against Violence against Women and Women against Violence and Pornography in the Media cropped up in the late 1970s, and pornography became a major target of feminist criticism. Prominent feminist scholars Andrea Dworkin and Catharine MacKinnon, for instance, sponsored legislation in various cities, including Minneapolis, to outlaw pornography by framing the issue not as one of decency or moral standards but as integral to the civil rights of women. Although the bill was overturned in the courts a year after its passage, the struggle over sexualized images of women continued to be a prominent battle line in the struggle over women's rights.

Controversies over explicit depictions of sex and the notion of pornography would, of course, continue to rage throughout the 1980s and '90s but, for the most part, mainstream American cinema was no longer interested in participating. Some turmoil would emerge in the late 1990s when the MPAA abandoned the category X, with its connotation of pornography, in favor of the supposedly more neutral NC-17, meaning "No children under 17 allowed." Films such as *Henry and June, Showgirls*, and the recent Bertolucci film *The Dreamers* all received this rating. Most directors, like Stanley Kubrick with his last film, *Eyes Wide Shut*, chose to edit their films rather than receive the now-dreaded NC-17, leading to more controversies about the power of the MPAA and its Code and Rating Administration's continuing power to censor films. Interestingly, as in the era of the Code, the vast majority of films targeted for the NC-17 rating have been those that depict sex and sexual activity.

Further complicating the sexual politics of the post-1970s was the emergence of the gay and lesbian rights movement. While there have long been voices urging greater rights and tolerance for gays and lesbians, such as the early Mattachine and homophile societies, the more spectacular and dramatic push for the rights of lesbian, gay, bisexual, and transgendered (LGBT) persons came after the Stonewall riots in 1968. The riots began in Greenwich Village after a fairly routine raid by police at a gay bar, the Stonewall. On this night, however, patrons refused to accept the regular harassment and arrests and, instead, took to the streets for a series of five nights of riots and battles with police that became the opening salvo in the more radical effort to secure rights for people of various sexual orientations.

Portrayals of homosexuality had created controversy for years, but in the post-Stonewall era, these controversies were often instigated by the LGBT community as they objected to the overwhelmingly negative and stereotypical ways they were portrayed. In 1980, for instance, two films, *Cruising* and *Windows*, were protested by members of the LGBT community because of the ways they linked homosexuality and violence.

By far the more incendiary of the two was William Friedkin's *Cruising*, based on a novel of the same name, which was in turn based on the real murders of gay men in New York City.[54] The film was crafted as a police procedural, with Al Pacino playing a detective sent undercover into the leather S&M bar scene of the gay community in search of a killer who murders his victims during or immediately following rough sexual encounters. While the violence within the film and the perceived reduction of the entire gay community to the smaller subset of S&M aficionados were cause for much protest, so too was the film's ending, which at least implies that a now sexually confused Pacino murders his kind and supportive gay neighbor. Reactions among the gay community to the novel were strong, and advance word that the film version would be shooting in New York City led to massive protests aimed at disrupting the shooting schedule and articulating the deep concern that the film not contribute to the demonization of the gay community.[55] Protestors shined mirrors onto sets, blew whistles during filming, and raged against the film in various public forums.

These protests had some effect. While Friedkin insisted that "*Cruising* is not about homosexuality," the angry protests of his film, even while in production, led the director to add an explicit statement to this effect that would run at the beginning of the film.[56] Controversies over the film did not end with this disclaimer nor were they limited to New York. In Boston, for example, the mayor's liaison to the homosexual communities asked a local theater owner for an advance screening of the film before it opened to the public. Outside theaters across the country protestors handed out leaflets reading "People will die because of this film," and as Vito Russo recounts, this may have been in fact the case: "In November 1980, outside the Ramrod Bar, the site of the filming of *Cruising*, a minister's son emerged from a car with an Israeli submachine gun and killed two gay men."[57]

The controversy surrounding *Cruising*, while certainly not the first of its kind, was one of the more spectacular moments of protest surrounding the portrayal of members of the LGBT community. Ironically, just a few weeks before the release of *Cruising*, United Artists released *Windows*, another film with a gay-related theme. Directed by Gordon Willis, it depicts a lesbian, played by Elizabeth Ashley, who is obsessed with her attractive next-door neighbor, played by Talia Shire. Her obsession with Shire's character is so great that she hires a tough taxi driver to assault the woman in the hopes that it will make her hate men and become a lesbian. David Denby famously denounced Willis's film, writing, "*Windows* exists only in the perverted fantasies of men who hate lesbians so much they will concoct any idiocy in order to slander them."[58]

Friedkin's *Cruising* did not fare much better with the critics. Vincent Canby blasted the film, contending, "Because *Cruising* was such a muddle-brained, nervously dishonest movie, it destroyed itself, rendering moot all questions about the film maker's responsibility to observable political and social truth."[59] Gay and lesbian protestors, however, did not agree that the film's failed quality evacuated the filmmaker's moral responsibility, and in the wake of the protests over *Cruising* a more galvanized movement emerged. As Russo notes: "*Cruising* was the last straw in a long stream of Hollywood horrors. Coming as it did in company with *Windows* and *American Gigolo*, it acted as a catalyst for a massive nationwide protest of the Hollywood treatment of gays."[60]

The complex sexual politics surrounding American film would continue into the 1990s and, for that matter, to the present day. Thus, when Jonathan Demme stepped upon the land mine of gender and sexuality with his 1991 thriller *The Silence of the Lambs*, he was following a long line of American filmmakers who have found their work provoking cries and accusations they had not anticipated. As we prepare to turn more fully to the controversies surrounding *Silence*, it is worth considering what lessons the history of sex and cinema can provide, and at this early stage in this book, it is worth drawing out some of the lessons that may be helpful throughout our exploration of film controversies. Here I want to attend to five such lessons learned.

First, the controversies over any type of film are largely defined in terms of who has the authority to redress grievances. In other words, people tend to complain to the institution they think can change things. The pre-Code era was rife with appeals to local, state, and even federal authorities to intervene in the regulation of film. Controversies during the period of the strong Production Code, however, were more likely to involve disputes over the PCA's, or at times the Legion of Decency's, authority and warrant for making particular cuts. The era immediately following the Code saw a gradual shift to what might be characterized as a "public relations" form of controversy—one aimed more at shaming a particular corporate entity, especially studios or theater chains.

In a way, these three broad phases might be considered judicial, regulative, and market focused. In the first phase, those embroiled in controversies over films were likely to appeal to legal frameworks for the protection of certain core social values—thus, an appeal to judicial authorities to render judgment concerning the legality of a given film. In the second phase, appeals were aimed at certain institutional entities but, importantly, entities devoid of specific powers of law. Here the focus was, in a way, less on the legal notions of right and wrong, or even cultural or social values, and more on the regulatory policies and procedures established by a specific entity, in this case the PCA. Thus, when Elia Kazan contested the cuts made to *Streetcar*, his argument was based not on issues of the First Amendment, as had been the case in previous decades, but on the right of the Legion of Decency to make cuts that were "not the recognized code of the picture industry." In the immediate aftermath of the Code, entering the third phase, there were certainly moments when the appeals were addressed mainly to legal institutions—especially with regard to pornography—but soon the focus of much of the protest shifted toward the underlying corporate motive of filmmaking, namely, profit. The protestors in the 1980s and '90s seemed increasingly aware of the power of negative publicity to shame a studio into backing away from particularly offensive stances; witness Friedkin's decision to place a disclaimer at the beginning of *Cruising*.

Certainly there can be no doubt that these different frameworks of authority are always overlapping and that, in this way, the three periods sketched out above are not distinct. Filmmakers in the 1920s were certainly motivated by corporate profit interests and sought to avoid negative publicity, just as filmmakers in the twenty-first century run the risk of ending up in a courtroom should they too drastically violate social norms and mores. But there does seem to have been a drift in recent years away from judicial and regulatory avenues and more directly toward a kind of public relations of shame approach.

A second major lesson to be derived from the history of sex controversies in film is the relationship between controversies and social norms. As I noted earlier in this chapter, sexuality seems to be a unique point of moral concern for the broader society, and controversies over representations of sexuality tend to focus on fairly abstract senses of morality and social norms. There seem to be two ways in which a particular film can provoke controversy in relation to these social norms. One, and perhaps the most obvious, is when films depict acts or attitudes that are in gross violation of existing norms concerning, in the present case, sex, sexuality, or gender. It is, as suggested in the introduction, an instance in which society's taken-for-granted assumption that no one would violate a particular social norm is shaken and people are drawn out to vocally and vociferously defend the norms and mores that they had previously believed went without saying. On the other hand, and perhaps not quite as obviously, there are also times when controversies erupt around the depictions of social norms that, while accepted by the vast majority of a society, are deemed harmful or limiting to a particular subset. This is clearly the case for both the feminist and gay critiques of films like *Snuff* or *Cruising*. The objection to both films was *not* that these films somehow cut against the grain of the regular social order but, rather, that they were depictions of precisely the normal patterns of society. The objection lay, therefore, not in the aberrance of the representation but in the oppressive social order accurately represented. The norm, in other words, was the problem—not necessarily the film.

A third lesson about the importance of controversies is that they draw other voices into the social dialogue about a particular issue, and this is a lesson derived from history. Thus, controversies over the white slavery films of the 1910s provided one platform through which social reformers and feminists could engage in the wider discussion of the social norms surrounding sex, gender, and sexuality. When Inez Millholland Boissevain wrote in the defense of films like *Traffic in Souls*, it was clearly not meant solely for the defense of these films but as an effort to challenge the existing strictures that limited public discussions of sex and sexuality, and when Elia Kazan took his complaint against the Legion of Decency to the pages of the *New York Times*, it served not only to promote his version of *A Streetcar Named Desire* but also as a challenge to the intertwinement of religion and Hollywood with regard to film censorship.

Thinking specifically about controversies over sex, gender, and sexuality, the history of controversies has served not so much to expand the public dialogue as to complicate it. With the introduction of new players, old participants are crowded out by the emergence of new interests. For quite some time, really throughout the period of the Production Code, one voice—that of the Catholic Church—held an especially important position in the various public discussions of sex and cinema. The emergence of new voices—the Beat generation, the Kinsey and Masters and Johnson reports, and others—served to shift the ground of public debate until by 1966 the voice of the Catholic Church and its conservative members was gradually crowded out. Soon, however, other issues and other controversies emerged. Feminists challenged the new sexualized cinema not on moral or religious grounds but on the basis of the civil rights of women. Thus, in an interesting twist of history, when some feminist critics were seeking to drastically restrict the production and dissemination of pornography, they found themselves in a political alliance with conservative religious leaders. Controversies, it would seem, make strange bedfellows.

The fourth element of the shifting dynamics of the sexual politics of film is the way that different elements of a film can become controversial. A simplistic attitude would be that films become more daring as time goes on, and at one level, this is true. When we watch early films, for example, the scandalous *Kiss* from 1896, the supposedly shocking element seems almost laughable. But this attitude may diminish the fact that it is not the films that change but our attitudes and points of view—here I cannot help but think of Doctor Oberholtzer's declaration in 1922 that surely audiences had seen every sexual thing that could possibly be shown.

Another thing we may miss with this "historical" point of view is the way that, as our viewpoints change, different elements of a given film may begin to stick out as provocative and disturbing. I can give two personal examples of historically noncontroversial films that, upon recent viewing, struck me as borderline offensive. The first is a timeless classic aired numerous times every year around Christmas time, Frank Capra's *It's a Wonderful Life* from 1946. By my count, there were no real scandals over this film in its time nor, for that matter, many since. But, looking through my twenty-first-century liberal eyes, I find the scene in which George Bailey angrily and violently shakes his wife jarring. I felt a similar reaction in a recent viewing of George Sydney's 1953 musical *Kiss Me Kate*, in the scene in which Howard Keel dramatically spanks Kathryn Grayson's character during their theatrical number. I suspect that my own sensitization to these moments of violence toward women was derived largely from the social changes wrought by controversies—controversies that occurred after those films were released but before my viewing of them. Controversies, in other words, can make viewing films a much more politically complicated endeavor.

Our fifth and final lesson from the historical controversies over sex and film is that films are, as suggested in the introduction, conceived as especially dangerous in American culture. At one level, it is odd that sex causes so much hysteria in American culture given the simple fact that none of us would be here if someone somewhere had not had sex. At a more interesting level, it is notable that film has historically been the most restricted of the media. Plays like *Tea and Sympathy* and even *Who's Afraid of Virginia Woolf?* were running on Broadway with little or no reaction, but when producers sought to bring these narratives to film, the moral guardians were provoked. This is not to diminish the long history of controversies over censorship in literature or theater, of course, but simply to observe that film has always been considered the most dangerous of these media of popular culture.

Here we can note two historical roots to this peculiar treatment of motion pictures. The first is that, as early as the first nickelodeon boom, cinema has been a form of mass entertainment. More than either literature or theater, although probably less than television, film is a medium of the masses, and it is precisely its populist character that has led many critics to fear that the messages it dispenses might be received uncritically by its audience. There is, in other words, a decidedly elitist strain in the attitude that film is somehow more dangerous. The second root, one deeply related to the first, is an abiding fear of visual representations. Seeing is, after all, tantamount to believing, and this fear of visual depictions in cinema can be traced all the way back to that legendary story of the Lumière brothers' threatening train. While the literal apprehension that filmic images might emerge into reality has subsided, if indeed it ever existed, there remains a clear worry that the images on screen will manifest themselves in the attitudes and behaviors of audience members. This attitude was expressed by Jane Addams in the earliest days of cinema when she voiced a fear that films would lead to bad behavior through mimicry. When protestors handed out leaflets outside showings of William Friedkin's *Cruising* proclaiming that "People will die because of this film," they were evincing a very similar concern.

Films, it would appear, are potentially very dangerous entities, but so too are controversies.

SEXUAL POLITICS AND *THE SILENCE OF THE LAMBS*

The spectacular controversy over *The Silence of the Lambs* that erupted outside the Dorothy Chandler Pavilion on the night of the 1992 Academy Awards follows along lines traced above. Fearing that the homophobic image of the "killer homosexual" would spark further repression and violence toward members of the gay, lesbian, bisexual, and transgendered communities, protestors targeted the film as dangerous. What makes this particular controversy so interesting as an example of the complex sexual politics surrounding film is that there were other fronts to this battle. In addition to contesting the attitudes of the dominant society and the film-making industry, those incensed by *Silence*'s homophobia also found themselves in a contest over interpretation with members of the feminist community, typically good allies in battles over sex and gender oppression. For many gay male critics, the film's antagonist, Buffalo Bill, was another in a long line of homophobic representations, while, for some feminist critics, it was more important that the film's protagonist, Clarice Starling, represented a strong female character overcoming the barriers of patriarchy. Of course, even within these two broadly conceived communities, there was not unanimity of opinion. For some gay critics, the outrage over *Silence* was just so much misplaced anger, anger largely sparked by the enormity of the AIDS crisis and the government's underwhelming response to it, and for some feminist critics, the lauded Starling was just a puppet of patriarchy. What becomes particularly interesting is the way a film like *Silence* could provoke such politically and emotionally charged responses from so many camps.

Clashes between feminists and members of the LGBT community, while not common, are not entirely unprecedented. Tim Edwards has thematized the occasional tensions between these communities along the lines of the difference between "sexual politics" and the "politics of sexuality." He explains that sexual politics tend to focus on the social oppression of gender roles whereby one's biological sex is used to overly determine one's social identity. In this line of critique, words like *fireman* engender a sexually oppressive politics in which a certain social identity— here, of a firefighter—is predetermined by one's biological sex—here, a man. Sex is problematic because it is used as the major defining characteristic of one's sense of self. Those engaged in the politics of sexuality, on the other hand, view sex and sexuality as one of the key defining characteristics of one's identity but want to argue that the limitation of sexuality to a single heterosexual orientation lies at the heart of a vast web of oppression.[61]

In early 1991, Jonathan Demme's film *The Silence of the Lambs* found itself landing squarely along the fault lines between gays and feminists and between sexual politics and the politics of sexuality. What made this controversy all the more poignant and bitter is that in many instances it pitted long-time political partners against each other. No longer was the battle simply against a sexually oppressive society; now it was also against those who were once considered friends and allies. While there have been and continue to be many differences among and between the gay and feminist communities, there have been more and deeper points of agreement. In the controversy over how to interpret *Silence*, however, the participants engaged not only in seeking to establish the rightness or wrongness of the film but also in challenging the interpretations of their traditional friends and allies. At times, the main question seemed to be not "How could they make such a film?" but "How could you not see how offensive (or uplifting) this film is to me?"

As a bit of background for those unfamiliar with the film, Demme's *Silence* is based on the novel of the same name by Thomas Harris and revolves around the Federal Bureau of Investigation's search for a serial killer. This killer, nicknamed Buffalo Bill, abducts female victims, kills them, removes portions of their skin, and then dumps their bodies in a river. The film later reveals that Bill is seeking to create a "suit" of women's skin to construct a new transsexual identity. FBI trainee Clarice Starling is sent by her superiors to interview incarcerated serial killer Dr. Hannibal "the Cannibal" Lecter to seek clues about Buffalo Bill. Through a series of harrowing interviews, Starling exchanges dark personal memories for information from Lecter. The plot gains momentum when

Catherine Martin, a U.S. senator's daughter, is abducted by Bill. Starling pieces together the clues given by Lecter and goes to confront the killer alone, eventually killing him in his dungeon-like basement. In the end, Starling rescues Martin and becomes a full-fledged FBI agent, and Lecter escapes to pursue revenge on his tormentors.

As noted earlier in this chapter, the film was remarkably well received by both audiences and critics, and its recognition by the Academy of Motion Picture Arts and Sciences is virtually unprecedented. The overwhelmingly positive reception of the film contributed, no doubt, to the viciousness with which critics of the film attacked it, and on the flip side of this dynamic, Adrienne Donald argues that "it's possible to see the Academy's decision to honor *The Silence of the Lambs* as the industry's professional refusal to bend to outside political pressure."[62]

The Gay and Lesbian Alliance against Defamation protested *Silence* because, as Executive Director Richard Jenkins explained, "The film is a continuation of Hollywood's appalling track record in portraying gays in negative ways ... and could potentially lead to gay bashing."[63] Writing in *The Nation*, film critic Stuart Klawans put his interpretation of the Buffalo Bill character quite bluntly: "The secret of Jack the Ripper has been revealed at last: He's a fag."[64] While a majority of feminist and female critics embraced Demme's film because of its strong female protagonist, other feminist critics responded negatively to the ambiguous relationship between Starling and her male "superiors," contending that she was far less liberated than she appeared.[65] Others felt that the film was still trapped in the traditional Hollywood vision in which women are the unique victims of sexualized violence and death. The dramatic contrast among reactions to Demme's film lends credence to Elizabeth Young's contention that *Silence* lies at the intersection of "the complex connections among feminist, gay male, and lesbian theories of difference."[66]

In the remainder of this section, I want to focus more closely on the internal microphysics of this controversy in order to gain some sense of how people argue for their interpretation of a controversial film.[67] In order to do this, I focus on one set of arguments issued about the film. As a reaction to the growing controversy, in March 1991 *The Village Voice* invited nine prominent critics to respond to Demme's film and "the fire it's ignited." The forum was titled "Writers on the Lamb: Sorting Out the Sexual Politics of a Controversial Film" and featured many of the better-known figures from the various sides of the dispute.[68]

In reading carefully through these responses—responses both to the film and to the various sides represented in the controversy surrounding it—three main approaches to engaging the question of interpreting the film emerge. At issue in this dispute is how the various communities ought to respond to the film and, perhaps as important, how the various sides in the dispute should relate to each other. In my reading of these nine brief essays, the authors base their argument for interpretation on

- the consequences of interpretation
- the question of authority
- the notion of subjectivity.

By exploring the ways people engage the issues of consequence, authority, and subjectivity, we may gain a clearer sense of how people seek to make sense of and resolve controversies over films.

Prominent gay activist and cultural critic Larry Kramer's is the first essay to appear in this series, and he utilizes an interesting amalgam of strategies to focus the reader's attention on the consequences of interpretation.[69] The focus here is on what happens when we accept a film like *Silence*. From Kramer's perspective, and that of others, choosing to keep silent over *Silence* can only lead to dangerous, even murderous, consequences. Other than a few opening comments disparaging the film's lack of believability, Kramer relies on the words of an external authority, "Dr. Richard Isay, who is a clinical professor of psychiatry at Cornell Medical Center and author of the book *Being Homosexual*."[70] Dr. Isay explains that "there is no doubt" the character of Buffalo Bill is depicted as a transsexual who is also a homosexual, at which point Kramer parenthetically reminds us that "most transsexuals are heterosexual" and that the character in the Thomas Harris novel is not a homosexual. The lengthy quotation from the psychiatrist expresses concern over the consequences of the "homophobic" characterization, which include playing on unconscious heterosexual hatred and diminishing the self-esteem of gay men.

Kramer's strategy is interesting. In a way, knowing that he has already become a clearly partisan participant in this dispute, he chooses to turn his response over to a more apparently neutral—here medical science stands both as neutral and as authoritative—voice who establishes two key "facts" about the film. First, that it does depict Buffalo Bill as a homosexual—unlike the original source novel—and, second, that the consequence of this depiction will be to further harm people already damaged by a homophobic society.

The dangerous consequences of interpretation are also played out in other responses, often in more grim and stark imagery. For example, Stephen Harvey, film curator at the Museum of Modern Art, paints a vivid and disturbing scenario in which Demme's film incites a "credulous homophobe out there in the dark."[71] Following a line of reasoning that traces back at least from Jane Addams through the protests over films like *Snuff* and *Cruising*, Harvey argues that the representations on the screen will play out in the real world through film's power to create mimicry in its audience.

A very different take on the issue of the consequences of interpretation is evident in the short essay by writer and art critic Gary Indiana.[72] In his essay, Indiana focuses on the consequences of the controversy itself:

> Given the hyperbolic, censorious reaction to *The Silence of the Lambs* from certain quarters, "debate" about the film's intentions and possible effects seems a moot issue. Instead, I think a discussion of the quality of the reaction may ultimately prove more useful to people concerned about this film.

The "gay community," Indiana contends, has encouraged the substitution of demagoguery for rational argument because of the twin specters of envying the straight community and mourning the tragedy of AIDS. Thus, Indiana bemoans "the style of argument that hypothesizes that because your friends are dying, your own lunatic ravings against the people you envy are haloed in nobility." Indiana parallels these interpretations of *Silence* with the rantings of McCarthy-era demagogues and likens the particularly vehement critic Michelangelo Signorile to "an especially unattractive infant proudly crapping his diapers in public."

Bracketing the irony of Indiana's hyperbolic response to these "over-reacting" critics, his comments focus squarely on the consequences of interpreting the film. For him, the failure of his community to engage in rational dialogue endangers the community as a whole. Failing to learn the lessons of the past leads gay critics to become "thugs" and "menaces" to the very community they seek to defend. Indiana laments, "I wish their friends better friends."

Despite differing interpretations of the film, Kramer, Harvey, and Indiana utilize the same basis for their comments: The profound consequences of interpretation for their community. These writers seek to oppose certain interpretations on the grounds of a collective well-being that consists of at least three layers: the dangerous material consequences of a homophobic society; the psychic scars suffered by gay males; and the fragile bonds of community.

Another prominent theme in these essays is the question of authority—whose interpretation should hold sway and what the consequences of this authority are. One of the most obvious sources for authority of interpreting the film is the author, here understood to be the director Jonathan Demme, and several of the essays take up Demme's position and responsibility in relation to the film. It is worth noting on this point that Demme had come out fairly early in the controversy saying that the serial killer Buffalo Bill was not a homosexual and pointing to one brief line in the film to that effect. His efforts to explain away the interpretation of Buffalo Bill as homophobic stereotype, however, were far from successful.

In his essay, Harvey mocks Demme's "hip" status, noting that "the people who made the film have such cool credentials—I bet some of their best friends are gay and everything," and the way critics "twist themselves into

pretzels" to defend Demme and the film from the charges of "a few laven-
der spoilsports." Harvey charges that Demme's attempts to defend the film
represent failure of both his ability—"Demme merits at best a C– in Mise-
en-Scene 101"—and his ethical responsibility. The film is, Harvey contends, designed to "extract maximum bucks from the broadest possible
public," and this design includes the use of homophobic clichés that may
incite violence against homosexuals. By exploiting the flames of homophobic prejudice in the name of profit, "Lecter and Gumb won't be the only
ones with blood on their hands."[73]

The Nation's film critic Stuart Klawans also writes about Jonathan
Demme's efforts to refute gay protests, but Klawans defends Demme while
condemning the film.[74] "[Demme] says he did not intend old Death Fag to
be seen as a homosexual, and I believe him, I don't understand, but I
believe him." What remains for Klawans to reason out for the reader is
how "a filmmaker of Demme's expertise" could have produced such a horrific misunderstanding. Two reasons for Demme's mistake are presented.
First, Klawans notes that, whatever Demme's artistic intentions, the image
of a "blond man in a nightgown" will not appear as a tortured soul but as
a "blond man in a nightgown." Second, and moving to a broader context,
he argues that the way images attain meaning is through repetition, "when
enough images have accumulated of blond men in nightgowns, all of them
meaning queen." Klawans concludes by arguing that Demme may have
intended to change these clichés but was ultimately unable to overcome the
unique hegemonic oppression of sexual orientation.

Novelist and activist Jewelle Gomez also focuses her concern on Demme
as filmmaker.[75] Noting the quirky charm of Demme's earlier films, she questions his decision to forgo character development in favor of "skillful editing
and gross generalizations" that leave the film lacking in depth and psychological sophistication. For Gomez, the speed and tightness of the film leaves
Demme "open to attack for contributing to the negative images of gay
men." While applauding the strong female character of Starling, Gomez
condemns Demme for choosing dramatic tension over political sensitivity.

Martha Gever, prominent lesbian activist and media critic, focuses her
essay on the character of Clarice Starling, though she rejects the idea of the
female FBI trainee as a feminist hero.[76] For Gever, Starling's success is a
result of her subjugation by patriarchal superiors: "No surprise, her heroic
trajectory is plotted by a pantheon of fathers." Between the "good daddies" of her father and Agent Crawford, and the "bad daddies" of Lecter
and Chilton, Starling is consistently outsmarted by the agents of a covert
patriarchal order. But the main thrust of Gever's argument in the essay is
to focus on the condemnation of gay male critics. She writes:

> The movie has even begotten the patronizing scolding of self-appointed
> daddy Larry Kramer, who accused all his gay children ... of complicity in

murder—including, apparently Jodie Foster, whose participation in the film he held up as an example of daughterly disobedience and betrayal.

The vitriolic condemnation of gay male critics, for Gever, is simply another form of male domination.

Film critic Amy Taubin follows a similar tack,[77] focusing her anger on the work of another prominent film critic, Ron Rosenbaum, who likened *Silence* to "soft-core gore-porn."[78] Such "ranting," Taubin contends, suggests that "the object of his wrath may have struck too close to home." Rosenbaum isolates a few seconds of clinically rendered death and expands them to encompass the entire film. Of course, Rosenbaum says his condemnation of the film is in the interest of protecting women from this kind of violence, a claim Taubin rejects: "Rosenbaum takes his role as guardian of the pleasure of *Mademoiselle*'s young readers very seriously. Unfortunately, his patriarchal self-interest blinds him to what women find so empowering," which is "a woman solving the perverse riddles of patriarchy—all by herself."

The remaining two essays are by women who defend *Silence* as an important expression of feminist strength. Additionally, both authors pursue their interpretation based upon the uniqueness of their own subjective point of view. Interestingly, these writers most explicitly deal with the growing rift between the divergent interpretations of *Silence*, demonstrating a clear sense of how much this controversy reveals about the divide between the various competing communities.

The tension between sexual politics and the politics of sexuality seems most apparent in the response of C. Carr,[79] a regular contributor to *The Village Voice*, who questions the axis of paternalist critics like Rosenbaum and gay advocates like Signorile, who called *Silence* "yet another lesson in Homophobia 101."[80] For Carr, the message of the film is clear and simple: "*Silence* is about femaleness as an embattled condition." As in Taubin's essay, Carr attends to the condemnations of the film and of its lead actress Jodie Foster: "Foster has been charged with homophobia by the gay press for the way [Buffalo Bill is] depicted, while the actor who plays him hasn't even been mentioned. And that should clue us in to the sexual politics in this entire debate." For Carr, straight and gay males are linked on an axis of patriarchal oppression. Rosenbaum's "twisted paternalism" fails to understand how women experience the text and seeks to place the blame for gender horror on the film's prominent female. Carr contends that women react so positively to *Silence* because "something in it rings true to what we experience every day."

The final essay, by feminist film critic B. Ruby Rich, most clearly exemplifies the strategy of interpretation based on subjective point of view.[81] Rich begins by noting that the film's "great accomplishment" has been ignored by the "exaggerated chorus sitting in judgment." *Silence* succeeds in breaking the cultural conflation of violence with eroticism by removing any sense of sex from its depiction of violence. The separation of violence and sexuality means "someone like me ... can last all the way to the end, secure in the knowledge that death but not defilement are on the agenda." Rich explains the split between gay and female communities by the difference between male and female points of view: "Male and female desires, fears, and pleasures have rarely coincided, so it should come as no surprise that dyke and faggot reactions to this movie are likely to diverge as well." Thus, in an important move, Rich suggests that the divide between men and women is a more fundamental difference than is the alliance between gays and lesbians fighting for the rights of homosexuals. In placing the primacy on her experience as a woman, Rich positions her essay within a world where "women are hunted and killed everyday," and from her perspective, a film that shows women fighting back and ultimately triumphing without "rely[ing] on a charming man" cannot be reduced to the "pass/fail score of one character." Rich concludes her essay with the only justification her interpretation needs, "Guess I'm just a girl."

The contributors to "Writers on the Lamb" articulate many of the arguments and emotions surrounding the controversial 1991 thriller and in so doing give us a useful vantage point for understanding the ways controversial films provoke audience members and challenge their preconceived notions about themselves, the world around them, and their friends and allies. As these writers observe, Demme's *Silence* clearly plays out differently when considered along the various intersecting lines of sex, gender, and sexuality. For many feminists, Clarice Starling represents the kind of atypical and progressive representation that should serve as a model for future filmmakers seeking to offer models of empowerment to women and not merely degradation. For many of the gay male critics, however, Demme's reliance on the old and overly established "gay male as psycho killer" motif—a theme greatly popularized in Alfred Hitchcock's *Psycho* and dozens of subsequent films—marks the film as politically regressive. In seeking to sort out the sexual politics of the film and its controversy, these writers try to come to grips with the potential consequences of both the film and the resulting dispute over its meaning, the question of who has both the authority and responsibility for interpreting the film, and the way their individual points of view challenge their previously held assumptions of unanimity and consensus.[82]

If we use this controversy as an object lesson for understanding the process of controversy over films, then a few points become important. First, in this exchange there was virtually no discussion of the film itself—in the sense of referring to specific scenes or using specific aspects of the film as evidence for claims about the film. The actual film almost stands outside the question of interpretation, and the focus is more on the interpreter than on the thing interpreted. This seems a persistent theme, one most dramatically evident in those numerous instances in which protestors of a film admit that they have never actually seen the film they are protesting. In this way, controversies over films may be less about the film than about what the film represents. That a filmmaker, and certainly one like Jonathan Demme, could make a film with such a depiction of a gay man (or a strong female) is more at issue than what is actually on the screen. Thus, in a way, controversial films are important not for what they depict on the screen, but for the assumptions they call into question and the kinds of responses they provoke.

A second point, more immediately related to the specifics of controversies over sex, is how deeply embedded notions of sex, gender, and sexuality are to notions of identity. While this seems an obvious statement, the amount of emotional and political energy devoted to protesting a filmic representation of gender and sexuality is telling. The vigor with which the controversy over *Silence* was pursued may hearken back to the peculiar divide between public and private. Sex, gender, and sexuality, being deeply intertwined with personal notions of ourselves and with our most intimately private acts, become heavily contested when put on display in public settings like movie theaters. There is a kind of exposure that occurs in the flickering light of the projector, and the things it reveals can be both troubling and dangerous.

The danger of film is a third and final lesson to be taken from these discussions. For these writers, to film is attributed a fairly impressive amount of cultural power. For some, this entails the capacity to uplift and empower a segment of the population, and for others, it entails the power to degrade. In the most dramatic instance, some attribute to film the ability to cause behavior in the external world—to encourage and incite actions of discrimination, harassment, and even violence. Of course, the other looming danger in these situations is that the resulting controversy may lead to a fracturing of community and a deep division among those who previously relied upon each other as allies in a broader struggle.

CONCLUSION

Jonathan Demme, at the very least, felt some level of chastisement from the controversy that surrounded his Oscar-winning film. His next film took up the issue of homophobia and discrimination through the poignant tale of a lawyer who contracts AIDS and finds himself shunned by his employer. The deeply affecting 1993 box office hit *Philadelphia*, which starred Tom Hanks and Denzel Washington, would garner an Academy Award for lead actor Hanks and go some way toward closing the gap that had opened between Demme and some members of the gay and lesbian community. Although he would deny that his choice of *Philadelphia* was driven by the controversy, there can be little doubt that, to many, this film felt like an apology.

Not surprisingly, controversies over sex, sexuality, and gender have continued in the years since *Silence* was protested at the Academy Awards. In 1995, for example, director Larry Clark shattered one of the few remaining taboos by painting a disturbingly graphic and amoral picture of adolescent sexuality in his film *Kids*. Some critics praised Clark's film for its honest portrayal of the urban "teenage wasteland," while others called it "truly shocking film, with gutter language unmatched in its volume and roughness, and a cavalier attitude toward sex that slithers beyond unbridled lust into the realm of irresponsible suicide." The Weinstein brothers, who had acquired the film for distribution through their Disney-owned production company, were forced to create a new and wholly independent distribution company—Shining Excalibur Films—just to distribute the controversial film.[83]

The twenty-first century has also seen its fair share of controversial films related to sex and sexuality. Surely the most spectacular controversy so far was that surrounding Ang Lee's 2006 *Brokeback Mountain*. Adapted from a short story by Annie Proulx, the film tells of a forbidden love affair during the early 1960s between two cowboys. Tracing their lives from their initial encounter throughout years of brief interludes together, the film paints a poignant and moving portrait of love denied and the cruelties of homophobia. While the film was a surprise box office smash—grossing more than $80 million—and garnered several Academy Award nominations with wins for direction, musical score, and writing, many critics felt that the film failed to live up to its potential. The mixed reactions were captured well by Scott Bowles, who wrote, "Admirers say the film is erasing Hollywood's homosexual stereotypes and raising consciousness of gay rights. Critics say *Brokeback*'s destiny is to be remembered more for its marketing than its artistic achievements."[84]

If the history of cinema is anything to go by, there will be numerous controversies related to sex, gender, and sexuality in the years to come, and each of these future controversies will be shaped not only by the film in question but also by the broader array of sexual politics of the time. The persistence of these controversies, however, should not suggest that they lack in importance. Rather, each controversy over sex and cinema helps to raise again the fundamental relationship between social morality, sexuality, and the ways we come to understand ourselves as social and sexual beings. In this way, the controversies regarding sex on film provide a useful marker of the deeper cultural tensions surrounding the relationship between our communal sense of morality and our personal sense of desire.

CHAPTER 3

Violence and Crime: Oliver Stone's *Natural Born Killers*

O n July 3, 1931, Mrs. William H. Taylor convened a meeting of the Better Films Committee of the Montclair Cultural Centre in Montclair, New Jersey. While committees focusing on the improvement of American cinema, or on the improvement of society through the promotion of uplifting films, were common throughout the United States, this committee's purpose was unique. The committee was called into session for the express purpose "to shape a united protest against underworld motion pictures." The impetus for this particular protest came from the tragic and untimely death of twelve-year-old Winslow Elliott just over a week before on June 23. Elliott had been playing with his sixteen-year-old friend William Harold Gamble when the older boy shot him to death. Gamble, it was reported, "was demonstrating 'how they did it' in a gangster film he had seen a short time before" when the gun he was using in the demonstration went off.[1]

The aftermath of this tragic shooting provoked discussion of two important social issues. The first, and the one most attended to by the police, was raised by the fact that the pistol used in this accidental slaying had been mail-ordered by seventeen-year-old Teddy Mohlman, a disabled friend of Gamble who had taken up target shooting as a hobby and had even purchased equipment to make his own ammunition.[2] The second issue, the concern over the gangster films that evidently inspired the events leading to this unfortunate event, was taken up with considerably more vigor by the community of Montclair. In addition to Mrs. Taylor's Better Films Committee, the shooting brought resolutions opposing gangster films from the Lions, Rotary, and Optimist clubs as well as the Kiwanis, and even the threat of legal action against Hollywood from the office of Mayor Charles G. Phillips.[3]

The death of Winslow Elliott added fuel to an already raging fire surrounding the impact of films on dangerous behaviors. As Richard Maltby
observes:

> Elliott's death escalated an already strident public discourse linking the public
> spectacle of crime to the movies, providing the press with the opportunity, as
> the *Literary Digest* put it, "to harp again on the type of pictures which are
> said to pervert the minds of the youth."[4]

The furor over this and other instances of violent criminal behavior apparently copied from film depictions led to various calls for an end to the large
and successful cycle of gangster films that been appearing since 1927. The
Elliott incident, for instance, led Warner Bros., one of the main producers of
"gangster films," to declare: "There will be no more gangster pictures shown
in Montclair in 1931." The Warner Bros. official went on to claim, "Such
films are practically at the end of their cycle. As far as I know, there are none
in production and none are contemplated."[5] So great was the general cultural concern over gangster films that this declaration came from Warner
Bros. in spite of the fact that the specific film linked to the shooting was one
of MGM's rare forays into the gangster genre, *The Secret Six*, directed by
George Hill and featuring an early performance by Clark Gable.

Fears about screen depictions of violent and criminal behavior had been
circulating long before the emergence of the gangster genre. Early reformers
feared that nickelodeons were dens of iniquity that would transform impressionable young people and immigrants into the kinds of criminals they
viewed on the screen. Sherman C. Kingsley, a prominent Chicago civic
leader, wrote after his 1906 study of the city's nickelodeon theaters that
"evil consequences have demanded the attention of juvenile and municipal
courts, probation officers and social workers."[6] Some argued that the power
of the visual spectacle created in its viewer an overwhelming impulse to
mimic the behavior, and they sought both to limit the amount of negative
behavior shown in films and to increase the number of "uplifting films" that
could serve as instructions in life and morality. Jane Addams, for instance,
opened a nickelodeon in 1907 with the hopes of demonstrating that films
could serve the ends of moral education. The theater closed three months
later due to a lack of both suitable films and attendance.[7]

In his 1915 book *The Individual Delinquent*, William Healy, director of
the Psychopathic Institute at the Juvenile Court of Chicago, wrote:

> The effect of moving pictures in starting criminalistic tendencies in children is
> almost always along such conspicuous lines that it is not necessary to cite
> cases. It is nearly always a boy who is affected and the impulse started is an
> imitative one. He proceeds to get weapons and cowboys clothes, and wants to
> make off for the plains. Or else he desires to become a soldier and get into
> warfare.[8]

The tendency in American films to dwell on the darker side of human nature—in relation to both sex and violence—was soon evident, and the focus shifted more to the effects of dangerous films and the inevitable call for their regulation.

Eighty years after Dr. Healy's declaration, Senator Bob Dole of Kansas stood in front of a crowd of political supporters holding up a copy of the *Boston Herald* with its front-page coverage of an elderly woman's murder at the hands of three assailants in Avon, Massachusetts. The purpose of this visual aid was to supply support for Dole's criticism of the violence in Hollywood films and, in particular, the 1994 film by Oliver Stone, *Natural Born Killers*. The paper reported: "Friends told police the trio regularly watched the movie on a videocassette one of the suspects purchased and drew comparisons between the characters in the film and themselves."[9] Dole's demonstration at this particular campaign stop during his failed effort in the 1996 presidential election underscored a message he had laid out earlier in a May 31 speech focused on the "nightmares of depravity" being created by America's entertainment industry. In that speech, Senator Dole specifically targeted Time Warner products such as the films Stone's *Natural Born Killers* and Tony Scott's *True Romance*, as well as musical groups Cannibal Corpse and 2 Live Crew. "A line has been crossed," Dole proclaimed, "not just of taste, but of human dignity and decency."[10]

This chapter is about the battles over this line, an ever-shifting line defined primarily by the kinds of behaviors considered appropriate and those deemed antisocial and dangerous. The specific notion of violence, the sense of social unrest and bodily assaults that motivated the comments by Dole, is a relatively new way of conceptualizing the line between appropriate and inappropriate behavior. Prior to the late 1950s, the general category of "violence" as a social problem would have been more often conceived in terms of "crime" or "delinquency." In many ways, as was evident in the last chapter's discussion of sex, the notion of violence has morphed throughout its long history, especially as it relates to the influence of film. In part this is due to the inevitable influence of history and the ways changes in the broader social network also alter our understanding of what constitutes normal and appropriate behavior versus what is cast as inappropriate and criminal.

Another contributing factor is the sense that the notion of violence is itself a remarkably fluid concept. Even within our contemporary understanding, we are left with numerous gray areas in defining violence. I recall an incident in which a professional hockey player was being charged with criminal assault for a particularly aggressive hit on an unsuspecting opponent. This struck many as an odd concept, especially those of us who have seen many professional hockey games. If hitting someone during a hockey game is considered an illegal assault, how large a backlog of cases will the National Hockey League produce from its long history of aggressive body checks and outright fistfights on the ice? What would one then make of professional football? Or, for that matter, of boxing? Clearly, our efforts to delimit the notion of violence are based on a wider and more complex network of ideas about what is appropriate or inappropriate, what is legitimate and what is illegitimate. As J. David Slocum observes, "Lurking behind many efforts to define acts of violence are the complex cultural processes by which some behaviors and actions are marked as 'violent' and others not."[11] In contemporary popular understanding, the criminal who robs a bank behaves violently, while the police officer who wrestles him to the ground does not. The protestors who hurl bottles at a corporate headquarters may be deemed violent; the national guard troops who disperse the crowd might not.

Controversies have historically emerged around films that depict criminal or violent behavior because these depictions have somehow crossed this ambiguous and shifting line between appropriate and inappropriate uses of force, at least in the opinion of some. In examining the history of these controversies, we will observe numerous points at which the line moved in such a way that things deemed perfectly appropriate in one era were seen as horrific in another. But, in spite of the shifting grounds upon which the public debates over violence in films have taken place, there are some relatively consistent features worth observing at the outset.

First, violence and criminality in films have consistently been conceptualized in terms of behaviors. While there are clearly other senses of violence—psychic, symbolic, economic, aesthetic, and so forth—in discussions about films, violence is almost always understood as the representation of specific behaviors such as robbing a train, or shooting or torturing someone.

Given this behavioral focus, it is not surprising that a second relatively consistent feature in the social controversies over violence in film is an underlying theory of mimesis or imitation. Viewing violent or antisocial behavior, the theory goes, will somehow lead the viewer to engage in similar behavior. Over the years, this theory has been raised in numerous and different ways—ranging from early psychologists who feared that cinema might have some sort of hypnotic effect to contemporary theories that viewing violence desensitizes us to it—but it remains consistent. In this way, one of the key features we find in our survey of controversies over violence—and something that will be a key feature in the case study of *Natural Born Killers* at the end of this chapter—is the focus on the glittering example of the "copycats" who, like William Harold Gamble, are perceived to have reenacted screen violence to murderous results.

A third feature, and one that helps to differentiate the kinds of disputes considered here from those in the previous chapter on sex, is that issues of criminality and violence have long been conceptualized in relation to social scientific or medical discourses. Whereas concerns over sex were often articulated through a discourse of religion and morality, violence and criminality, with their behavioral definitions, have consistently been understood as medical, psychological, or sociological issues that require a "solution."

Fourth and finally, just as violence has been consistently seen as a medical or scientific problem, its regulation has been mainly motivated by desires for social control. More so than sexuality, violence stands as a potential threat to the very fabric of society, and the capacity to differentiate legitimate and illegitimate uses of force lies at the very heart of the notion of government.

The desire to regulate violence, however, runs counter to an equally strong desire to view it. As Thomas Schatz aptly puts it, "Movie violence in America has involved, since its inception, something of a holy trinity of necessary participants: a culture industry determined to depict and exploit it, moviegoers equally determined to experience it and social watchdogs determined to regulate it."[12] The tension between social restrictions on violence and our cultural attraction to it dates back well before the invention of film. David Trend contends, "Violence has always figured prominently in storytelling. Violent imagery has been around since hunters began scratching accounts of their exploits on the walls of caves."[13] Even a cursory survey of mythology, literature, theater, and the visual arts provides ample evidence that violent acts have played a prominent role in both our real and our symbolic history. Where would Shakespeare have been without the bloody battles, swordfights, and tragic suicides that mark his distinguished body of work?

Film has been no different. From the early one-reelers to the modern three-hour digital epic, cinema has been deeply interested in depictions of violence. Filmmakers and film theorists have long recognized this deep connection between cinema and violence. William Rothman argues that this connection was well understood by one of the pioneers of early cinema, D. W. Griffith:

> Griffith envisioned film as possessing the power to whip viewers into a frenzied state, to cause viewers to lose their moral compass and give in to what is base in human nature. In Griffith's vision, movies have a voracious appetite for violence, as human beings have; violence is internal to film's nature, as it is internal to human nature.[14]

Early filmmakers like Luis Buñuel, whose 1929 debut *Un Chien Andalou* contains the iconic "eye-slicing" scene, and Russian filmmaker and theorist Sergei Eisenstein understood the power of film to affect the audience as an fundamentally violent act, and this theoretical notion has been more recently advanced by French philosopher Gilles Deleuze, who argues that the experience of cinema produces "a shock to thought, communicating vibrations to the cortex, touching the nervous and cerebral system directly."[15]

While many of these theories work at a very abstract level, there is a clear and everyday sense of the truth that viewing a film is a matter of sub-jecting oneself to the at times brutal control of another. As Noel Burch observes, "Whatever his level of critical awareness, a viewer, face to face with the screen, is completely at the mercy of the filmmaker, who may do violence to him at any moment and through any means."[16] Perhaps because of the existentially violent (or at least potentially violent) nature of film, filmic depictions of violence have fairly consistently provoked controversy.

A HISTORY OF CONTROVERSIES OVER VIOLENT FILMS

Death looms large in the earliest cinematic efforts. It is worth noting that the early days of cinema coincided with a suddenly expanding interest in spiritualism in the aftermath of the Civil War, and the relatively new tech-nologies of photography and then film were soon exploited by purveyors of spiritualism to provide evidence of spectral visitations. Early filmmakers such as Georges Méliès and George Albert Smith made films that focused on the contemporary fascination with life after death, though often with a tongue-in-cheek attitude, as in Smith's 1897 *Photographing a Ghost* in which the uncooperative spirit refuses to stay put for the hapless photographer.[17]

The fascination with death was not, however, limited to the afterlife. The moment of bodily death was also a cause of much public interest in the waning years of the nineteenth century. Thomas Edison's studio, for instance, produced a series of films attending to death. The topics of these films ranged from killing animals to the reenactments of famous execu-tions. The focus on the body and its real, scientific limitations set these films apart from the earlier, albeit often facetious, attention to the spirit-ual. As Lisa Cartwright notes, "The one-minute *Electrocuting an Elephant* documents the moment of the elephant's death. But, more importantly, it also documents public interest with scientific technology and its capacity to determine the course of life and death in living beings."[18] In addition to the actual death of a living being caught in that 1903 film, Edison's studio reenacted deaths in such films as *Execution of a Spy* (1902) and *Execution of Czolgosz with Panorama of Auburn Prison* (1901). Leon Czolgosz had been convicted of the assassination of President William McKinley and was electrocuted in 1901 in the New York State Prison in Auburn. Edison's stu-dio reenacted both the assassination and the execution.[19] The popular sub-genre of "execution films," Mary Ann Doane notes, "manifests an intense fascination with the representation of death."[20]

This early interest in death was accompanied by a similar interest in vio-lence done to the body. Silent films were, essentially, about the body—its movement and the things done to it—and so these films often attended to sudden and blunt things happening to people. This depiction of violence did not necessarily involve a harsh or brutal tone. "Sight-gag and slapstick comedy," William Everson observes, "were essentially a matter of violence."[21] Mack Sennett's Keystone Cops, for instance, engaged in numerous over-the-top displays of physical misadventures. The protagonists of early comedies were often subjected to numerous ordeals.

Concerns over the effects of filmed violence were expressed at an early date with regard to the real violence depicted in boxing films. The most vociferous objections to boxing films would emerge in relation to race during the reign of African American champion Jack Johnson and concerns that films of these bouts, like the 1908 film of the Johnson–Burns fight, would stir racial turmoil. But red flags about the social impact of screening boxing matches—even between two white boxers—were already being raised as early as the 1896 filming of the Corbett–Fitzsimmons fight.[22] Social critics feared that the exhibition of any boxing films might teach both children and immigrants that physical violence was an acceptable method for dealing with others and, as such, as early as the turn of the twentieth century, critics were calling for regulations of films depicting real violence.

These initial explorations of death and violence, however, caused nowhere near the public outcry that the depictions of violence in relation to crime did. While the most prominent cinematic crime genre was that of gangster films, beginning in 1927, the depiction of crime in American films already had a lengthy history. Larry Langman and Daniel Finn, for instance, compiled more than two thousand titles in their comprehensive *Guide to American Silent Crime Films* and persuasively argue that the foundation for the gangster film was well established in the silent films of the early 1900s.[23] With the introduction of crime films came an accompanying public outcry. By 1907, the popular trade magazine *Motion Picture World* was warning that children might be led astray by crime films, citing an example of two young girls whose shoplifting was attributed to seeing a film about a thief.[24]

Worries over the social impact of crime films soon found a forum in legal courtrooms, and the earliest court-adjudicated case related to film censorship involved two films that depicted crimes: *The James Boys in Missouri* (1908) and *Night Riders* (1908), two early westerns. When exhibitor Jake Block was denied a permit to show these films by the Chicago police censor board, he filed an appeal with the Illinois Supreme Court. Block's lawyers advanced arguments that would become common in subsequent controversies over violence in films. First, they argued that the films were "reproductions of parts" of plays about the same subject matter that were being staged in Chicago theaters. In other words, the violent acts being depicted on the screen were already being represented in other, unregulated media. Second, they argued that the acts of criminality depicted in these films were part of the "American historical experience" and therefore could not

be deemed "obscene" or "immoral."[25] Filmic depictions of violence and
criminality, these lawyers argued, could not be deemed inappropriate if
they were, first, similar to depictions in other media and, second, drawn
from real lived experience. In essence, films were mirrors reflecting society
and thus could not be blamed for the unpleasant images they revealed.

The lawyers' line of reasoning, however, was rejected by the Illinois
court, which ruled that government had a responsibility to "secure decency
and morality in the moving picture business, and that purpose falls within
the police power." Further, the court ruled that the need to restrict film
was especially important because "the audiences include those classes
whose age, education and situation in life especially entitle them to protection against the evil influence of obscene and immoral representations."[26]
Like the arguments advanced in defense of these early westerns, the court's
decision also anticipated the kinds of responses made by those who would
in the coming decades seek to limit the filmic depictions of violence. Society has a right to protect itself, the reasoning went, from the potentially
corrosive effect of these spectacles of criminality, and these images are
dangerous primarily because there are some in society who might fall
under their "evil influence."

The concerns over crime in films would continue throughout the early
decades of cinema. In 1912, another spectacular copycat case was reported
in the *Philadelphia Record* when a young boy's death during a failed train
robbery was attributed to the boy viewing *The Great Train Robbery* in a
nickelodeon in Scranton, Pennsylvania—in spite of the fact that the short
film was not playing in Scranton at the time.[27] In 1913, the city of Detroit
banned films showing scenes of police corruption or scenes revealing how
to commit crimes.[28]

The clear pattern that emerges from these early disputes over film violence is that the concern is not so much about the depiction of violence as
the representation of criminality and antisocial behaviors. Thus, Detroit's
ban on depictions of the police as corrupt reveals a desire not so much to
limit the violence on screen as to reinforce the legitimacy of social and
moral order. This reasoning is given its most clear articulation in a 1922
ruling by the Illinois Court of Appeals on Chicago's prohibition of the western *The Deadwood Coach*. In its ruling, the court argued:

> Where "gun-play," or the shooting of human beings, is the essence of the play
> and does not pertain to the necessities of war, nor to the preservation of law
> and order, is for personal spite or revenge, and involves taking the law into
> one's own hands, and thus becomes a murder, the picture may be said to be
> immoral; it inculcates murder.[29]

In spite of the array of social interests lined up in opposition to films
about crime and violence, and the wide legal and political powers at their

disposal, the public's hunger for representations of crime and violence continued to motivate filmmakers to produce these films. The most enduring
and potent form of early film violence had its roots in a 1912 film by the
groundbreaking film director D. W. Griffith. *The Musketeers of Pig Alley*
tells the story of a proper lady and her attempted seduction by a young
street thug. Filmed on location in a real urban alleyway and employing
actual street toughs, Griffith's film, while essentially still in his standard
"damsel-in-distress" mode, stands as the first American gangster film. As
Jonathan Munby comments, "The gangster's world is replete with bars,
alleys, dance halls, guns, cops, loyal sidekicks, and rival gangs. Behind the
veneer of realism lies a whole host of conventions that would come to dominate the gangster cycle."[30]

The gangster film emerged in its more recognizable form in 1927 with
Joseph von Sternberg's *The Underworld*. This film tells the story of gangster "Bull" Weed, his moll "Feathers," and a down-and-out lawyer he
pulls from the gutter, with the moniker "Rolls Royce." The film was
designed, in Sternberg's words, as "an experiment in photographic violence
and montage."[31] Released by Paramount without much fanfare, the film
was a breakout hit and essentially saved Sternberg's floundering career
and made silent film actor George Bancroft into a star. Sternberg's film is
a masterpiece of cinematography and of narrative development, and if the
cinematic motifs of the gangster films were already rendered in Griffith's
Musketeers, they were first perfected by Sternberg.

The emergence of the gangster film as its own increasingly popular and
unique genre, however, was the result of more than just cinematic artistry.
With little doubt, the legal state of Prohibition—the outlawing of alcohol
import, sales, and possession by the Eighteenth Amendment and the Vol-
stead Act—was a major factor. The illegal smuggling of alcohol and the
operation of illegal speakeasy drinking establishments provided much of
the impetus for the emergence of the real-life gangster into public con-
sciousness. In 1929, historian and socialist activist Waldo Frank observed
the prominence of the celebrity status of gangsters, noting that crime had
become "a cult so potent and popular that it outdoes politics and vies with
sport in its rank in the public prints."[32] The gangster film added considerably to this already spectacular cult status.

In addition to the difficult legal conditions of Prohibition, there were also
other cultural factors related to the popularity of the gangster genre. In his
influential 1948 essay "The Gangster as Tragic Hero," Robert Warshow
argues that the gangster represented an opposition to the "the qualities
and the demands of modern life" and thus satisfied a deep desire by Americans in the 1920s and '30s for a symbolic escape from their increasingly
modernizing and industrializing world. In this way, the gangster figure
helped Americans deal with the inherent tension between their desire for
social order and their desire for unbridled freedom. In an oft-quoted

passage from this essay, Warshow declares, "The gangster is the 'no' to that great American 'yes' which is stamped so large over our official culture." The navigation of this tension was particularly interested in the violent aspect of these films. Warshow argues, "Our response to the gangster film is most consistently and most universally a response to sadism; we gain the double satisfaction of participating vicariously in the gangster's sadism and then seeing it turned against the gangster himself."[33]

The vicarious experience of sadism and the seeming celebration of violent crime worried many of the opponents of the increasingly popular gangster films. These opponents, in turn, put pressure on the various agencies responsible for maintaining decency in films, and during the late 1920s, the emerging gangster film received considerable attention from local and state censorship boards. In his excellent book *Classical Film Violence*, Stephen Prince observes:

> Local censorship of screen violence showed clear patterns. Censor boards eliminated scenes in which guns were flourished on-screen.... Violence that smacked of sadism—fights that involved choking or kicking—was actionable, as well as extreme forms of torture and scenes showing the response of the victims of violence.[34]

A uniform policy was clearly needed and the action of local censorship boards revealed a nascent policy in the works. Interestingly, the earliest efforts by William Hays and the Studio Relations Committee to develop a set of moral guidelines—the 1924 "Formula" and the 1927 list of "Don'ts and Be Carefuls"—largely ignored violence and treated criminality with only the lightest regard. These early guidelines focused almost exclusively on issues of sex and religion. But the growing popularity of the gangster film—as well as the celebrity status of real-life gangsters—led to calls for a Hollywood crackdown on violence and criminality in films.

The emergence of "talkies" in 1929 exacerbated the growing public concern over gangster films, and 1930 saw the premiere of the first and most influential of the new generation of these violent films with Archie Mayo's *The Doorway to Hell*. Publicized as a story "snatched from today's headlines" with the tagline "The picture gangdom dared Hollywood to make," *Doorway* was an enormous hit for Warner Bros. and was quickly followed by more recognizable titles like *Little Caesar* and *Public Enemy*.[35] But it is *Doorway* that broke new ground and helped to establish many of the standard elements of the gangster genre—even clichés like keeping a tommy gun in a violin case and the mobster impulsively flipping a coin. It also provided James Cagney with his second film appearance and a chance to settle into the gangster role that would make him a star.

The growing tension between the condemnation of violent gangster films and their popularity was most poignantly revealed in the stories of copycats, fans who were so enamored with the violence in the pictures that they chose to replicate it. The shooting of Winslow Elliott by a playmate reenacting a scene from *The Secret Six* in 1931 was preceded by another spectacular copycat situation in New York City. Young hood Francis "Two Gun" Crowley, a nineteen-year-old bank robber, was apprehended by the police, but in the midst of their arrest, he pulled a second gun from his inside coat pocket—hence the moniker "Two Gun"—and shot a detective before escaping a massive siege of the building.[36] For two months, Crowley roamed the city amid a massive manhunt, but in May he was finally surrounded by police in a gun battle on West 90th Street. Prior to being overcome by tear gas and being taken by the police, Crowley wrote a letter explaining that his crimes were inspired by "the new sensation of the films." Ironically, as Richard Maltby observes, "Crowley was electrocuted before he could discover that he had, in return, inspired Hollywood," for within a year the story of his capture would be woven into Howard Hawks's *Scarface*.[37] Among the unlikely critics of gangster films and their possible consequences for young viewers was notorious gangster Al Capone, who wrote in July 1931, "These gang pictures—that's terrible kid stuff. Why, they ought to take them all and throw them into the lake. They're doing nothing but harm to the younger element of this country."[38]

Capone, of course, was not alone in his concern and condemnation. The gangster was joined by groups like the Legion of Decency, the Daughters of the American Revolution, the Protestant League, and the Police Benevolence Association in opposing the popular film genre. In the face of this growing social controversy, Hays and the Motion Picture Producers and Distributors of America (MPPDA) began a major public relations effort in defense of Hollywood.

This effort had two major strategies. The first was to declare that the gangster film was actually an effective tool against real-life gangsters. Hays himself declared that Hollywood had made great strides in diminishing the celebrity status of real gangsters "by showing he can't win and by ridicule."[39] Hays argued, and indeed his office put explicit pressure on directors to conform to this reasoning, that gangster films from Hollywood inevitably revealed the gangster as weak and spineless and, ultimately, punished for his wicked ways. Various experts were also hired by the MPPDA to provide a kind of apologia for these popular films. Carleton Simon, a prominent criminal psychologist, was employed by Hays as a special consultant and wrote a short piece in defense of the gangster fascination by arguing, "Whetted by newspaper accounts of similar occurrences, the public seeks vent for its curiosity to have a clearer understanding and a closer perspective as to the causes that lead to gang feuds."[40] In an additional part of this public relations strategy, the Hays office used the furor over gangster films to further install itself as both chief protector of Hollywood's interests and chief censor of its products, using the controversy to

promote the new Production Code, which was first written in 1930. In light
of various studies that claimed films were contributing to juvenile
delinquency—studies like those funded by the Payne Fund, notably Henry
Forman's 1933 *Our Movie Made Children*—Hays hired noted police reformer
August Vollmer to defend Hollywood. Vollmer wrote that "films which have
dealt with the subject of crime within the social safeguards imposed by the
motion picture Production Code were deterrents, not incentives, to criminal
behavior."[41]

The second major strategy was to declare a moratorium on gangster
films, arguing that the genre had run its course and that Hollywood was
no longer interested in producing such films. This strategy was used, it is
worth recalling, in the case of the slaying of Winslow Elliott when
Warner Bros. officials claimed that "such films are practically at the end
of their cycle," and even Jack Warner himself, patriarch of the studio,
declared in 1931 that he refused to allow his fifteen-year-old son to
watch such films and that his studio, the leading purveyor of gangster
films, would stop producing them.[42] Interestingly, these declared moratoriums failed to stop the production of gangster-themed films, even by
Warner Bros.

In spite of the declared desire to quell the production of gangster films
and to require that they be presented as morally uplifting object lessons
that crime doesn't pay, the 1930 Production Code, which came into rigor-
ous enforcement in 1934, says very little about crime and violence. There
are prohibitions against showing brutal murders "in detail," against illegal
drug use, and against showing details of criminal procedures, as well as
admonitions against making revenge a theme in tales set during modern
times. The use of guns, a major source of protest during the late 1920s and
early 1930s, was to be "restricted to essentials." When contrasted with the
more detailed and explicit admonitions against portrayals of sexual relations and perversion, it was clear to all involved that the strict period of
the Production Code was ultimately more about sex than it was about
violence.

In spite of the MPPDA's reluctance to act, the increasingly violent real-
life gangster drama being played out in the streets of America intervened.
In May 1934 in Oklahoma, notorious bank robbers Bonnie and Clyde were
gunned down in a hail of bullets during an ambush by federal agents.
Accounts of their violent deaths fueled newspaper headlines that cried out
that "crime doesn't pay" and even sent explicit messages to other gangsters
to be warned as they were next on the FBI hit list. The even more dramatic
spectacle of the death of John Dillinger on July 22, 1934, machine-gunned
down outside a movie theater in Chicago—ironically after viewing the
1934 gangster film *Manhattan Melodrama* starring Clark Gable—caused
even more public outcry against film's glamorizing the gangster lifestyle.[43]
These events proved a tipping point for the lengthy public relations battle

over the virtue (or vice) of the gangster film, and on July 15, 1935, William Hays declared a complete moratorium on the Hollywood gangster film.

It is worth here noting that the gangster films were not alone in their spectacular displays of violence or as objects of cultural concern. Westerns, as far back as the 1908 *James Boys in Missouri*, were remarkably violent and seemed to create direct connections between masculinity, violence, and revenge.[44] In contrast to the consternation over gangster films, however, there was relatively little public outcry over westerns. Another film genre that received little critical censure over violence was the inherently violent genre of war films. Graphic violence was generally allowed in films about war and depictions of combat—the particularly gruesome 1930 film *All Quiet on the Western Front*, for example, raised very few concerns at the Production Code Administration (PCA) offices. The lack of outrage over these two genres reinforces a broader sense that critiques of violence were not so much about the depiction of violence itself as they were about the prosocial versus antisocial tone of the violence. Westerns and war films generally reinforce the social values of moral order and authority; the use of violence in these films is, for the most part, ultimately about protecting society rather than destroying it.

The genre other than the gangster film most often targeted for condemnation over violence also emerged at about the same time as the modern gangster film: horror. The American horror film emerged in its proper form in 1931 with the twin specters of *Dracula* and *Frankenstein* released within months of each other by Universal Studios. Earlier films had contained horrific images—films like *The Phantom of the Opera* (1925) and *London after Midnight* (1927), for example—but the truly supernatural gothic tales that would become the foundation for the horror film began with these two Universal films in 1931. They were quickly joined by a host of other similarly gothic and monstrous films such as Paramount's *Dr. Jekyll and Mr. Hyde* (1931).[45]

During their initial emergence in 1931, the enforcers of the newly adopted Production Code paid relatively little attention to the sudden spate of horror films. The Studio Relations Committee, for example, recommended a number of changes to the script for *Dr. Jekyll and Mr. Hyde*, but many of these focused on suggestions of sex rather than violence.[46] For the most part, these films fell outside the general guidelines of the Code at that time. As David Skal observes, "There was nothing in the Production Code about vampires."[47]

Local and state censorship boards, on the other hand, were considerably more concerned about these gruesome creatures from the grave, and many of their concerns related to the violence and brutality depicted in these films. James Whale's film *Frankenstein*, for instance, was the subject of considerable censorship action—most notably and protractedly in Kansas.

These cuts were largely, though not exclusively, focused on acts and aspects of violence and cruelty. As Stephen Prince contends:

> The film's physical detailing of violence, its marking of pain and rage as an emotional and bodily experience, and its placement of this detailing within a morbid story of grave robbing and vivisection, are what elicited the Kansas censors' judgment that *Frankenstein* was a film of "cruelty" and the ensuing protest action by other censor boards and community organizations.[48]

Interestingly, the controversies over *Frankenstein* were not finished. The film was rereleased in 1938 in a clever pairing with its monstrous sibling *Dracula*, and the double feature created an impressive frenzy at the box office. The *New York Times* reported that the pairing sold out theaters in cities like Seattle, Los Angeles, and St. Louis for weeks and that in Salt Lake City, "Four thousand frenzied Mormons milled around outside, finally broke through the police lines, smashed the plate glass box office, bent in the front doors and tore off one of the door checks in their eagerness to get in and be frightened."[49] The frenzy, however, proved too much for some of the residents of White Plains, New York. Katherine Vandervoort, director of attendance for the local school district, wrote a letter to the MPPDA reporting hysterical reactions from the local schoolchildren and threatening action from the National Federation of the Parent Teacher Association.[50]

The vast majority of controversies over violence during the 1930s and 1940s, however, remained centered around the gangster film. Not surprisingly, the 1935 moratorium on gangster films was utterly ineffective in containing narratives about gangland violence and crime. Hollywood studios developed two strategies for continuing to cater to the public's obsession with gangsters that mirrored their earlier PR efforts. First, Hollywood began repackaging the narrative of the gangster within what Fran Mason calls the "social gangster film.' In these films, the gangster is shown as a kind of social warning against turning to a life of crime, and the narratives are subtly coded to suggest that the tough persona of the gangster belies his inner weakness. Often in these films, the gangster is juxtaposed with a more socially appropriate and morally strong character. In Archie Mayo's 1936 *The Petrified Forest*, for instance, Humphrey Bogart's gangster plays against the optimistic poet portrayed by Leslie Howard. Bogart's eventual death in the film seems to suggest the superiority of the poet's perspective. Perhaps more famously, the 1938 film *Angels with Dirty Faces*, directed by Michael Curtiz and starring James Cagney, pairs the tough guy gangster with the morally superior priest Father Jerry, played by Pat O'Brien. The emphasis on crafting Cagney's character Rocky as a "crime doesn't pay" lesson is clear in the initial response from the Production Code to the script, ironically submitted by Jack Warner, whose pledge to make no more gangster films apparently didn't last too long. In the letter to Warner from PCA head Joseph Breen, Breen insists, "It is important to avoid any flavor of making a hero and sympathetic character of a man who is, at the same time, shown to be a criminal, a murderer, and a kidnapper."[51]

The second strategy to avoid controversies over gangster films was to recast these narratives from the perspective of the law enforcement agencies pursuing them. If tommy gun–wielding gangsters were offensive to public sensibilities, then tommy gun–wielding federal agents might be acceptable. Thomas Schatz calls this particular generic twist the "gangster-as-cop" narrative.[52] The prototypical film in this variation is the 1935 William Keighley film *G-Men*, which focuses on the classic gangster actor Cagney's turn as a tough street kid turned government agent (or "g-man"). Here the violence, revenge, and brutality are apparently sanitized by virtue of their commission in the name of the law, and to a large extent, it proved successful in calming public fears about the gangster films. A 1938 editorial in the *San Antonio Light* exclaimed, "Every member of congress ought to witness at least one exhibition of 'G-Men,' the new motion picture." The reason for this recommendation was the need for Congress to support the federal law enforcement officials in their battle against crime, and "realistic ... scenes of crime suppression" would remind the legislators that "our violent and hideous crimes have been realistic" as well.[53]

The editors of the *San Antonio Light* were not alone in their praise of this new form of gangster picture, as *G-Men* and many of its progeny were passed with only minor changes by the PCA and local censor boards. Interestingly, many of these films contained scenes of violence that were technically in violation of the Code and in previous films had been heavily censored by local and state boards. What set these new films apart from their violent predecessors was that the violence was perpetrated by the heroic law enforcement agents rather than by glorified criminals.

Glorification of gangsters, however, was far from over, and the postwar period saw another spate of gangster films beginning with the 1945 biopic *Dillinger*. Concerns about the new wave of gangster pictures emerged almost immediately. Only a few months after the film's release, syndicated Hollywood columnist Louella Parsons declared, "I certainly hope the success of the 'Dillinger' picture at the box office doesn't start a trend of gangster movies. We have outgrown them."[54] According to screenwriter W. R. Burnett, plans for an earlier film about the notorious gangster had been floated at Warner Bros., but "the next Monday the studio had 1,400 telegrams from women's clubs and other busy bodies all over the country asking them not to make the picture."[55] While Warner Bros. backed away from the project, a few years later in 1945 the King Brothers produced a low-budget version of the gangster's life, and the film, much to Louella Parsons's regret, went on to big box office success and even an Oscar nomination for Best Screenplay.

The new cycle of gangster films, no longer focused on moral lessons or glorifying federal officers, once again met with considerable public condemnation. An article in the *South Bend Tribune*, in Dillinger's home state of Indiana, attributed the recent rise in juvenile delinquency to the film, arguing that there was "proof of the bad influence of crime pictures of the *Dillinger* type."[56] Public sentiment again, ironically, turned against the very successful new cycle of gangster pictures. Popular syndicated columnist and radio personality Erskine Johnson led a campaign in 1947 against plans for a biopic of the life of Al Capone. His campaign brought numerous letters of support, which he promptly printed in his column: "The American Legion Auxiliary of the Roy W. Kelly Post No. 90, Ashland, Wis., voted strongly protesting against the filming of Al Capone's life as a movie"; "We the Woman's Council of the First Christian Church of Longview, Wash., opposed the filming of the life of Al Capone."[57] By December 13 of that year, Johnson was able to declare victory: "Well you did it. One million, one hundred seventy-six thousand readers of my column and listeners to my radio show deluged movie czar Eric Johnston with letters and petitions protesting the filming of the life story of Al Capone." The pressure brought to bear on Johnston, president of the Producer's Association, eventually led to the outlawing of "films dealing with the life of a notorious criminal" and films whose titles suggest "occupations unsuitable for the screen." The popular columnist could even report a letter of congratulations from a Minnesota district judge, who wrote to "thank you for your courageous stand against the story of Al Capone reaching the screen."[58]

The "ban" of 1947, however, proved no more effective than the similar moratoriums of 1931 or 1935. In 1948 alone, such gangster classics as John Huston's *Key Largo* and Abraham Polonsky's *Force of Evil* appeared, followed in 1949 by Raoul Walsh's *White Heat* and in 1950 by another Huston classic, *The Asphalt Jungle*. The story of Capone's life would appear on-screen in 1959, starring Rod Steiger in the title role. The popularity of the new film noir genre, with its bleak and often brutal story lines and dark cinematography, combined with the general decline in box office revenues and the increasing competition with television meant that the groups seeking to expunge violence and crime from the movie screens would face an impossible task. This did not, of course, mean that opponents of violence and crime would not continue to attend to the depictions of violence on the silver screen, and numerous controversies erupted during the 1950s, especially around films thought to promote juvenile delinquency.

The controversies over violence and film often erupted around the influence of violence on children. Thus, because the postwar era saw a major increase in the number of young people, the arrival of these children at adolescence in the mid-1950s led to increasing concern for the impact of violent entertainment. This bubble generation appropriated ideas of violence and crime in new ways with the rise of the troubled teenage rebel in such films as the aptly titled *Rebel without a Cause* (1955) and *The Wild One* (1953) and with the rise of their troubled stars, James Dean and Marlon Brando, respectively. Of this era, Richard Witcombe observes:

> The war babies were growing up. There was a new phenomenon emerging in Western societies, the sexually alert, economically independent "teenager," a traumatic figure for middle-aged middle America, as the new stars and the reactions they produced showed all too well.[59]

A tidal wave of public concern over juvenile delinquency soon swept across the entertainment industry, ranging from psychiatrist Frederick Wertham's proclamation that comic books were contributing to juvenile deviance and delinquency to Senate hearings about Hollywood and juvenile delinquency.[60] Indeed, the concern of middle-aged Middle America was great enough to pressure the PCA to declare a moratorium on juvenile delinquency films—a familiar, though largely ineffective strategy—in 1956.

For present purposes, the more relevant historical developments during this period were the decline in the Production Code's authority and the increasing interest of the federal government in violence as a broader social problem. As outlined in chapter 1, major industrial changes eroded the Production Code's authority in the 1940s and 1950s. The breakup of the studio monopolies and the practices of block booking opened up a greater possibility that films could be released and exhibited without the PCA's Seal of Approval. The end of World War II also brought a revival in various foreign national cinemas and an increase in imported films that were not subject to the strictures of Hollywood's voluntary code. Further, the 1952 ruling in *Burstyn v. Wilson* recognized that films were afforded a level of First Amendment protection, thus beginning the long process of dismantling of the local and state censorship boards.

Federal interest in crime and juvenile delinquency as they related to film reached its zenith in 1955 when Senator Estes Kefauver, who interestingly had previously held heavily publicized hearings on organized crime, held hearings on the problem of juvenile delinquency and the role of the media in contributing to it. "The predominance of brutality in both movies and television," the report read, "is making our Nation's youth insensitive to human suffering."[61] Indeed, it was this commission's investigation that led Hollywood to declare its 1956 moratorium on juvenile delinquency films.[62] Governmental interest in violence also began to take a decidedly social scientific approach as the U.S. government in the 1950s and '60s turned increasingly to social psychologists to understand and resolve various social problems. Social psychologists such as Paul Lazarsfeld became involved in numerous studies of the effects of mediated violence on actual behavior. In 1971, André Glucksman reported on the number of studies of media and violent behavior in young people: "The UNESCO Bibliography lists 500 titles, but the Karl Heinrich Bibliography published in 1959 has 2500."[63]

Violence became a broad social concern during the 1960s. Martin Baker argues that "the notion of 'violence' as a concept with explanatory force emerged in the late 1950s to early 1960s. Beginning in the US, it took form as a response to social changes and political unrest."[64] As Baker suggests, much of the concern about violence was focused on social unrest resulting from struggles over civil rights and, later, the Vietnam War, but issues of juvenile delinquency and questions about violence in the media also were grouped under the broader concept of violence. Reflecting on the perceived increase in violence during the 1960s, historian and social critic Arthur Schlesinger Jr. wrote, "In recent years the movies and television have developed a pornography of violence far more demoralizing than the pornography of sex."[65] The relationship between film violence and real violence was very clear, although it is beyond our scope to determine whether the media was promoting violence or merely reflecting the social reality outside the theaters—or perhaps both. By decade's end, the 1960s could rightly be called the decade of American violence, as this ten-year span was rife with massacres, riots, combat atrocities, and assassinations.

On-screen, the decade began with one of the most shocking and successful films in Hollywood history, Alfred Hitchcock's *Psycho*. The notorious history of *Psycho* has, of course, been recounted and analyzed numerous times, but is nevertheless worth recalling here. After directing more than forty feature-length films, Hitchcock feared he had become predictable, and by this time, he was even the host and producer of the popular *Alfred Hitchcock Presents* television series. Hitchcock also feared he was being outstripped by competitors like the French director Clouzot, whose *Les Diaboliques* garnered him the moniker "the French Hitchcock." At Hitchcock's urging, his assistants searched for more extreme material and came across the novel *Psycho* by Robert Bloch, a little-known book based on Wisconsin serial killer Ed Gein and featuring gruesome scenes of bodies being preserved and shocking—for the time—sexual perversions like transvestitism.

Paramount, Hitchcock's studio, made it abundantly clear that they did not want him to make this film. As *Psycho* author Bloch would later recall, "Paramount absolutely didn't want to make it."[66] The studio's aversion to the project led it to grant Hitchcock a minuscule budget of just $800,000, less than a quarter of the budget allotted for his previous film, and to refuse him space in the Paramount studios for his production. Hitchcock refused to be thwarted and shot the picture on his television lot at Universal and with much of the crew from *Alfred Hitchcock Presents*. The resulting film produced a shockwave through American culture and raised the bar for shocking film violence for generations of American filmmakers.

Time magazine called *Psycho* "a spectacle of stomach-churning horror," and the *New York Times* declared it "a blot on an honorable career."[67]

Audiences, on the other hand, flocked to Hitchcock's Grand Guignol even enduring the unheard-of practice of standing in line to enter the theater. Prior to *Psycho*, films were shown on a continuous loop, with A and B pictures separated by shorts and serials; audiences were permitted to enter the theater at any point during the showings. But in an inspired gesture toward the novelties and gimmicks of contemporary theater practices, Hitchcock refused to allow patrons to enter after the beginning of *Psycho*. While this "gimmick" would change the way audiences watched movies, the most relevant impact of *Psycho* for our purposes was on the aesthetics of film violence. The shocking shower murder and the twisted linkage of sex, violence, and the American family represented a fundamental shift in representations of screen violence in American cinema. Contemporary audiences were so taken with *Psycho*—screaming, laughing, throwing popcorn—that even Hitchcock himself was surprised, even inquiring with the Stanford University Psychology Department about the possibility of a study to understand the hysterical reaction to the film.

Interestingly, and as a testament to the Production Code's inability to deal with violence per se, when *Psycho* was screened for the PCA, the recommended cuts related only to sexual elements—a passionate kiss, shots of nudity in the infamous shower scene, and the like. Cuts related to violence were made to Hitchcock's film, but these were suggested not by the PCA but by the Catholic Legion of Decency, which insisted that the murder of the detective Arbogast be made less graphic and that Norman not be shown with blood on his hands as he cleans up the scene of his "mother's" crime. Before long, however, the 1960s would witness the decline of both of these watchdog agencies.

Within six years, the PCA would meet its Waterloo over the battles concerning *Who's Afraid of Virginia Woolf?* The formerly powerful censorship agency was replaced in 1968 by the ratings system, which opened the floodgates for increasingly graphic and violent films. The transition years were especially marked by anxiety over violence. For example, *Variety* declared 1967 "the Year of Violence," in large part due to two bloody box office champions.[68] The more successful, though often neglected, of these films was Robert Aldrich's *The Dirty Dozen*, in which a group of U.S. servicemen, all sentenced to death or life imprisonment, are given one last chance at redemption through a suicide mission into Nazi Germany. The film's impressive cast included Lee Marvin, Ernest Borgnine, football star Jim Brown, John Cassavetes, Telly Savalas, and Donald Sutherland. It was nominated for four Academy Awards—including a Best Supporting Actor nomination for Cassavetes—and won the Oscar for Best Sound Effects, but the film's larger notoriety was based on its graphic scenes of violence and brutality.

Scenes of combat violence had, of course, long been acceptable in American cinema, but Aldrich's *Dirty Dozen* went far beyond the typical shooting and bayoneting scenes of previous films. In one of the more notorious sequences, German officers, as well as women, are doused with gasoline and then ignited by hand grenades while trapped in an underground bunker. Scenes like this, according to a *New York Times* survey of psychiatrists, led to concerns about "the accentuation of violence by television, films, newspapers, and magazines, and particularly the impression this makes on children." *Times* film critic Bosley Crowther worried that "by habituating the public to violence and brutality—by making these hideous exercises into morbid and sadistic jokes, as is done in 'The Dirty Dozen'— these films of excessive violence only deaden their sensitivities and make slaughter seem a meaningless cliché," and Legion of Decency leader Martin Quigley argued that "on TV and in too many films, killings are piled on killings, new and extraordinary means are found to kill and maim. An appeal is made to sadism and perversity."[69] Some commentators even blamed the film for contributing to the race riots in Detroit that year.

In spite of the criticism and controversy, *The Dirty Dozen* was the top grossing film at the box office in 1967, and it was accompanied in theaters by a cadre of violent films, including Sergio Leone's spaghetti western *A Fistful of Dollars* and another World War II film, Cornel Wilde's *Beach Red*, which the Legion of Decency rated Condemned. But by far the most controversial, and arguably influential, violent film of that year was Arthur Penn's *Bonnie and Clyde*. Penn's depiction of the notorious outlaws Bonnie Parker and Clyde Barrow combined graphic violence with romance and comedy, and the film received a host of Academy Award nominations, including nominations for Faye Dunaway (lead actress), Gene Hackman (supporting actor), and Warren Beatty (lead actor) and Oscar wins for Estelle Parson (supporting actress) and Burnett Guffey (cinematography). It was the graphic violence in the film, however, that grabbed many of the headlines. The slaughter of Bonnie and Clyde at the film's climax was more than most audiences had ever experienced, due especially to the extensive use of squibs—small explosive charges with "blood" packets—placed on the actors themselves, creating an especially graphic depiction of bullets hitting flesh.[70] So great was the pressure from some groups against these violent films that the National Association of Theater Owners declared in September 1967, "The kind of sadism and viciousness that used to be considered 'shock value' is now being escalated to the extent that pressure is developing from community groups and national organizations in protest over the excess."[71]

The causes of this increasing screen violence were, undoubtedly, many. Some attribute it to the increasing power and influence of independent directors. With the decline of the studio system, directors became more central to the making of films, and the desire of a generation of filmmakers to push the boundaries without a nervous studio boss peering over their shoulders was clear. Directors such as Arthur Penn, Stanley Kubrick, and notably Sam Peckinpah utilized their independence to stretch the previously established boundaries of narrative form and aesthetic acceptability. Others contend that the rise in on-screen violence was merely a reflection of the rise in violence off-screen. Robert Aldrich defended his *Dirty Dozen* by arguing, "For better or worse, force has made this country function.... This is a country which reacts to force."[72] Jack Valenti, only two years into his job as president of the Motion Picture Association of America (MPAA), argued that the violence in films paled in comparison to the violence depicted each night on the television news:

> For the first time in the history of this country, people are exposed to instant coverage of a war in progress. When so many movie critics complain about violence on film, I don't think they realize the impact of thirty minutes of the Huntley-Brinkley newscast—that's real violence.[73]

Still another justification was provided by Geoffrey Shurlock, chief of the soon-to-be defunct PCA, who noted, "I hate violence myself. But as long as the public accepts it, I will have to approve it in films."[74]

The notion of violence had always been articulated in relation to other cultural values. During the gangster film cycles of the 1930s and '40s, violence was understood negatively in terms of criminality. In this understanding, violence was dangerous so long as it contributed to the glamorization of the unlawful. In a way, this view made sense given the precarious nature of law and order during the boom days of the Roaring Twenties and, perhaps even more so, the dark years of the Great Depression. However, when violence was rearticulated in the service of law and order—in the "g-men" cycle of films and, for that matter, in films portraying war—it became acceptable. A similar trend can be seen during the 1950s when the use of violence in relation to teenagers in the "juvenile delinquency" cycle of films seemed to glamorize antisocial behavior among the young: the violence—articulated as "juvenile delinquency"—was again viewed negatively. So, too, in the late 1960s, during a period of increasing American violence at home and abroad, a concern for violence was voiced, but now it was understood as a more general category of physical action against others. This broader sense of violence—one not limited to tommy guns and gangsters—may have arisen partially in response to the perception that violence was becoming an increasingly common political tool—both for those in power and those in opposition. Student protests against the war and civil rights marches against institutional racism were often met with violent responses from the government and turned into chaotic street battles. As social critic Todd Gitlin observed, "The rhetoric of showdown and recklessness prevailed."[75]

The tumultuous decade of the Sixties achieved its zenith in 1968. In that year, the war in Vietnam reached its tragic crescendo with the largest insertion of U.S. troops, the highest death tolls, and the bloody onslaught of the Tet Offensive; two harbingers of peace and social change were gunned down—Martin Luther King Jr. on April 4 and Bobby Kennedy on June 4; and the protests outside the Democratic National Convention in Chicago descended into bloody chaos. In response to the violent nature of the times, President Lyndon Baines Johnson established the National Commission on the Causes and Prevention of Violence, and a portion—though in fairness a very small portion—of the committee's attention was focused on Hollywood.

MPAA president Valenti was called to Washington to testify before the presidential commission. During his appearance, he noted, "The problem of violence was one of the principal matters that occupied my attention when I first became president of this Association," adding, "It is only one, I might say, because it's only one part of the human condition."[76] These two themes would dominate Valenti's remarks. First, he declared that the MPAA was deeply concerned about issues of violence. Indeed, Valenti noted a voluntary letter signed by some 350 writers, producers, and directors pledging to avoid needless scenes of violence in light of the horrible assassinations of 1968. Second, he pressed the point that violence was a fundamental facet of the human condition and, as such, because many contemporary filmmakers were committed to offering mature and sophisticated explorations of the human condition, violence was a necessary ingredient.

The solution, according to Valenti, lay in reconsidering the audiences for these mature and sophisticated explorations. Films were no longer, he noted, one size fits all. "Motion pictures do not appeal to a single audience. There is no mass audience today."[77] The key to Valenti's proposal was that if movies were no longer designed for a unified and uniform audience, then the means of controlling films could not be unified or uniform. The one-size-fits-all construction of the Production Code was outmoded, and the solution lay in a system of categories that would align films with their appropriate audiences. Films would be rated with, initially, four ratings— G, for general audience; PG, for parental guidance recommended; R, for restricted (those under 17 admitted only with an accompanying adult); and X, meaning adults only. Thus, the death of the Production Code Administration—in many ways killed by the controversies over on-screen violence—saw the birth of the Code and Ratings Administration (CARA) and the motion picture rating system that continues to the present day.

In terms of violent films, the end of the Production Code truly opened the door. Among the first films to come blazing through was a small, independent horror film produced by a group of industrial filmmakers in Pittsburgh titled *Night of the Living Dead*. Released in 1968, the film that launched the career of horror auteur George Romero broke a number of barriers in relation to graphic violence. In spite of its negligible budget, the film's brutality, graphic images of cannibalism, and bleak, even nihilistic, ending produced strong reactions among many viewers. Perhaps most famously, popular movie critic Roger Ebert bemoaned the savagery of this film. Ebert in particular observed the way the independent and unrated film was, perhaps foolishly, distributed among matinee creature features and poignantly recounts watching the film while surrounded by terrified, sobbing young children whose parents had deposited them at the theater with little concern about what was playing.[78]

Even for films that went through the new ratings system, violence continued to be a difficult issue to classify. As a case in point, Sam Peckinpah's *The Wild Bunch* began production before the ratings system was established but was released under CARA with an R rating in 1969. Peckinpah's gritty story about a group of aging outlaws who seek out one last big score in the waning days of the Old West pushed the boundaries of violence on American screens. Syndicated Hollywood reporter Bob Foster declared:

> Never in all the years of television, even in the coverage of the Vietnam and Korean War, has so much violence been packed into two hours. *The Wild Bunch* is nothing but a series of gunfights, blood-curdling, blood-filled shoot outs and profanity carried to its extreme.[79]

Critic Judith Crist contended that the film's violent ending was "the bloodiest and most sickening display of slaughter that I can ever recall in a theatrical film."[80] Of course, these critics and most audiences saw an edited version of the film—preview audiences in Kansas City saw a thirty-five-minute longer version and reportedly left the theater in disgust. According to Frank Miller, "The theater was picketed the next day."[81]

The Wild Bunch and *Night of the Living Dead* opened up a new era in violence on-screen. Indeed, Marsha Kinder has argued that Peckinpah's *Wild Bunch*, along with other films of that era such as the earlier *Bonnie and Clyde* and the later controversial 1972 Stanley Kubrick film *A Clockwork Orange*, would establish the fundamental narrative structure of violence in American cinema for the next thirty years. In her reading, the violence in these films erupts in ways similar to musical numbers during a musical film—as orchestrated spectacles whose elegance and choreography supersedes the narrative function the violence itself serves.[82] This glorification of the spectacular moment of violence and the expansion of special-effects-driven gore established an aesthetic foundation for the cinematic violence in the years to come and would also become a prominent target for social critics.

Peckinpah continued to push the envelope of violence in his subsequent film *Straw Dogs*, released in 1971. This film, which starred Dustin Hoffman and Susan George, follows an American mathematician and his English wife as they return to her village. Animosities related to class and sex emerge as the mathematician raises the ire of the local villagers with his pompous attitude. The underlying tensions erupt when the wife's ex-lover and a group of his ruffian friends rape her and, later, when a local mentally disabled man is accused of murder and takes refuge with the mathematician and his wife. The angry local men return to seek revenge on the accused murderer, and the tensions explode into a symphony of violence. *Variety* declared, "Director Sam Peckinpah indulges himself in an orgy of unparalleled violence and nastiness with undertones of sexual repression in this production."[83] Wrapped up in the carnage are disturbing messages about masculinity—Hoffman's character seems to mature into being a "man" during his violent retribution—and female sexuality—the rape sequence has been often cited as one of the most disturbing scenes in film history and is accused by many of eroticizing rape.[84] On the first point, Pauline Kael, for instance, wrote that the film's purpose seems to be "to demonstrate that David [Hoffman's character] enjoys the killing, and achieves his manhood in that recognition."[85]

The combination of sex and violence had a long standing in American films, but the escalation of this relationship in the films of the early 1970s provoked considerable reaction. Peckinpah's film was followed by another film that featured rape at the center of its narrative, Stanley Kubrick's *A Clockwork Orange*. Kubrick's film received both harsh condemnation—including an X rating from the CARA—and strong praise, being nominated for the Academy Award for Best Picture and winning the New York Film Critics Circle's Best Picture in 1971.

A Clockwork Orange is an adaptation of the novel by Anthony Burgess. Set in the near future, the film follows a young punk named Alex who enjoys classical music and committing horrific acts of violence and rape with his gang, referred to as "droogs." After being arrested, Alex is sent to prison and enrolled in a rehabilitation program that, essentially, conditions him to have an intense physical aversion to violence and sex. In addition to the intensity of the scenes of violence, Kubrick's film is marked by its distant and ironic tone—sequences appear in slow motion, the classical soundtrack provides an oddly incongruous background, and one of the more infamous scenes involves Alex bursting out with "Singin' in the Rain" during a vicious assault on a writer and his wife.

The protests against *Clockwork* were intense in the United Kingdom, where the film was linked to a number of copycat crimes, including a rape in which the assailants were reportedly singing "Singin' in the Rain." The film was pulled from theaters in the UK and not rereleased there until 2000. In the United States, several newspapers, including the wide-circulation *Detroit News*, refused print ads for the film, citing its X rating and disturbing content.[86]

Perhaps the most lasting and disturbing cultural impact of both *Straw Dogs* and *Clockwork* is their legitimization of a brutal aesthetic of sexual violence, which would be taken up with increasing graphicness in numerous later films, ranging from Hitchcock's *Frenzy* (1972) to Meir Zarchi's *I Spit on Your Grave* (1978). The period of the 1970s would see a dramatic rise in films portraying violent rape. As critic Sarah Projansky notes, "the sheer number of representations of rape that have appeared on screen since the 1970s" can be seen as "a sustained definition of women as sexually victimized and a sustained cultural assault on women."[87] It is also worth recalling here that it was during this period of the early 1970s that the increasingly vocal feminist movement began to turn its critical eye toward the depictions of sexualized violence against women, as discussed in chapter 1.

The period between 1967 and 1971 marked an important and contentious turning point in American screen violence. *Bonnie and Clyde, The Wild Bunch,* and *A Clockwork Orange* were not simply violent films, they were *masterfully* violent films directed by three of America's most successful auteurs. These films did more than merely push the boundaries of violence on-screen—they created a visual aesthetic of violence, mayhem, and brutality that would have a lasting influence. Writing in 1975, Rick Witcombe insisted, "Movies like *Straw Dogs* and *A Clockwork Orange* have treated human savagery so penetratingly and resoundingly, for both public and other film-makers, that it almost becomes impossible to push much further."[88] Throughout the 1970s, however, filmmakers continued to push the boundaries in horror films like *The Texas Chainsaw Massacre* (1974), which *Harper's* called "a vile piece of sick crap with literally nothing to recommend it," and Romero's splatter-fest *Dawn of the Dead* (1978).[89] Other genres also embraced the rising tide of violence, especially tales of wronged men seeking revenge, as in the series of *Dirty Harry* films and the urban vigilante tale of *Death Wish* (1974), of which even the novel's author, Brian Garfield, protested its glamorization of violence.

The public's taste for particularly graphic and chaotic films would wane to an extent in the 1980s—John Carpenter's graphic 1982 masterpiece *The Thing* was generally reviled by critics as an orgy of violence and avoided by the mass public, which chose to envision its alien invaders as the cuddlier *E.T.* However, violence continued into the 1980s in a series of films that Susan Jeffords has referred to as "hard body" films.[90] These films, starring the likes of Arnold Schwarzenegger and Sylvester Stallone, featured big men with rippling muscles, combat training, and lots of guns. While the public enthusiasm for this particular brand of violence was high, there were lingering concerns about the effects of this kind of action violence on young people.

The tipping point in this debate came with two 1984 films from Steven Spielberg—*Gremlins*, which he produced, and *Indiana Jones and the Temple of Doom*, which he coproduced and directed. So concerned was Paramount about the violence in *The Temple of Doom* that it added a notation that "the film may be too intense for younger children," but this notation was not sufficient for the many parents, who took their children to see an adventure featuring Indiana Jones paired with a young Indian boy. Spielberg himself suggested to the MPAA that the broad category PG was insufficient for modern films, and from that suggestion emerged the PG-13 rating, which recommends special parental guidance for children under thirteen years of age.[91]

While the violence of the 1980s might have been somewhat subdued—or at least was brought into the service of righteous police officials and revenge-seeking military veterans—the 1990s saw the reemergence of the more chaotic and brutal elements of the 1970s with the rise of what J. David Slocum has called "the new violence." Filmmakers embracing this new graphic and brutal aesthetic included Abel Ferrara, whose *King of New York* (1990) and *The Bad Lieutenant* (1992) gesture back toward the grittier films of the 1940s and '50s, and perhaps most notably Quentin Tarantino, whose *Reservoir Dogs* (1992) simultaneously evokes heist-gone-bad films like John Huston's *The Asphalt Jungle* and the exploitation films of the 1970s. In many ways, Tarantino became the patron saint of the new violence, and the success of *Reservoir Dogs* and his follow-up *Pulp Fiction* (1994) solidified him as the hippest of the hip new violent Hollywood directors. But Tarantino's most controversial turns in cinema, thus far at least, have come from his work behind the typewriter rather than behind the camera. In the mid-1990s, two Tarantino-penned films emerged into one of the most public and protracted battles in the culture wars: the Tony Scott film *True Romance* (1993) and, with even greater intensity, Oliver Stone's *Natural Born Killers*.

VIOLENCE AND *NATURAL BORN KILLERS*

The movie that would become the most controversial violent film in recent memory began life as a treatment titled *The End of the Road*, written by Roger Avery. When Avery's friend and occasional writing partner Quentin Tarantino finished reworking the script, it was some four hundred pages long. The two writers then proceeded to separate elements of the story—writing first the script that would become Tony Scott's *True Romance* and then putting together the remaining scenes and dialogue and turning them into what would serve as the initial step toward Oliver Stone's *Natural Born Killers* (hereafter, *NBK*).

The script that would become *NBK* was shopped around Hollywood without any success until it ended up in the hands of Sean Penn, who promptly handed it on to Stone. Stone was preparing to shoot *Heaven and Earth* in Thailand and committed to making *NBK* his next film. However, the initial Tarantino screenplay wasn't yet acceptable to Stone—the narrative structure did not follow any clear chronological order, and the characters of Mickey and Mallory, the spree-killing couple at the center of the story, were mainly seen from the point of view of others. Producers Jane Hamsher and Don Murphy brought Dave Veloz on board to rewrite the script, providing a more coherent first act and fleshing out the two main characters. Tarantino was so incensed that he demanded he be listed only as "story by Quentin Tarantino" and would later publish his original version of the script, claiming that it was superior to the version filmed by Stone.[92]

In discussing his interest in making *NBK*, Stone declared, "I wanted to have fun. I really wanted to do a combination of a road movie, like *Bonnie and Clyde*, and a prison film, like *The Great Escape* or *Papillon*."[93] Stone's "fun" film, however, soon turned into what some critics called the most expensive mainstream experimental film ever made. With more than three thousand cuts—the average film has about six hundred—and featuring subliminal shots, religious and Native American spiritualism, animated sequences, and backdrops filled with hallucinatory images that serve as a "psychological" setting for the characters, Stone's *NBK* set out to craft an entirely new aesthetic for film violence. After making the film, Stone declared, "*Natural Born Killers* will be fresh in 20 years. I don't quite see anyone else making films like that. It's a new grammar."[94] What emerged from the making of *NBK* was a film that sought to critique mainstream America's love affair with violence and violent imagery by overloading their sensory intake with what one critic called "sheer carnage ... unrivaled in American film."[95]

Throughout much of his career, Oliver Stone has been known as a "cinematic provocateur," as critic Daniel Green puts it.[96] These provocations have not been without their consequences, and several of his films have become embroiled in controversy. Stone's *Platoon* poignantly mirrors his own horrific experiences as a soldier in Vietnam and paints a grim picture of America's zeal for war. His 1991 film *JFK*, which portrayed District Attorney Jim Garrison's pursuit of the alleged conspirators in the assassination of President John F. Kennedy, created a firestorm of controversy over the historical accuracy of his conspiracy narrative.[97]

On the surface, *JFK* and *NBK* have very little in common other than provoking controversy. The former is a studied and meticulously plotted historical detective film that blends the appearance of real historical evidence with fictionalization to craft a compelling case for the conspiracy theory of JFK's assassination. *NBK*, on the other hand, is an anarchic and surreal depiction of human violence taken near, if not actually, to its limits. However, in other ways, *NBK* follows along naturally from Stone's previous works. David Courtwright, for instance, argues that "*NBK* really belongs to Stone's Vietnam oeuvre" in its critical take on the dark, violent side of human nature.[98] Similarly, Green argues that the film "depicts with horrifying force the sorry state to which America has descended in the generation following the Kennedy Assassination."[99]

The basic plot of *NBK* is, in spite of all its aesthetic innovations, fairly straightforward. The film begins with our protagonists, Mickey and Mallory, slaughtering the patrons of a gritty roadside diner, after which we flashback to their first meeting in a segment patterned after an episode of *I Love Lucy*, complete with laugh track. This episode is also deeply disturbing, however, as it recounts Mallory's abusive home, complete with sexually abusive, alcoholic father and negligent mother. After Mickey is sent to prison by Mallory's father—accused of grand theft auto—he escapes, and the duo's murderous journey begins with the slaying of her parents. The pair's rampage becomes the focus of intense media glamorization, mainly through the person of television hack Wayne Gale, and we are shown various adoring fans. In the midst of their rampage down Route 666, the pair encounters a Native American mystic and we see, via hallucination, Mickey's broken childhood. After this episode, the pair are apprehended by an equally violent and corrupt police officer and taken to prison. Once in prison, television anchor Gale arranges an interview with Mickey— aired after the Super Bowl—the live broadcast of which sparks a violent, blood-soaked riot in the prison, which oddly also houses Mallory. The duo escapes by taking Gale hostage before unceremoniously killing him and is last seen driving off into the sunset surrounded by a group of children.

NBK opened at number one at the U.S. box office and lingered in the list of top money earners for several weeks. By the end of its run, it had earned a little more than $50 million, making it a modest hit.[100] Critics were deeply divided by the film. The critic for *Time* declared the film "daredevil fun of the sort that only Stone seems willing to provide in this timid film era," and Todd McCarthy, writing for *Variety*, called the film "a scathing indictment of a mass media establishment that caters to and profits from such starmaking." On the other side, David Denby felt the film was "an ejaculatory farce, but without satisfaction or rest," and Janet Maslin condemned the film's glorification of the sadistic killers and their "exhilarating freedom." Writing in *Rolling Stone*, Peter Travers insisted that "Stone's hypocrisy is galling" and declared, "Stone calls this bile satire.... Stone turns his film into the demon he wants to mock: cruelty as entertainment."[101]

My own sense of *NBK*, for what its worth, follows along with the more negative assessments. Stone said the film had a Jungian psychology, "with a little Nietzsche," and in that regard I can only recall Nietzsche's warning that whoever fights monsters must be careful not to become one. While the anarchic and transgressive spirit of *NBK* seems promising, in the end it seems to me the film becomes what it seeks to critique—another glorification of violence and incivility and nihilistic narcissism.

But the focus of this chapter is not on my assessment of the film or even the assessment of its contemporary critics. The heart of the controversy surrounding *NBK*, as has been the case for many controversial violent films, was whether it encouraged the violent behaviors it depicted and sought to criticize, and in this way the controversy over *NBK* is a good and representative example of many of the tensions surrounding depictions of violence throughout the history of film. Debates about *NBK* stirred up questions about whether film ought to be considered an art form or a commercial commodity—a debate that dates back to the 1915 *Mutual v. Ohio* decision—as well as the peculiar dichotomy between violence that is approved for social purposes and violence that is condemned as antisocial— as seen in the applause that greeted the replacement of gangsters with g-men in the 1940s.

The Massachusetts murder case that Bob Dole touted as proof of the danger that "nightmares of depravity" like *NBK* and *True Romance* would spur individuals to violence was, sadly, not an isolated incident, and it can be argued that *NBK* has been cited as a direct inspiration by more criminals than any film in history. Peter Schweizer, writing in *National Review*, claims that the film contributed to more than a dozen murders around the world, including the decapitation of a thirteen–year-old girl by a fourteen-year-old boy in Texas, the murder of a stepmother and half-sister by a teenager in Utah, and a killing spree by a young couple in France that left five dead.[102] In Chicago, there were reports of a trio of would-be burglars whose leader reportedly watched *NBK* several times before their spree and another group of teenagers who blamed the film for their robbery of a grocery store.[103] A couple in Georgia reportedly watched *NBK* nineteen times in a row and then, as Courtwright notes, "embarked on a crime spree that included carjacking, theft, kidnapping, and murder." They even "used Mickey's and Mallory's names in correspondence to each other after they were apprehended."[104] The film was even implicated in the tragic shooting spree by Eric Harris and Dylan Klebold at Columbine High School.[105]

The ensuing controversy over *NBK* can be seen to operate on three different, though interrelated, levels. The initial level includes the remarks from Kansas senator and White House aspirant Dole and the reactions to his condemnation of *NBK*. A second level of the controversy was begun when popular novelist and attorney John Grisham not only condemned Oliver Stone's film but also suggested that the film be held liable for some of the copycat crimes it allegedly inspired. This condemnation led directly to the third level of controversy, which took place in a series of court battles that reached all the way to the Supreme Court over Stone's responsibility for a copycat crime.

At the initial political level, Senator Dole's polemic against Hollywood instigated one small skirmish in the broader battle for the White House in 1996 and the even broader "culture wars" of the early 1990s. The culture war, conceived as a struggle between progressive liberals and social conservatives to control the wide-ranging values and norms of the culture, has been ongoing throughout American history, but it certainly reached a fevered pitch during and immediately following the Reagan era. President Ronald Reagan forged his political base out of a union between socially conservative religious fundamentalists and fiscally conservative, promilitary conservatives. This union became increasingly vocal during the Clinton administration, as President Bill Clinton became an attractive target for those who felt America had "lost" its deeply held and religiously based values. The skirmishes of the culture wars centered largely around those segments of society that overtly transmit values—notably, education, the media, and law. The battle cry of social conservatives often focused on taking back these institutions for "family values."

As James Hunter writes in his seminal book *Culture Wars: The Struggle to Define America*, "The contest to define reality, so central to the larger culture war, inevitably becomes a struggle to control the 'instrumentality' of reality definition."[106] Naturally, Hollywood was a key target and Dole's polemic against films like *NBK* and *True Romance*, as well as against music like Ice-T's song "Cop Killer," fit clearly within the broader political rhetoric of the New Right. Indeed, Ralph Reed, the Christian Coalition's executive director, called Dole's "Nightmares of Depravity" speech a "defining moment of his candidacy" and felt that, with that speech, Dole "clearly recognizes not only the importance of the religious conservative vote, but understands the broad appeal that can be gained by making themes about culture a centerpiece of his campaign."[107] Dole, though a longtime major player in the Republican Party, had not been seen as an especially strong proponent of the religious right's agenda. But, in the aftermath of major victories for Republicans in the 1994 congressional elections, Dole used his attack on Hollywood as an attempt to ride the tide of the culture wars and gain momentum in his bid to remove Clinton from the White House.

Dole's attempt was, of course, ultimately unsuccessful, as President Clinton won reelection with a fairly healthy 70 percent of the electoral vote, but for a while Dole was successful in shifting the national attention to questions of the entertainment industry's responsibility in relation to violent materials. Interestingly, Clinton had already raised the issue of media violence months before Dole did, in his 1995 State of the Union Address in which he urged efforts to "understand the damage that comes from incessant, repetitive, mindless violence."[108] Clinton would also later champion the V-chip, a device designed to help parents regulate what their children could watch on television—and that took its "V" from the concern over violence in American media.[109] The 1990s were filled with similar debates and initiatives as numerous politicians took up the question of media violence, and in 2000, a Senate hearing investigated whether Hollywood was intentionally marketing violence to children.[110]

Dole's critique of *NBK* was not without its own critics. At least three responses were offered by supporters of the film, and these are illustrative of deeper tensions surrounding questions of violence in film. The first response to Dole was based on his selective condemnation of Hollywood. Beyond singling out films like *NBK* and *True Romance*, Dole explicitly pointed his finger at Time Warner—the corporation responsible for these and other violent films and music. His critique did not, however, extend to other contemporary violent films like the Schwarzenegger vehicle *True Lies* or the Bruce Willis film *Die Hard with a Vengeance*. Critics of Dole's narrow polemic noted that those films not only starred prominent Hollywood Republicans—Schwarzenegger and Willis—but were also distributed by Twentieth Century-Fox, a company owned by conservative media mogul Rupert Murdoch. Dole's selectiveness thus seemed designed to raise the violence issue without angering powerful supporters of his campaign. As Henry Sheehan noted at the time, "Clearly Bob Dole is no fool. But just as clearly, he's no moral arbiter, either."[111]

Beyond the intriguing tangle of political bedfellows, Dole's choice to denounce *NBK* and later praise *True Lies* may also be motivated by the ways in which violence is depicted in these films and the ends toward which it is put. Kimberly Owczarski makes an important observation about Dole's critical rhetoric when she notes that the film *True Lies*, which Dole praised, "is so normative that it does not disjoint the viewer from the narrative," whereas *NBK* "does jolt the viewer, and, in so doing, causes the viewer to think about the action onscreen."[112]

Three important points can be raised from this observation. First, the film *True Lies* presents violence largely in the service of law and order—Schwarzenegger is a secret agent who inflicts enormous and cartoonish levels of violence on terrorists who threaten America—while in *NBK*, violence is not only antisocial but also anarchic—Mickey and Mallory's killing spree seems to serve no end other than their own narcissistic lust for destruction. The tension between prosocial and antisocial violence mirrors that of earlier eras and raises the difficult question of whether we are willing to accept horrific acts of violence if they are said to serve our "national interests."[113]

A second objection was raised by those who questioned how Dole could condemn media violence while continuing to support the National Rifle Association and a broader agenda to keep firearms readily available. As critic Roger Ebert complained, "Dole's appeal to conservative voters requires a selective use of issues: yes to guns, no to movies depicting them."[114] In this complex contradictory stand on violence, we see reflected the long-standing concern that somehow films are more dangerous than material objects. The violent film threatens to infiltrate the very psyche of the nation and for this reason requires more careful control than the actual physical means for inflicting mass violence on others. This logic—that culture is ultimately to blame for violence rather than the ready availability of firearms—was remarkably pervasive throughout this period, as debates about the spate of high school shootings seemed more focused on films, music, and video games than on the firearms used in their commission.

A third objection to Dole's critique of *NBK* was raised by his admission that he had never seen the film but had merely "read a bunch of reviews."[115] On this point, Ebert blasted the presidential candidate, recommending: "First, you have to see the movies. Then you have to think about them."[116] Once again, as with the first objection to Dole's comments, we find here echoes of earlier debates. For Ebert, one of those who praised Stone's violent film, *NBK* was a satirical critique of media violence, and Dole's failure to recognize this was due, in large part, to his failure to engage the film at any meaningful level. This line of reasoning mirrors that of the William Hays claim that gangster films were a deterrent to crime: in both instances, it was claimed that violence was being portrayed in a negative light.

The long-standing historical question remains, however, as to whether depictions of violence can remain negative or, as in this instance, the violence being critiqued becomes glamorized. Jane Caputi puts the question well: "How is *Natural Born Killers* not part of 'the media' that creates such cultural bankruptcy? Does it simply reflect that condition, or does it work to conjure the murderous future it so saucily envisions?"[117] For many of Dole's supporters, the answer to this question was clear—*NBK* was responsible for provoking violence in the real world. Representative J. C. Watts Jr., for instance, laid the blame for the Columbine shootings squarely at the foot of Oliver Stone. The film, he argued, had inspired the two teenage killers who had made "a religion out of violence. Their high priest seems to have been Oliver Stone."[118]

The charges against *NBK* were not confined to the oratorical flourishes of politicians but also extended into a broader cultural struggle over questions of violence, media, and responsibility. The cultural tussle over *NBK* was most dramatically encapsulated in the highly publicized debate between Stone and an unlikely critic, bestselling novelist and attorney John Grisham. While Grisham made his fortune from novels about crime and legal intrigues—for example, *The Pelican Brief* and *A Time to Kill*, as well as their movie adaptations—he became one of Stone's staunchest and most public condemners. In a 1996 issue of *The Oxford American*, a literary magazine he publishes, Grisham not only charged Stone with responsibility for copycat crimes but went on to suggest the legal strategy of filing what would amount to a product liability suit against the film's producers.

The arguments Grisham advanced are instructive for our thinking about the dynamics of controversies related to violence in film. Grisham's essay begins with his recollection of living in the small town of Hernando, Mississippi, and his acquaintance with a local cotton gin owner, Bill Savage, and then moves to a harrowing description of Savage's senseless murder and the seemingly unrelated shooting of a woman in Ponchatoula, Louisiana.

The shootings of Savage and the woman, Patsy Byers, who survived her shooting though remained paralyzed, Grisham reveals, were related. Two teenagers from Oklahoma, nineteen-year-old Sarah Edmondson and her eighteen-year-old boyfriend Ben Darras, had left their homes in an aimless drive toward Tennessee before engaging in the brief crime spree that would leave Savage dead and Byers disabled. After their arrest, the two young lovers turned against each other, and each blamed the other for the crimes.

Grisham derived the motivation for these crimes from statements made by Edmondson: "Ben loved *Natural Born Killers*, and as they drove to Memphis he spoke openly of killing people, randomly, just like Mickey spoke to Mallory."[119] This and other crimes, in Grisham's estimation, can be laid directly at the feet of Oliver Stone and the Hollywood institution he represents, and in the final pages of his essay, the novelist searches for ways to rectify the situation. One means of redress—a boycott—was dismissed by Grisham as ineffective. The second suggestion was to sue.

> Think of a movie as a product, something created and brought to market, it is only one small step away. If something goes wrong with the product, whether by design or defect, and injury ensues, then its makers are held responsible.[120]

A massive liability judgment would, in Grisham's estimation, be the most effective means of stopping the flow of violent images upon the screens, and it was this suggestion that inspired the family of Patsy Byers to file a lawsuit against Stone and Time Warner.

Grisham's essay is another interesting example of some typical appeals issued against violent films. The argument that films be seen as products—products that can be defective and dangerous—harkens back to the logic of early-twentieth-century jurists who saw films as "mere entertainment" but also recognized its potential for "evil influence." Additionally, in an interesting wrinkle to the standard argument about "glamorizing violence," Grisham's essay comes back time and again to the audacity of these crimes. Grisham's accusations against the film and the criminals inspired by it are framed by how offensive the flagrant flaunting of moral standards are: "Soon the two youths began *bragging* about their exploits"; Sarah is quoted as saying, "Ben *mocked* the noise the man made when Ben shot him." It is not so much the crimes that strike such a chord with Grisham as it is the blatant disregard for moral standards and the lack of remorse or regret. Grisham sees the source of this mocking cruelty in Stone's film: "You see, the character Mickey in *Natural Born Killers* felt much the same way. He sneered and laughed a lot when he killed people, and then he sneered and laughed some more after he killed them."[121]

The traditional objection about glamorizing violence is involved here—Grisham writes that "Oliver Stone is saying that murder is cool and fun"—but there is another dimension that focuses on the spectacular—literally the spectacle—nature of the violence. Ultimately, the offensive audacity is not just that of the characters or of the copycat killers but of Stone and his Hollywood compatriots who seem unable to control themselves. While Grisham's legal solution—dealt with below—did not prove effective, the incendiary charges against Stone raised by Grisham did spark even further debate about the film as the duel between the novelist and the filmmaker was covered by popular magazines, including *Vanity Fair*, *Time*, and *The Village Voice*.

As a final comment on Grisham's polemic against Stone, it is worth observing what many others noted, namely, that Grisham seems an odd critic given his own role in producing narratives of violence and crime. Stone responded to Grisham's accusations against him by charging that "Grisham is a hypocrite," observing that his books have featured murders, adultery, and vigilante killings.[122] Grisham's hypocrisy, like that of Dole, stems from his dual sense of violence. Violence in the service of law and order is, in Grisham's sense, appropriate and laudable; however, violence as a disruptive force is to be condemned. As Joel Black notes in his perceptive reading of Grisham's essay, "According to [Grisham's] ethic, displays of physical violence and abuses of justice are acceptable as long as the Law reestablishes and re-asserts itself at the end."[123]

In a way, the law did assert itself in the protracted controversy over *NBK* when the liability case brought against Stone and his producers by Byers wound its way through the court systems. The teenage killers, Edmondson and Darras, received justice in the courts, both sentenced to thirty-five years for the shooting of Byers with an additional life sentence for Darras in the slaying of Bill Savage. So, too, did Oliver Stone, though his case took considerably longer. After the "incitement lawsuit" was initially dismissed by District Judge Robert Morrison, the Louisiana appellate court reinstated the case. Stone and Warner Bros. appealed this decision all the way to the U.S. Supreme Court but found no relief, and the case made its way back to the 21st Judicial District Court. The plaintiffs charged that Stone and Time Warner were guilty of inciting the shooting of Patsy Byers and that *NBK* was not entitled to First Amendment protection because, first, it incited violence and, second, the film should be regarded as obscene.

The accusation by Byers's attorneys was not without precedent. There have been numerous previous cases charging some artist with responsibility for actions alleged to be inspired by their art. Rock musician Ozzy Osbourne, for instance, was sued by the parents of a teenage suicide victim who claimed his music led to their son's death. However, in almost all of these cases, the courts have ruled against the plaintiffs and in favor of the protection afforded artists under the First Amendment. The courts have relied upon an argument established in *Brandenberg v. Ohio*: that inflammatory speech cannot be prohibited unless it clearly incites illegal behavior. This legal reasoning argues that "the mere tendency of speech to encourage unlawful acts is not a sufficient reason for banning it."[124] The same reasoning that protects inflammatory messages from prior restraint also extends to protection against liability for acts said to be inspired by the message. As Helen Anderson notes, "Producers and sellers of art and entertainment are not liable for the actions of those who consume their products."[125] Not surprisingly, Byers's attorneys were unable to offer evidence of a clear intent to incite, and therefore, on March 12, 2001, the court dismissed the lawsuit against Stone and Warner Bros.[126]

Although Stone and his film were cleared, at least two interesting legal legacies from this controversy remain. First, while the court continued its precedent of ruling against liability charges against artists, there continues to be interest among some parties in finding ways to link liability for violent crimes to media makers. John Charles Kunich, a law professor at Appalachian Law School, has argued for a "shock tort," that is,

> a cause of action based on acts of violence causally linked to the perpetrator's exposure—especially if a minor—to shockingly violent forms of mass entertainment that, on their face, appear to be calculated primarily to appeal to persons with an appetite for killing or sociopathic behavior particularly of an unlawful nature.[127]

Along similar lines, Rick Caballero, the attorney who represented the Byers family in the action against Stone, expressed hopes that the case might be picked up for review by the Supreme Court and that the case might be used to expand the legal notion of obscenity. Caballeros explained, "If we could get the Supreme Court to include violence in the obscenity standard, we can make it [graphic violence] a community standard."[128]

A second legal wrinkle related to the struggles over violence in *NBK* is that the courts have allowed evidence of a defendant viewing the film to be admitted in criminal trials. As Anderson reports, "A fascination with, or just a taste for, the movie [*NBK*] has been used against criminal defendants in a number of cases." She goes on to detail instances of the viewing of *NBK* being used as evidence in murder cases in Georgia, Louisiana, Massachusetts, New Mexico, North Carolina, Oregon, and Washington. The notion that the act of watching a film like *NBK* can be used as evidence of a criminal intent or state of mind is a perplexing take on the relationship between film and behavior. When the courts conceive this relationship in terms of the producer, the causal link is perceived as weak, and the producer's right of expression trumps whatever "mere tendency" to cause violence may be discerned. However, when framed in terms of the consumer of violent media, the courts seem to view the link between media and violence as markedly more plausible. As Anderson puts it:

> The basis for admission of evidence of the movie, or the defendant's fascination with it, seems to be an assumption of a causal link between the movie

and crime—a link that has been rejected in the suits by crime victims against producers of the movie.[129]

Thus, in the contemporary legal wrangling over violence in media, there seems to be a new and unique distinction being developed between the producer and consumer of violent media, a distinction that may continue to shape controversies over violence in film in the years to come.

CONCLUSION

Controversies over violence in film date back at least as far as those related to sex and, in many ways, have had as big an impact on the broader mechanisms of film production, viewing, and regulation. However, the broad survey of the history of controversies over violent films suggests that these disputes have followed different cultural contours than those related to sex. Where sex and sexuality seemed largely understood in relation to questions of identity and morality, the controversies over violence appear to be more focused on the deep question of social order and governance. Violence in the service of law and order has almost without exception been sanctioned—even when explicitly violating censorship codes—whereas violence depicted as a source of disorder and criminality has almost always been the subject of public censure, and at times censorship.

One of the questions I have intentionally avoided in this chapter is whether or not violent films and media actually *do* contribute to violent behavior in society. This matter has received mountains of attention from social scientists and public policy makers, and the various conflicting results from numerous studies have contributed to a wide and lively public debate.[130] Not surprisingly, much of this debate has centered around the influence of violent media on children, and this has been a fairly consistent trend in debates about film violence since the beginning of cinema. The most dramatic and publicized of the copycat cases throughout the history of violent films have been those related to children, including William Harold Gamble in 1931 or Sara Edmondson and Ben Darras in 1995. The ultimate answer, if such is even possible, to the question of whether the media led these children and countless others to commit violent crimes is, for present purposes, less interesting than the reasons that this question is posed in the first place and, perhaps most importantly, the way this question is framed in light of contemporary political struggles. As a clarifying example, in both the case of Gamble and that of Sara Edmondson and Ben Darras, one of the alternative issues raised was the ready availability of firearms, which were indispensable in the commission of these crimes. However, in both cases, the public debate about the role of film quickly drowned out this other conversation. The desire of politicians, reporters, and social scientists to point their fingers at popular entertainment as the culprit is an interesting and instructive consistency.

If the study of controversy—which is to say a systematic focus on under-standing the ways people argue and deliberate during times of contro-versy—has any merit, then it must be as a way of understanding the contours of public debate. Attention to these deliberations, literally the rhetoric of the controversy, should draw our attention as much to the ques-tions raised as to the answers proposed.

CHAPTER 4

Race and Ethnicity: Spike Lee's
Do the Right Thing

lthough it is a bit embarrassing to admit now, the thing I remember most about first viewing Spike Lee's 1989 film *Do the Right Thing* was being afraid. The film had been surrounded by incendiary press accounts and reviews since its debut at Cannes. While Lee's film lost out for the top award that year to Steven Soderbergh's *sex, lies, and videotape*, it certainly received the most press attention, and critics like David Denby—who claimed Lee was "playing with dynamite in an urban playground"—and Jeanne Williams were soon condemning the film as nothing but a provocation to racial violence.[1] Jack Kroll, writing in *Newsweek*, worried that the film would put "dynamite under every seat." Joe Klein, in *New York* magazine, objected to "the dangerous stupidity of Spike Lee's message."[2] Those warnings echoed in my head as I sat in a theater crowded with patrons of various races. Lee would later comment that the negative publicity surrounding the film had hurt it at the box office because "it scared white audiences away from the film"—and as one of the white audience members who overcame the negative hype, I can understand Lee's assessment.[3] Of course, fear has always been at the heart of race relations in America, both the fear of people from other races and, for white liberals like myself, fear that our actions might be perceived by others as racist. Trapped within these conflicting sets of fear and guilt, I recall glancing around the audience at the urban cinema where I had come to watch Lee's incendiary polemic, and it seemed to me that others were experiencing a similar sense of trepidation.

Of course, the dire predictions of critics—and my own personal fears—did not come to fruition as there were no major incidents of violence or unrest attached to Lee's film, but that fact should not lead us to immediately dismiss those apprehensions as baseless. The controversy over Lee's *Do the Right Thing*, as with the controversies over many films representing race and ethnicity, was largely driven by these predictions of unrest that come from and fuel the fear of the film as harbinger of violence. But, where does this fear come from? Given the already tense racial climate in America in the late 1980s—a state of tension existing arguably since the nation's inception—why would a movie be perceived as particularly dangerous?

At this point in this book, these questions should seem familiar. Throughout the history of cinema, films have been perceived as dangerous and provocative, and the cinematic messages about sex or violence or race as somehow more potent and potentially disruptive than those rendered in other media. Of course, controversies over race and ethnicity in film have their own unique history, and the dangers perceived in these films are also unique. Whereas controversies over sex have seemed to orbit around notions of morality and identity and controversies over violence tend to engage issues of social stability and order, controversies over race invoke their own unique sense of danger—a danger centered on the issue of difference.

As Gerald Butters Jr. notes, "The trope of race has been a powerful form of difference in American film. Racial differentiation creates societal Others."[4] In this sense, the "Other" is not simply someone who is not Us, but someone who is distinctly not *like* us—whose presence makes our similarities clearer by their dissimilarity, or at least our perception of their dissimilarity. As cultural critic Kenneth Burke perceptively observed, one of the most powerful ways to create a sense of "us" is to contrast "us" with "them." In American culture, and certainly in American cinema, race and ethnicity have been among the most common visual means of demarcating "us" from some Other. Following Burke's thinking, the creation of an Other is not merely a demarcation or a means of defining "us" but also creates a sense of fear of that Other whose difference from us defines them. The separation created by this division between "us" and "them" and the fear it generates, in turn, lead to anger and resentment directed toward those who are, by definition, not like us.

These observations, of course, are probably not especially earth shattering, and I acknowledge that critics of race relations over the past hundred or so years have made abundantly clear the ways that representations of various races contribute to our deeply stratified society. Writing in 1903, renowned African American intellectual W. E. B. Du Bois declared, "The problem of the Twentieth Century is the problem of the color line"; sadly, his assessment may be accurate for the next century as well.[5] But one additional idea—though, again, not one that is especially unique to this writing—should help to push our thinking about race and film a bit further. The idea is this: There is a fairly clear cinematic sense of who "we" are versus who "they" are, and this unspoken and generally taken-for-granted assumption of who constitutes the "we" is those of European ancestry, whom I will call whites.

The privileging of a white point of view is not unique to cinema, but it is pervasive. Ella Shohat and Robert Stam have noted that in most American media, "Europe is seen as the unique source of meaning, as the world's center of gravity."[6] Even though the United States is one of the few nations not founded on a notion of ethnicity or race—but rather on a constitutional framework of law—it is a nation that has consistently and aggressively privileged the perspective and social position of those descended from particular European ancestries.

Of course, even this sense of what constitutes "European ancestry" has been a moving target. At time, those of Irish or Italian descent were not considered "white," nor were those from Portugal or from eastern Europe. The fluidity of the boundaries around this privileged European social position is telling in two regards.

First, it reminds us that the very notion of "white" is constituted not by some essential quality or lineage that delineates a White race, but rather, as noted above, is constituted by the Others who are defined as not white.[7]

The second idea suggested by the fluid boundaries around whiteness is the degree to which whiteness is a privileged site. The reason the lines demarcating "white" from "nonwhite" are important is because of the level of privileges and social currency given to those considered white. These unstated privileges range from very real and powerful protections, such as not having to fear being pulled over by the police solely because of one's race and not having to fear being denied housing, to more mundane but still potent issues such as always being able to consume media written by and for white people.

The notion of "white privilege" is a powerful concept because it reframes debates about issues of race and racism so that these debates no longer focus attention solely on the victims of racial oppression. There has been for many years an unfortunate tendency for discussions of racism to focus primarily on how the victims "fail" to achieve social and economic parity. This insidious logic of "blame the victim" also allows members of the privileged race to relieve themselves of responsibility. If, many of us think, we don't actively deny housing to members of another race or use racial slurs, then we are, by our definition, not "racist." Defining racism solely in terms of active behaviors allows the vast majority of us who are not actively involved in acts of discrimination to ignore the problem and, in that insidious logic noted above, to leave the problem of racism for those oppressed by it to solve.

Conceiving racism in terms of white privilege reminds us that systems of racial oppression and racial privilege are inextricably linked, so the privileges enjoyed by one group are necessarily implicated in the oppression endured by another. In this way, as sociologists Michael Omi and Howard Winant famously declared, our understanding of race creates a "racial formation" that is involved in almost every social institution, ranging from the symbolic (like films and television) to the material (like housing and health care). As Omi and Winant observed, "Race is a matter of both social structure and cultural representation."[8]

Understanding this racial formation through the notion of white privilege also underscores the ways in which white privilege is rendered invisible by both the social institutions that provide it and the cultural representations that support it. White actors, for instance, are never called "credits to their race." Indeed, in many ways, whiteness is not even considered a race at all but is defined instead as the "norm" against which all other races are contrasted. This invisibility allows the privileges of white people to be perpetuated and institutionally supported without calling attention to them because there is no white race to privilege, just other races who are "behind."[9]

This brief consideration of white privilege brings us to an important implication of white privilege for controversies over film. The boundaries around the invisible formation of white privilege are constant sources of conflict and controversy, although, given the invisible nature of white privilege, these contests are almost always defined in terms of the Others who object to their position in society. But, conceived in terms of issues of whiteness and white privilege, the controversies over race and ethnicity in film are not solely about how a certain group is represented in film but about who has the authority over representation of the Other and, for that matter, who gets to define "the Other" in the first place. In American society, this authority has centered almost exclusively within the cultural privilege of whiteness, and it this authority that has been at the center of most debates about race and representation.

A HISTORY OF CONTROVERSIES OVER RACE AND ETHNICITY IN FILM

As David Bernardi observes, "Race has been and continues to be a fundamental part of U.S. cinema."[10] Sadly, this history has not always been a positive one. Racist depictions are evident from even the earliest short reels of the 1890s, in films like *The Chinese Laundry Scene* (1896) and *Chicken Thieves*, an 1897 Edison film built around the stereotype of a thieving African American male and concluding with a white farmer firing his shotgun at the retreating thief. While the racist roots of American film cannot be justified, in some important ways they can be understood to be derived from broader cultural trends occurring during the birth of the modern cinema.

The turn of the nineteenth century was a particularly turbulent period in American history and one in which the pressing questions of enfranchisement were being posed in dramatic and difficult ways. If the eighteenth century was the revolutionary point of origin for the American idea, articulated in the Declaration of Independence and later the Constitution, then the nineteenth century was the period in which the revolutionary idea was being brought into practice. Founding a government on the idea of universal legal and political equality was relatively easy in concept, but in practice it was difficult. The Civil War represents, perhaps, the most dramatic moment in which the principal of "liberty and justice for all" was tested and, while the war and Lincoln's proclamation of emancipation were successes, the subsequent period in which racist social institutions and practices were allowed to essentially recreate a plantation system in the South put the American ideal to great test. As Butters notes, "The late nineteenth and early twentieth centuries also witnessed some of the worst racial violence in U.S. history."[11] He cites racial riots in such towns as Wilmington, North Carolina; Springfield, Illinois; and Brownsville, Texas as well as the rapid growth in lynchings of African Americans during this period.

Of course, American racial tensions were not solely about relations between whites and African Americans but also included those of most other races considered nonwhite. While Chinese immigration had been encouraged in the 1860s and '70s in order to facilitate western expansion, by 1882 Congress had passed a law barring Chinese immigrants from entry into the country. A similar concern was raised about Japanese immigration into western American cities. The fear of Japanese immigration reached its peak in 1906 when a controversy over segregated schools in San Francisco—where Japanese students were not allowed into schools designated "whites only"—led President Theodore Roosevelt to negotiate his famous "gentlemen's agreement" with the government of Japan to voluntarily limit Japanese emigration into the United States. Tensions with those of Latin American descent were also high, as the United States engaged in the Spanish American War in 1898, and the destruction of Native American cultures was rapidly reaching its zenith during the late nineteenth century.

As early as 1912, the film western was romanticizing the killing of Native Americans with particular emphasis on the death of Col. George Armstrong Custer in 1876. Of the rapid growth in films depicting Native Americans as villains, Allen Woll and Randall Miller observed that "little attempt has been made by filmmakers to understand Indian motivations for action, as virtually all activities are characterized from the white man's point of view," and, in general, we can take that tendency as a given in almost all the depictions of other races in the earliest decades of American cinema.[12]

The dominance of the "white man's point of view" relates to the fact that early cinema, dating from the rapid growth of nickelodeons in 1905, was primarily a venue for the lower classes and immigrant populations.

Sharon Kleinman and Daniel McDonald note the "strange irony that many of the early silent films, which were heavily viewed by immigrant audiences, reflected the xenophobic, anti-immigrant, and anti-Black views prevailing in the American zeitgeist."[13] The gross caricatures of nonwhite races thus functioned to reinforce the broad assimilationist ideology in America—all are welcome so long as they give up their cultural traditions and meld into mainstream American society.

Regarding the ideological function of early films, Butters contends:

> As a "poor man's entertainment," therefore, these films need to be considered in relationship to issues of class. Appearing in a decade in which millions of first- and second-generation immigrants were attempting to climb the American ladder of social mobility, films with African American portrayals [though I think we can also add Latino, Chinese, Japanese and Native portrayals] tended to solidify "whiteness," stretching the boundaries to include the masses of newcomers who were attempting to become "American."[14]

Even a cursory glance at the depiction of nonwhites in these early films reveals a staggering array of the most base and horrific stereotypes imaginable—from the series of "watermelon" films from Edison and Lubin studios, with their crude caricature of voracious African Americans played for "comedic" value, to the use of the racial slur "greaser" in relation to Latino Americans.[15]

It is worth noting here that films did not necessarily invent these early vulgar stereotypes. Vaudeville, pulp novels, magazines, cartoons, and folktales all contributed to the cardboard-cutout caricatures of various races and ethnicities—from the Irish being drunks to Polish Americans lacking intelligence to Native Americans being murdering savages.[16] Early films made these stereotypes more striking and visually marked. Silent films, of course, work almost exclusively in the nonverbal, visual medium wherein physical appearances and actions stand in for characterization. While the roots of these stereotypes were laid in American popular culture long before the advent of cinema, the growth of silent films disseminated them in a highly efficient mass system that would create a visual typology of racism that has continued in American cinema to this very day.

As I hope to demonstrate in this historical survey, this racism did not go unnoticed or uncontested. The history of racial representation in American films, as I suggested earlier, is a history of contests over the authority to craft representations.

At the outset of this history, it is worth acknowledging one of the difficulties unique to considering controversies over race, namely, the multiplicity of issues invoked with the mere mention of the word *race*. Notions of sex and violence are, as I suggested in the previous chapters, fluid and dynamic, but at any given point in time, discussions of "sex" generally point toward the same set of issues. In discussing race and film, there is a difference. Discussions of representations of, say, African Americans may have a very different valence than conversations about Latinos—and, indeed, this was often the case.

Until relatively recently, there were few discussions of "race," as a general concept, in relation to film. Rather, the particular controversies over racial representations tended to be specific to the representation and the race represented. As such, it will be necessary to move among different racial communities and consider the various trajectories of their struggles over representation. As noted above, at the heart of all these discussions is the unstated and taken-for-granted centrality of white privilege, and it will be important for us not to lose track of that, either. Indeed, as I think will become clear throughout this section, the various, often diverging paths of struggles over racial representation tend to have one thing in common: their paths are largely dictated by the efforts of the white majority to maintain its authority over issues of representation and privilege.

1897–1914

Among the earliest films with racist depictions were those aimed at Chinese and Japanese immigrants. The backlash against the Chinese, who had been eagerly brought into America in the early 1800s but then banned from immigrating in 1882, created a host of culturally biased stereotypes. As Eugene Wong argues:

> Culturally biased perceptions of the Chinese as uniquely non-Western in dress, language, religion, customs and eating habits determined that the Chinese were inferior.... The assumed unassimilability of the Chinese was attributed to their racial and cultural characteristics, with scant attention paid to the fact that few whites encouraged them to assimilate, while many active discouraged their assimilation by legal and illegal means.[17]

This cultural bias against Chinese immigrants translated easily onto the screens of early nickelodeons in films like *The Yellow Peril*, a 1908 production depicting a Chinese servant who provokes his master's violent scorn. The tension surrounding cultural assimilation was also evident in films like D. W. Griffith's *That Chink at Golden Gulch* (1910), in which a Chinese character (played by a white man in "yellowface") is rescued from cowboy bullies by a young woman to whom he then pledges his loyalty. He later thwarts a bank robber by cutting off his braided hair in order to subdue the robber and subsequently turns the reward money over to the young woman and her fiancé. Beyond the visually stereotypical depiction of the titular protagonist—including intertitle cards reading, for example, "Charlie Lee wishee much glad you two"—the narrative's story line underscores the assimilationist ideology at work in these early films. The acceptable place in American society for Charlie Lee is one of subservience to the whites whom he both serves and fears. Perhaps the most important part of this subservient depiction is the erasure of any hint of sexual desire on the part of the Chinese character. Miscegenation, a topic that looms large in early fears about racial depictions in film, was deeply taboo in American culture, and depictions of nonwhites had to be either desexualized or have their sexual desires punished. In Griffith's early film, the prior strategy is utilized. As Daniel Bernardi reads this film, "Less a character and more a caricature, the Chink is de-masculinized in a way that justifies his eventual servitude and ensures that his intentions are not read as sexually transgressive."[18]

While Chinese communities in America did not accept the racial slurs and demeaning depictions, the more dramatic protests against early racist cinema came from the Japanese community, who had the advantage of being supported by a more powerful home government. By the early years of the twentieth century, the nation of Japan had transitioned fairly smoothly to westernization and had itself become a major geopolitical power—engaging in extensive military campaigns throughout the Pacific, including the Sino-Japanese War of 1895, in which Japan gained control over Korea, Taiwan, and other principalities of China, and perhaps more dramatically, the Russo-Japanese War in 1904–5, in which Japan essentially defeated the Russian military in China. In the United States, the growing power of the Japanese government led to slightly more delicate treatment. As Wong observes, "Although there was a limit to which the Japanese might resort against persecution of Japanese nationals in America, the Japanese government's willingness to protest strongly any demonstration of anti-Japanese behavior or sentiment was seriously acknowledged by American officials."[19]

Although the U.S. government took a more cautious stand in dealing with Japan, American cultural racism saw little distinction between Japanese, Chinese, Koreans, or others from the Pacific region. The blurring of nationalities into a single Asian stereotype, unsurprisingly, did not sit well with the Japanese government, which sought to maintain Japanese superiority in the eyes of the American government. However, these efforts met with a clear rebuff in the Immigration Law of 1924, which excluded Asians from any nation from citizenship in the United States.

The legal exclusion of people of Asian descent was motivated by numerous economic, racist, and political factors, and the depiction of these peoples in American cinema contributed to the general racist attitude. This cultural bias against those of Asian descent was wrapped up in an older Western myth of the "Yellow Peril." Gina Marchetti describes this myth:

> Rooted in medieval fears of Genghis Khan and Mongolian invasions of Europe, the yellow peril combines racist terror of alien cultures, sexual anxieties, and

the belief that the West will be overpowered by the irresistible, dark, occult forces of the East.[20]

The theme of the Yellow Peril led Hollywood films to portray characters of Asian descent as, in the worst cases, threatening or, in most other cases, either bumbling clowns or subservient exotics. In almost every instance, the depiction of Chinese or Japanese characters emphasized their difference and provided a cultural foundation for other institutional forms of discrimination.

Not surprisingly, these cultural forms of prejudice did not go without response. In addition to various protests by the Japanese government against instances of discrimination against its émigré population, the Japanese American community began forming a strong alliance against discrimination and prejudice through connections with both the Japanese government and groups of prestigious pro-Japanese white Americans.[21]

Another development was the use of film by the Japanese government in other parts of the world to propagate its own vision of Japanese supremacy in Asia. Thomas F. Millard, writing in a 1907 edition of the *Washington Post*, remarked upon the spread of films depicting Japanese victory over the Russians. His concerns reveal the strange dynamics surrounding race and film:

> A Chinese or Indian coolie cannot be reached by literature as a rule, except indirectly; but he is absolutely open to impression from pictures which represent action, the authenticity of which he does not dream of questioning, and which shows the white race he has so long respected and feared beaten at war by a dark-skinned brother.[22]

There is an odd irony in an American commentator condemning the Japanese government for seeking to use cinematic images to create a vision of racial superiority—a condemnation that required turning a blind eye to the similar American efforts both at home and abroad.

These two examples—protests against racist depictions and the use of film to provide counterdepictions—are indicative of the general responses to controversies over race and film. The first response was to vocally condemn the slurs depicted on the screen, and the second was to take up the instruments of cinema and seek to initiate a new filmic discourse through which to create a different vision. In the case of Japan, this effort was facilitated by a strong national government that could both lodge official protests against unfair representations and produce counterpropaganda.

A similar situation arose in relation to Latin Americans during this early period. As early as 1907, American films were referring to Mexicans with the derogatory racial slur "greasers," and the depiction of Mexicans and other Latinos as violent, deceptive, and barbaric soon became a staple of the burgeoning western genre.[23] By 1913, the Mexican government had lodged its first official protest of an American film, condemning the 1913 Universal documentary picture *Madero Murdered*, about the murder of revolutionary leader Francisco Madero at the order of military leader Victoriana Huerta, who later became leader of Mexico. The Huerta government's protest of *Madero Murdered* was not the only objection to Hollywood depictions of Mexico and Mexicans, and these protests would set the stage for a complete Mexican ban on U.S. films that took effect in 1922, beginning a period in which America's cultural attitude toward Mexico and its Latin American neighbors would change dramatically.

Before turning to some of the dramatic sea changes that occurred during the 1920s, one other racial group deserves attention: African Americans. With little doubt, in the long history of American racism and the mechanisms of white privilege, those of African descent have been among the most oppressed. The tragedy of the enslavement of Africans and the horrible legacy of continued institutionalization of racism has marked this nation's history perhaps more than any other theme. The period following the Civil War and the end of legalized slavery led not to enfranchisement of the freed African Americans but instead brought about deep levels of resentment and animosity through the failed efforts of Reconstruction and the passing of Jim Crow laws, ordinances that served to reinstate economic, political, and cultural oppression against African Americans. It was during this period of the late nineteenth century that American cinema was born, roughly thirty years after the end of the Civil War and fewer than twenty years after the abandonment of the civil rights efforts of Reconstruction.

Early cinema, as mentioned earlier, borrowed heavily from existing forms of popular culture and adopted their racist stereotypes of African Americans. In his influential book *Toms, Coons, Mulattoes, Mammies, and Bucks*, Donald Bogle traces the history of various stereotypes of African Americans, ranging from the ostentatious urban "Zip coon" to the overly sexualized "buck," and observes the way these figures emerged from vaudeville and pulp novels to take their place as cinematic representations of African Americans. Arguably the most popular form of American vaudeville entertainment was blackface—a show derived from minstrel shows in which white performers would darken their face, often with burnt cork, and engage in "comedic" skits denigrating African Americans. In his book *Love and Theft*, Eric Lott argues that blackface entertainment served as a means of protecting white power and privilege by symbolically controlling and containing the cultural practices of African Americans through theatrical modes of ridicule. As he puts it, for white audiences, blackface entailed "a self-protective derision with respect to black people and their cultural practices that made blackface minstrelsy less a sign of absolute white power and control than of panic, anxiety, terror and pleasure."[24] This desire to contain African American culture through the lampooning it flourished in American cinema.

The cinematic representation of African Americans often took on a strikingly ghoulish and vicious tone. Thomas Edison's studio, for instance, distributed a short film entitled *Ten Pickaninnies* in 1908 in which ten African American children are killed by various means (one is eaten by an alligator and another stung to death by bees). More disturbing still was a film released by Biograph in 1898. Titled *An Execution by Hanging*, the short documentary depicts the execution of an African American male in a Florida jail and demonstrates not only the fascination with death in early silent films—discussed at more length in the preceding chapter—but also the degree to which violence visited upon the body of African Americans, especially males, fit in with a broader cultural form that helped to shape both American racism and American cinema.

During the first decade of cinema, these depictions were in some ways countered by other comparatively uplifting depictions of African Americans—such as Edwin Porter's 1903 *Uncle Tom's Cabin* or documentary reels featuring African American soldiers, including Lubin's 1898 *Colored Invincibles*, which depicted troops aiding Theodore Roosevelt's Rough Riders. However, these depictions were overwhelming outweighed by negative depictions, particularly after the fiftieth anniversary of the Civil War brought a wave of nostalgia for the "Old South." As Thomas Cripps, one of the true pioneers in the study of African Americans in film, observes:

> After 1910 the celebration of the Civil War removed almost all authentic depiction of black Americans from the nation's screens, the semicentennial serving as an inspiration to put aside realism in favor of romantic nostalgia as a mode for presenting Negroes in film.[25]

While the often shockingly racist depictions caused some outcry among the African American community, by far the most controversial films of this period were those depicting African American heavyweight boxing champion of the world, Jack Johnson. As noted in chapter 1, Johnson's rise to global prominence as the world champion caused shockwaves in American culture, and one of the chief points of concern was the films that captured his dominance and allowed it to be disseminated throughout the country.

Johnson achieved prominence in 1904 when he became the number-one contender for the heavyweight title, but current champion Jim Jeffries refused to fight the African American. However, when Canadian Tommy Burns became champion in 1906, Johnson followed the new champion and persistently demanded his title shot, which he got on December 26, 1908, in a fight that left Burns bloodied and on the canvas and Johnson the first African American champion of the world.[26]

Johnson's victory was enough to cause turmoil in the white-dominated American culture, but his personality added considerably to the consternation.

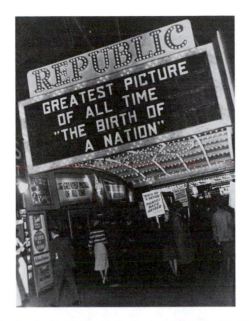

Protests against *The Birth of a Nation* helped to establish the NAACP as a major force in cultural politics. © Corbis.

During the mid-1970s, some women's organizations framed pornography as a violation of women's rights. © Bettmann/Corbis.

Martin Scorsese's *Last Temptation of Christ* became an early battleground in the culture wars. © Gary Wagner/Sygma/Corbis.

Charges of anti-Semitism were leveled at Mel Gibson's *The Passion of the Christ*. © Chip East/Reuters/Corbis.

The character Jame Gumb, played by Ted Levine, was seen by many critics as a homophobic stereotype. Orion Pictures Corporation/Photofest. © Orion Pictures Corporation.

Oliver Stone's critique of American violence was accused by some of promoting the very violence it sought to condemn. Warner Bros./Photofest. © Warner Bros.

Mookie (Spike Lee) and Sal (Danny Aiello) face each other after the film's dramatic climax. Universal Pictures/Photofest. © Universal Pictures. Photographer: David Lee.

The graphic suffering of Jesus, played by James Caviezel, raised questions about the film's spiritual aims. Newmarket Films/Photofest. © Newmarket Films. Photographer: Philippe Antonello.

In an era when the only "positive" roles for African Americans were as servants or soldiers, Johnson was a decidedly more provocative and flamboyant character. As Butters observes:

> Jack Johnson also presented a public persona that was absent from the American cinema and almost nonexistent in mainstream American public life.... Johnson liked to wear colorful clothes and drive sports cars. He regularly flashed around money and frequently kept the company of white women. Johnson was boastful, proud, arrogant, and loud, qualities that defied how white society wanted the African American to behave.[27]

White commentators were quick to call for a "great white hope"; even writer Jack London made an explicit appeal to Jack Jeffries to come out of retirement and face Johnson.

What made Johnson's victory even more troubling to whites was that it was captured on film, and in 1909 *Johnson-Burns Fight* was being distributed around the country. The film caused a growing level of concern among white audiences, who had conceived the heavyweight boxing championship as the exclusive purview of their own kind. Out of this assumption of superiority, the *Johnson-Burns Fight* film was generally withheld from distribution in African American communities, but such was not the case with the second Johnson fight film, *Johnson-Ketchel Fight*, in which Johnson again demolished a white opponent, this time producing an iconic image of the champion standing against the ropes, hand on hip, while the white fighter lies unconscious beneath him.

The defeat of Stanley Ketchel by Jack Johnson led to the showdown that most commentators had been hoping for since Johnson became champion. The fight between Jack Jeffries and Jack Johnson was arranged in the dusty town of Reno, Nevada, and held on July 4, 1910. Publicity for the fight made it clear that this was to be considered a racial showdown between Johnson and Jeffries, who was described by columnist James Corbett as "all that is powerful and brutish in the white man."[28]

After fifteen rounds, Johnson defeated Jeffries and retained his heavyweight championship. Throughout the country, the fight had been closely followed by those huddled around radios and in theaters where the fight was announced round by round, and with its culmination, celebrations broke out throughout African American communities. Tragically, these celebrations were accompanied by violent riots aimed at African American communities in many major cities and, as Butters puts it, "innocent black men and women were beaten because Johnson had defeated Jeffries in the ring. At least eighteen African Americans were killed."[29]

By most accounts, the calls for the banning of *Johnson-Jeffries Fight* began within twenty-four hours. American cities from Cincinnati and Baltimore to New Orleans and Atlanta quickly moved to ban the film. The reasoning provided for these bans is instructive in thinking about the controversies over race and film in terms of white privilege. In Baltimore, for example, a spokesperson for the Board of Police Commissioners insisted, "We have a large colored population here and the exhibition of the pictures might cause racial troubles." This fear seemed largely unfounded, given that most of the trouble caused on the night of the actual fight was directed at the African American community, but even in Washington, D.C., a city that did see unrest on the evening of the fight, there was fear that the exhibition of the fight film might provoke a repeat of violence.[30] Indeed, this fear that the images would provoke another round of unrest was at the heart of a national campaign against the *Johnson-Jeffries* film led by the Christian Endeavor Society. Its secretary, William Shaw, proclaimed in a widely circulated message, "Race riots already have followed the announcement of the negroes [*sic*] victory. Moving pictures of prize fighting will create more violence."[31] In a particularly graphic version of this argument, the mayor of Louisville, Kentucky, contended, "It is not difficult to foresee what will happen if the fight pictures are shown. Prejudice existing for scores of years will rear itself and flourish again in crime and blood," and the governor of Missouri sought to ban the film in order to avoid "race controversies and disturbances."[32] While the direction of the violence is not explicitly stated, the continued invocation of the "colored population" and the "prejudices existing for scores of years" suggested that the real fear was that Johnson's victory would incite African American violence against white oppression.

The efforts of white authorities were generally successful. The *Johnson-Jeffries Fight* film was banned in virtually every part of the South, as well as in many major cities throughout the rest of the country.

In locales where the film was not banned, the rationale given by authorities was as instructive as the reasons given for banning the film elsewhere. For instance, the chief of police in Milwaukee claimed, "There is no specific law by which to stop promoters from bringing the fight pictures here." This was an excuse invoked by a number of municipalities—although many others were not troubled by their lack of statutory authority and banned the film anyway. The governor of Indiana, Thomas R. Marshall, complained, "Personally I think the exhibition of the Jeffries-Johnson pictures should be prevented. They will lead to trouble, riotous conditions and, possibly, murder. But as governor, I doubt the utility of an executive to issue an order or proclamation not authorized by statute." A different reason for allowing the fight was offered by the acting mayor of Omaha, Nebraska, who exclaimed, "I have seen innumerable views at moving picture shows which tend more to moral decadence than the views of the fight would."[33]

The African American press, however, recognized that the banning of the film had less to do with fears of violence than with the desire to limit images of an African American proving his superiority to the Great White Hope. No such hue and cry had been issued in protest of the violence done to African Americans through harassment, murders, and lynchings—a point driven home by a headline in the *Richmond Planet*: "Hypocrisy That Shames the Devil." The editors of the *St. Paul Appeal* contended that

> the apparently country-wide objection to the exhibition of the Johnson-Jeffries fight pictures comes more from race prejudice than from a moral standpoint. Who believes for one minute, that had Jeffries been the victor at Reno, there would have been any objection to showing the pictures of him bringing back "the white man's hope"?[34]

While the *Johnson-Jeffries Fight* film did appear on screens throughout the country, the long-term impact of the controversy was severe. Motivated by fears that Johnson's prowess would continue to grace the silver screen, Congress pushed for legislation outlawing the importation and interstate transfer of fight films, in what would become the Sims Act. Much of the rhetoric surrounding the Sims Act, as discussed in earlier chapters, dealt with issues of violence and the impressionable nature of children. However, the main focus of the act was, with little doubt, on Jack Johnson and the particularly dangerous images of African American empowerment. In debate concerning the bill, a representative from Ohio specifically questioned the racist motivation for the bill, asking if "it were more indefensible for a white man and a black man to engage in a prize fight than two white men," to which a Georgia supporter of the bill responded, "No man descended from the old Saxon race can look upon that kind of contest without abhorrence and disgust."[35]

As noted in chapter 1, the passage of the Sims Act opened the floodgate for legislative regulation of films and helped to solidify the definition of film as commerce, which could thus be regulated by federal bodies. The controversy surrounding the Sims Act reveals the broader struggle over who would have authority over representations of Others and how deeply implicated the notion of white privilege was with issues of film regulation.

1915–1930

The first two decades of American cinema had seen numerous controversies surrounding race and film—ranging from protests by national governments like Mexico's to the efforts of African American communities to be allowed to view films of their heavyweight hero's boxing triumphs. But, in many ways, the foundational moment for controversies related to racial representations in film was, with little doubt, the 1915 epic by David Wark Griffith, *The Birth of a Nation*. *Birth* has rightly been hailed by film scholars as a seminal film in the history of the medium, pushing the boundaries of cinematography, plot structure, and editing further than any film beforehand. That said, the film is also one of the most revolting and pernicious statements of American racism that has ever been captured on film. While earlier films had laid out a vile caricature of African Americans, Griffith's film crafted a visually stunning and compelling narrative in which the emancipation of African slaves was the "original sin" from which the nation must free itself. Indeed, one of the opening scenes depicts Africans being auctioned at a slave sale and the intertitle card reads, "The introduction of the African to American shores laid the seeds of national tragedy."

The effectiveness of Griffith's film lay in both its epic scope and its ability to focus on a core set of characters with which the audience established an intimate relationship. The story of the Civil War and Reconstruction is told through the lives of two interrelated families—the Stonemans, a Northern family that favors abolition, and their Southern cousins the Camerons, who own a plantation. In part 1 of the three-hour-plus film, originally shown in two parts separated by an intermission, the Stoneman and Cameron families meet in the Camerons' South Carolina home and the idyllic conditions of the antebellum South are depicted. The Civil War then divides the families, and the action is often intercut between male members of the two families as they engage in various large-scale battles. The first half ends with the assassination of Abraham Lincoln and the rise of the Radical Reconstructionists.

The second half continues to follow the fortunes of the two families. The Camerons are reduced to poverty and harassed by the horrifying caricatures of African Americans—all the principal African American characters were played by white men in blackface because, Griffith claimed, he could find no qualified African American actors to play the parts—while the Stonemans come to South Carolina to oversee Reconstruction and support the villainous freed Africans and their cunning mulatto leader Silas Lynch as they turn the South into a land of chaos and barbarism. The climax of the film comes with a typical melodramatic rescue, though this time it is the Ku Klux Klan, led by one of the Camerons, who rides in to save white families, especially women, from the horrible clutches of the brutal former slaves. The film ends with two marriages between the Stoneman and Cameron families and a vision of Christ leading the nation to peace.

Whatever its place in film history as innovating narrative structure and filmmaking technique and helping to set the foundation for the predominance of feature-length films, at the time of its release, *Birth of a Nation* was seen by many as a film about one thing: a defense of white privilege and dominance. From it source material—two novels, *The Clansman* and *The Leopard's Spots*—by white supremacist Thomas Dixon, to its casting of only whites in blackface for the principal African American roles, *Birth* was a visual depiction of a harsh brand of "race radicalism" in which the only solution to America's racial problems lay in removing African Americans from American soil.[36] The sad legacy of the film is that it led to a rebirth of the Ku Klux Klan, which used the film as a recruiting tool throughout the 1920s.[37] In the longer term, as Manthia Diawara argued, "*The Birth of a Nation* constitutes the grammar book for Hollywood's representations of Black manhood."[38] Thus, both politically and cinematically, *Birth* solidified a visual and cultural framework of white racism and established a cultural narrative in which whiteness had to be defended against the danger of African American blackness.

But there is another legacy of Griffith's *Birth*, a legacy of protest and response that galvanized the African American community in ways the filmmaker could not have foreseen. As Butters argued, "The controversy over *The Birth of a Nation* marked a radical change in the relationship between African Americans and the cinematic medium."[39] On both the political and cinematic fronts, the African American community was strengthened by its response to this film to a degree that previous films and previous controversies had not even begun to approach.

In terms of the political response, the controversy over *Birth* led numerous public figures to denounce the film—the Chicago social reformer Jane Addams, for instance, called it a "pernicious caricature of the Negro race"—and solidified the foundations for the recently formed National Association for the Advancement of Colored People (NAACP).[40] Established in 1909, the NAACP quickly grew to a nationwide organization with a widely circulating journal, *The Crisis*, that served to disseminate the organization's opinions. In 1915, however, the organization was still generally scattered and fragmented across its various branches. The inflammatory nature of *Birth* prompted these various branches, as well as other related organizations, to form a unified front.[41]

The African American newspaper the *Chicago Defender* called the film "one of the most infamous assaults upon the womanhood and manhood of the Afro-Americans ever attempted to be presented" and conjectured that it was "designed to stir up race prejudice." The paper also noted that it would be the NAACP that "will undoubtedly be called upon to exert every effort to prevent the production of 'The Birth of a Nation' in Chicago."[42] In Boston, the NAACP organized an effort to buy up all the tickets, but when "several thousand Afro-Americans gathered early in front of the theater, money in hand, to buy tickets ... they were refused," leading to a conflict that saw hundreds of uniformed police beat the crowd back.[43] Formal protests were also organized in other cities, and the NAACP published various tracts and pamphlets denouncing the film and questioning its historical accuracy. Interestingly, the protests were strong enough to lead Griffith to meet with NAACP president Moorfield Storey and even to offer him $10,000 if he could identify any historical inaccuracies—an impossibility given the way the film fictionalizes most of the historical figures.[44]

Much of the protest sought to ban the film from exhibition, and in some states this was successful. The organization pushed the National Review Board, the early voluntary censorship board, to ban the film outright and also worked to pressure state and city censorship boards to ban the film. The NAACP and related groups expressed fear that the film would stir racial hatred and further encourage white violence against African Americans, already at horrific levels nationally. However, in spite of the unprecedented level of organized resistance provided by the African American community, *Birth*'s overwhelming popularity among white audiences led many municipalities to allow its exhibition.

In thinking about controversies over race in film in terms of white privilege and the symbolic creation of whiteness, the defense of *Birth* from members of the dominant white community becomes more interesting. For example, when the NAACP and other organizations pushed for the city of Chicago to ban the film, the courts were called upon to intervene, and in his decision, Judge William Fennimore Cooper provided a telling argument in favor of the film:

> This ground that it will engender race animosity is based purely on assumption. To find that this is a good objection to the allowing of the injunction this court will have to assume that our white citizens will not know or appreciate the fact that the days as presented in the play were early in the first years of the last half century. This court will have to assume that they who will witness the play will be so stupid that they will be unable to comprehend that the people represented on the film were of two or three generations ago. And that they do not, and will not, appreciate the fact that in the succeeding time the negro race has advanced almost immeasurably.[45]

The reasoning here stands in stark contrast to that employed by governmental institutions just three years earlier when the topic had been whether or not to allow the screening of the *Johnson-Jeffries Fight* film. In that earlier instance, the assumption that the filmic images would provoke unrest and violence had seemed more credible, where in considering *Birth*, the images of racial violence were presumed innocent until there was actual evidence of their inflammatory nature. On another level, it is also revealing that the white audience is afforded a greater capacity to see beyond the illusion of film and separate the dramatic actions from real life, while in the previous controversies numerous public officials had openly feared that the boxing film would deceive African Americans with the illusion of social superiority.

In those municipalities where *Birth* was banned, public officials faced harsh criticism from their white constituents. In Lowell, Massachusetts, the mayor's decision to ban the film was characterized as pandering to the African American voters, "for nobody is to be offended during these campaign days."[46] Numerous residents of Ohio chose to bus to other states to view the film and subsequently publicized their praise of Griffith's film and their consternation at the decision of the Ohio Board of Film Censors to ban the film. Coretta Coblentz of New Madison, Ohio, for example, wrote to the *Lima Sunday News*, "Why such a clean, moral play should be barred from the State of Ohio is beyond my comprehension," and she and many of her compatriots provided overwhelming praise for the film, almost universally declaring it the greatest film they had ever seen.[47]

In fairness to this praise, many writers seemed to focus on the film's antiwar message. Edna Simmons, for instance, wrote, "Who would not choose peace rather than war after seeing this wonderful play?" But other defenses of the film embraced its racist attitude. Bessie Smith of Gibons-burg, Ohio, wrote that the film "showed how brutish negroes can act," and Catheryn Dyer confessed, "I was always against the Ku Klux Klanners until I saw the play. If it had not been for them I don't know what would have come of the world."

Interspersed within this praise for the film's racist depictions and the Ku Klux Klan were assertions that the film was not racially biased. In a front-page piece praising the film, Utah's *Ogden Standard* boldly proclaimed:

> There is nothing in the whole production to stir up race hatred. There is bound to be resentment against the radical abolitionists who took advantage of the poor and bleeding south but there is nothing to stir up hatred toward the black race.[48]

What becomes clear in even a cursory examination of these responses is that the criteria for determining whether a film might "stir up race hatred" are based on the broader culture of white privilege. Films that threaten the supremacy of whiteness are considered too dangerous, while films that depict white dominance are not.

Efforts to halt the exhibition of *The Birth of a Nation* were largely unsuc-cessful, and the film would go on to become not only one of the most suc-cessful films of that era but also one of the most influential. In some ways, the most interesting impact of the film was on African American filmmak-ing. May Childs Nerney, a leader of the NAACP who had pushed for the film to be "suppressed altogether," soon recognized that the only real response to Griffith's film was to produce equally spectacular motion pictures as a coun-terpoint, and soon numerous African American filmmakers began taking up the challenge of rebutting Griffith's racist vision.[49]

The first African American filmmaker, William Foster, had been making films since 1912, and his vision of making films that were simultaneously profitable and uplifting of his race became a founding principle for most African American production companies. Within five years of Griffith's *Birth of a Nation*, fledgling African American production companies such as the Lincoln Motion Picture Company, the Colored and Indian Film

Company, and the Frederick Douglass Film Company were producing films like *Realization of the Negro's Ambition* (Lincoln, 1916), which tells the story of a young African American civil engineer who, after various melodramatic adventures, discovers oil on his father's farm and ends up married with family, farm, and wealth, and the Douglass Company's *The Colored American Winning His Suit* (1919), in which Bob Winall, an African American law graduate from Howard University, thwarts a plot to frame his fiancée's father and wins her hand.

The push for African American–produced films grew out of the controversies over representation, which motivated much of the public pressure put on African American audiences to patronize these films. For example, in a 1921 edition of the *Baltimore Afro-American*, readers were told:

> The worst enemy of the race producer is the race movie fan himself. Colored Americans are governed by the standards set by white producers and because the films have not measured up to these standards, they are scoffed at and sometimes boycotted altogether. The cinema game within the race is in its infancy and it is within the power of every race fan to crush it in the cradle.[50]

The challenges facing African American–produced films, and even African American–themed and –cast films produced by white independent producers, were substantial. White theaters would generally not book such films, and while there would eventually be dramatic growth in the number of theaters catering to the African American community, the growth was relatively slow. But in spite of these difficulties, by 1921 there were more than three hundred theaters in the United States catering primarily to African American audiences; this year also saw the highest level of African American films in distribution.[51]

It is not the case that all the films produced by African Americans were universally accepted as uplifting and appropriate. In some instances, white community members protested certain African American films, and in other instances, the African American community found itself divided by questions of the appropriateness of the filmic representation of their race.

Arguably the most provocative, popular, and divisive African American filmmaker was Oscar Micheaux, a fascinating historical figure who went from a successful stint as a South Dakota homesteader to best-selling author and then pioneering filmmaker. Micheaux's silent films focused on such controversial topics as lynching and the practice of light-skinned African Americans "passing" as whites. As an example, Micheaux's 1920 film *Within Our Gates*, which deals with racial violence and lynching, was intensely controversial in both white and African American communities and faced numerous challenges from local censor boards. But, of all the films produced during the post-*Birth* period, *Within Our Gates* can be seen as the most direct response.

In his masterful exploration of Micheaux's body of work, J. Ronald Green argues that this unflinching depiction of racist violence can be "reasonably accepted as a direct rebuttal to Griffith's sensibilities and politics," and Butters has called this film "a turning point in the history of African American cinema in its bold and frank presentations of race relations in the United States."[52] Tellingly, this view was shared by some contemporary audience members. In a letter to the editor of the African American *Chicago Defender*, Willis N. Huggins not only declared Micheaux's film the embodiment of "the spirit of Douglas [*sic*], Nat Turner, Scarborough, and Du Bois, rolled into one" but also observed the way the film provided a clear and compelling response to Griffith's earlier film:

> "The Birth of a Nation" was written by the oppressors, to show that the oppressed were a burden and a drawback to the nation, that they had no real grievance.... "Within Our Gates" is written by the oppressed and shows in a mild way the degree and kind of his oppression.[53]

The film is an intricate story involving an African American woman, Sylvia, who seeks to better herself through education, and a dispute between an African American cotton farmer and a wealthy white landowner that leads to murder and a horrific sequence of lynch mob violence against the innocent African American family. One of the later sequences, in which the lynching of the African American family is intercut with an attempted rape of Sylvia, seems markedly similar to the dramatic cross-cutting that characterizes the climax of *Birth of a Nation*.

Reactions to *Within Our Gates* were dramatically mixed. The film faced considerable problems with censorship boards and was edited and reedited throughout its distribution period to accommodate the various board concerns.[54] Reactions within the African American community were also mixed. In part because of the violent race riots that had engulfed Chicago in the summer of 1919, the release of *Within Our Gates* seemed poised to reignite the still-smoldering racial tension. The end of World War I had seen many African Americans returning from military service to find themselves back among violent racial oppression and limited economic opportunities. For some commentators within the African American community, Micheaux's representation of tension and violence seemed too close to the mark for comfort.

These concerns were shared by the Chicago censorship board, which struggled over the film for two months—viewing edited and reedited versions before finally approving the film for exhibition. The film premiered in Chicago on January 12, 1920, at Hammond's Venodome and by all accounts drew record-breaking crowds, in part due to the clever marketing by which Micheaux exploited the film's trouble with the censors. In a piece about the film appearing in the *Chicago Defender*, the film was touted:

This is the picture that it required two solid months to get by the Censor Board, and it is the claim of the author and producer that, while it is a bit radical, it is withal the biggest protest against Race prejudice, lynching and "concubinage" that was ever written or filmed.[55]

The record crowds were accompanied by some African American protestors who believed the film too radical and inflammatory—although many of these protestors had not seen the film and were relying on secondhand information. There were even reports that some of these protestors, upon seeing the film, changed their minds and embraced it as "perfect in-as-much as the showing up of a certain class of both the white and our Race is done."[56]

The success of *Within Our Gates* helped to solidify Micheaux's place as America's most prestigious and most provocative African American film-maker, and his later films, especially during the silent era, would continue to provoke controversy. He took up issues such as religion, in the 1924 *Body and Soul*, which was the debut film for Paul Robeson, and passing in *The House behind the Cedars*, also from 1924.

The two strategies outlined above are indicative of the general trend of African American responses to filmic racism during the 1920s: Organizations such as the NAACP continued to protest films with negative racial depictions, and African American filmmakers produced a variety of films designed both as critiques of white racism and as moral lessons for the "uplift" of the race. These two trends were part of a major effort to contest the white culture's claim to represent not only itself but also other races, and the voices of protest—whether from picket lines or pamphlets or the silver screen—created an important dynamic in which African Americans would both contest and compete with filmic representations of race relations.

The first tactic, political protest, would survive unabated through to the present day, but the second, African American filmmaking, became almost completely dormant by the end of the decade. There were many causes for the decline in African American–produced independent films, including difficulties acquiring financial backing, competition with better-funded white films, and the Great Depression. But perhaps the greatest single cause was the advent of sound technology in films. The increased cost associated with filming with sound was more than most African American production companies could afford. Furthermore, the expense of outfitting theaters with sound technology was greater than most theaters catering to African American communities could bear. By 1931, the age of African American silent film was at an end, and the next decades of American filmmaking would see a dramatic consolidation of filmmaking in the white studios of Hollywood.

While the emergence of the African American response to racist film was perhaps the most dramatic of the era, there were major controversies surrounding other racial and ethnic communities during this period as well. In New York City, for example, Joseph V. McKee, president of the Board of Aldermen, introduced an amendment to the censorship code barring films in 1927 that "are immoral, indecent, or tend to ridicule, disparage or hold up to obloquy or contempt any race, creed or nationality, or are calculated to arouse racial, national or religious prejudice." The amendment was supported by various Irish organizations, including the United Irish American Societies and the American-Irish Vigilance Committee, and was motivated by their perception of negative Irish portrayals in contemporary films such as *Irish Hearts* and *The Shamrock and the Rose*.[57]

Another ethnic group also had considerable problems in the aftermath of World War I: Germans. Animosity toward Germans and German Americans was high in the years after the war, and German films became a target. The debut of *The Cabinet of Dr. Caligari* in 1920 was met by an angry mob of veterans, who became so threatening that the screening was scrapped by the theater owner out of fear.[58] A similar fate met the Ernst Lubitsch film *Madame DuBarry* (aka *Passion*) in 1919. The controversy over its German origin in St. Louis led to the film being "hurriedly taken off and hushed up like a scandal in the family," according to a 1921 edition of the *Lincoln State Journal*.[59]

Controversies over other racial representations were also complicated by national ethnicities and even more so by the intricacies of geopolitics. Hollywood was engaged in increasingly distorted caricatures of Chinese and Japanese villains, especially in serials such as *The Yellow Menace* and *The Exploits of Elaine*. The tensions around this anti-Asian sentiment came to a head with the popular serial *Patria*. Produced by William Randolph Hearst, who had developed intensely anti-Japanese sentiments, *Patria* recounts a supposed Japanese plan to invade the United States with the assistance of Mexico. The serial, released in 1919, came at a particularly difficult time in U.S.–Japanese relations due to tensions over Japanese immigration as well as struggles over Pacific hegemony. In an unprecedented move, President Woodrow Wilson wrote to Hearst, arguing that the serial was "extremely unfair to the Japanese and I fear that it is calculated to stir up a great deal of hostility."[60] Hearst bowed to the pressure, and the films were withdrawn and reedited to downplay the focus on the Japanese invasion plot and, instead, emphasize Mexico as the principal villain.

While shifting the focus from Japanese villainy to Mexican scheming helped to alleviate tension with Japan, it did not do much for relations between Hollywood and Mexico. Hollywood films had long portrayed Mexicans and other Latin Americans in negative terms, typically as cunning and violent outlaws and thugs. The prominence of these racist depictions led in 1922 to a sweeping Mexican ban on U.S. films with racist depictions. In February of that year, the Mexican government issued a statement to Hollywood companies declaring, "The Government of Mexico will find it

necessary to stop the importation to Mexico of all films produced by companies which may continue to manufacture films derogatory to Mexico."
The ban was sweeping enough to include all films produced by a company,
even those not exported to Mexico, in an attempt to prevent films sent to
other countries from including negative portrayals of Mexicans. This harsh
measure was designed to stop what one Mexican official described as "the
usual portrayal of the Mexican in moving pictures ... as a bandit or a
sneak."[61] The measure had an immediate impact on Hollywood, which
was involved in strong efforts to increase their importation of films into
Mexico and other Latin American countries, and the potential of a Mexican
ban was seen as a potentially devastating economic blow.

Before the end of the year, however, the ban was rescinded after Hollywood sent a delegation to Mexico to insist that American films would curb
their anti-Mexican tones, declaring that "no pictures which would be offensive to Mexicans would be exhibited." Members of the delegation included
John C. Flinn and John L. Day Jr. of Famous Players–Lasky Corporation,
which had produced a number of the offending films, and B. J. Woodie,
personal assistant to the newly appointed president of the Motion Picture
Producers and Distributors Association, William Hays.[62] Hays's office had
worked hard behind the scenes to arrange this promise of better treatment
in order to hold off the economic consequences of a total Mexican ban, but
during the 1920s, his office had virtually no power to enforce this promise
and, as such, the depiction of Mexicans and other Latinos saw, as Gary
Keller puts it, only "shallow and cosmetic" changes.

The superficial response to Mexico's concerns about Hollywood racism
would be transformed in the 1930s by two important factors. One would
be the creation of a new enforcement mechanism for Hays's office, the
advent of the Production Code Administration in 1930. The second would
be the increased emphasis on U.S. alliance with its southern neighbors with
the reemergence of conflict in Europe and around the world.

1930–1956

The Production Code Administration held deep yet ambivalent views
about racial representations. On the one hand, for some groups, the PCA
showed considerable concern. As I discuss in more detail presently, Latinos
were afforded substantially more cinematic protection than other groups,
due to economic and, later, political concerns. On the other hand, some
groups, such as African Americans, received remarkably little support from
Hollywood's new regulatory agency. As well, existing racial tensions were
dramatically transformed by other major historical events—first by the
tumult of World War II and later by the dramatic increase in the visibility
of the civil rights movements. Yet in spite of the changes to the American
film industry—both internal and external—controversies over racial

representations continued to emerge, and these can be seen as related mainly to questions of white privilege and the authority of white culture to dictate the terms for representation of other racial groups.

The Mexican ban on derogatory Hollywood films in 1922 had a longer-term effect than the initial and largely empty promises of William Hays in the same year. The development of the Production Code Administration, discussed in more detail in chapter 1, provided a more effective mechanism for enforcing restrictions on Hollywood representations, and the economic incentive to maintain good relations with the Latino market provided an impetus for change. Alfred Charles Richard Jr. concludes from his comprehensive study of PCA documents related to Latino imagery:

> In the twenty years between 1935 and 1955, the Hays Office shaped the silver screen's Hispanic image by insisting on the removal of what was currently considered to be offensive Hispanic imagery. Literally thousands of script changes were suggested to and forced on film makers which affected the stereotype.[63]

In the early years, the PCA's work consisted mainly in removing the racial slur "greaser" and softening the stereotype of the Mexican bandit. Additionally, the PCA was heavy-handed in enforcing changes to films like *Heroes of the Alamo*, in which it required that scenes of Mexican soldiers slaughtering Texans be removed as well as other scenes demeaning to Mexicans, including the line "Any Texan [could] lick ten Mexicans, single-handed."[64]

The incentive to promote a more positive representation of Latinos was increased with the beginning of military tensions in the Atlantic and Pacific. President Franklin Roosevelt's first inaugural address announced the desire to implement a policy of being a "good neighbor" to the nations to America's south. The "Good Neighbor Policy," designed to foster positive relations, began taking an effect in Hollywood as early as 1938, and it became a more fundamental part of the Production Code in 1940 with the creation of the Office of the Coordinator of Inter-American Affairs (CIAA). Headed by Nelson Rockefeller, whose family had extensive holdings throughout Latin America, the CIAA established the Motion Picture Society for the Americas (MPSA), whose membership paralleled that of the Motion Picture Producers and Distributors Association (MPPDA) but also included government-appointed officials and heads of various professional guilds. While the MPSA was a voluntary nongovernmental agency, its influence on Hollywood studios was immense and immediate. As Richard notes, "Within a month all of the major production companies instituted subcommittees which met weekly to exchange information about their studio's respective pictures with Latin content."[65] In 1941, Addison Durland, a Cuban-born journalist working with NBC, was recruited to become the

Latin American specialist with the PCA, and soon Durland's influence led to a reduction of the more vulgar stereotypes and provided a more nuanced authenticity to Hollywood representations of the varied countries and cultures of Latin America.[66]

The CIAA and MPSA changed the images of Latinos not only through censorship and enforced editing but also by promoting more positive images. One of the more prominent forms of this positive good neighbor policy was in the growth of Latin American musicals during the final years of the war and into the next decade. The Latin musicals encouraged a positive image of Latinos and also allowed for cinematic romantic relationships between North American whites and Latin Americans—something that was strictly forbidden between whites and other races in other Hollywood films. As Richard observes, "Possibly the most important metaphor [the Latin musicals] projected was that of one people within two hemispheres, individually different, but who could share love and friendship to ensure inter-American security."[67] Interestingly, while the MPSA was disbanded at the end of the war and the CIAA absorbed into other governmental agencies, the Production Code Administration continued to foster the Good Neighbor Policy—now that the positive image was written into the PCA's regulations, it would continue on until the mid-1950s. Indeed, Durland remained in his post until 1951.

The war created numerous complications surrounding the representation of race, many of which were indicative of the nebulous nature of the conception of whiteness. Germans, for instance, became an increasingly popular target for ethnic slurs and negative representations. Indeed, the negative depiction of Germans before the U.S. entry into the war was so prominent that the Senate held subcommittee hearings on whether or not Hollywood was "war-mongering." Wendell Willkie was hired by Hollywood to represent its interests, and he turned the tables on the isolationist senators by insisting that if the main question was whether Hollywood hated Hitler then "there need be no investigation. We abhor everything Hitler represents."[68] Concerns about Hollywood's negative depictions of Germans in general and Nazis in particular were also taken up by U.S. Ambassador to Great Britain Joseph Kennedy. Kennedy was greatly concerned that the United Kingdom would not hold out long against the Nazis and that the United States needed to be prepared to make peace with Hitler. He brought this message to various Hollywood studio executives during private dinners in which he lectured them on the importance of maintaining peace with Germany and of American films remaining neutral.[69]

The events of December 7, 1941, put an end to these concerns, and the floodgate of negative depictions of America's enemies was opened. Perhaps not surprisingly, the negative images of the Japanese were even more vicious and derogatory than the depictions of the Germans. Given a history of some sixty years of racist caricatures of the Japanese, Hollywood had a backlog of images of the "yellow peril," and the 1940s saw these released at a furious pace. Films such as the 1942 Paramount release *Wake Island*, a Pacific battle film featuring Marines, were used in recruiting, and the ruthlessness of the Japanese characters depicted in the 1944 film *Purple Heart* led critic Louella Parsons to proclaim, "I defy anyone to see this picture and not want to go out and kill, single-handed, every Jap."[70] Interestingly, however, even the unrelentingly negative portrayal of the Japanese during the war was influenced by the subtleties of racial politics, as the Office of War Information put pressure on Hollywood to drop the racial slur "yellow" from its vocabulary for fear of offending the allied Chinese.[71]

Concerns about keeping allied nations positively inclined toward the United States also impacted the Hollywood image of Latinos; however, the favorable image of Latinos crafted under the auspices of the CIAA, MPSA, and PCA was not without racial controversies. One sensitive issue was the presence of people of African heritage in films set in Latin America. Cultural elites in Argentina, for example, were offended by one of the first Good Neighbor musicals, *Down Argentine Way* (1940), starring Carmen Miranda, whose Hollywood career was instigated to further the policy. The offensive content was the inclusion of a musical dance number featuring the African American dancing duo the Nicholas Brothers, which Argentinean officials feared would give the impression that Argentina was a nation of "Indians or Africans." A similar scene in Miranda's second feature, the 1941 *Carnival in Rhythm*, was subsequently cut.

As Brian O'Neil notes, the policies of Addison Durland, intended to promote a more positive view of Latin America, led him to "reconfigure Latin America as modern, clean, and especially in the cases of Brazil and Argentina, European in complexion."[72] This observation is informative with regard to the broader notion of whiteness and white privilege that lies at the heart of many controversies over racial representation, namely, the fluidity of the notion of whiteness as a racial category. The "whitening" of Latin America during the Good Neighbor Policy years suggests the degree to which the notion of whiteness is always open to negotiation and amendment, but perhaps more importantly, the alterations or expansions of who gets to occupy—even temporarily—the position of white cultural privilege are made with an eye toward maintaining that white privilege. The efforts to "clean up" the image of Latin Americans—which, in fairness, consisted of both eliminating some vile stereotypes as well as the far less noble process of erasing people of African descent from representations of these nations—was undertaken with the specific goals of, first, maintaining strong sales in the region and, second, preserving strategic political alliances during the period of the war.

Another unfortunate aspect of whiteness revealed in the controversy over Carmen Miranda's first film was the clarity with which whiteness was countered most clearly by "blackness"—the representation of African Americans. While the PCA and its various governmental collaborators found it useful to promote a positive image of Latinos, the same was not the case for African Americans, who continued to receive unfavorable representations on film. In the period surrounding World War II, some of the more harsh stereotypes disappeared, but so too in many cases did the portrayal of African Americans on-screen at all. Roles for African Americans were so limited that in 1942 leaders of the NAACP met with Hollywood studio executives to discuss the dearth of opportunities for African American actors. In spite of the promise by studio executives to create more African American roles, the promise yielded only a handful of all-African American musicals such as *Stormy Weather* (1943) and some roles in war films like *Bataan* (1943). As O'Neil observes, "As far as the vast majority of Hollywood's wartime films were concerned, African Americans simply did not exist and when they did, it was almost always in short musical numbers."[73]

Illustrative of the difficult position African American actors faced was the situation surrounding David O. Selznick's *Gone with the Wind* in 1939. While the production offered numerous employment opportunities for African American actors, the roles were largely distasteful in their re-creation of plantation-era slave positions. As Leonard Leff and Jerold Simmons recount, "By February 1939, black publisher Leon Washington had circulated a petition among 'colored maids' to boycott *Gone With the Wind*."[74] Controversies surrounding *Gone with the Wind* also encompassed the use of the "n-word," which Selznick seemed insistent upon featuring in the film. PCA head Joseph Breen resisted the inclusion of the racial slur out of concern that it might spark protests and relented only when Selznick promised that the offensive word would be used solely by African American characters. This compromise, however, met with considerable resistance from the African American cast members themselves. Butterfly McQueen complained so much that she later recalled being told "Mr. Selznick would never give me another job." But the resistance proved effective, and Selznick later relented to using instead the slightly less offensive term "darkie."[75] He also wanted to avoid too much confrontation with the PCA in anticipation of the battle he would later fight, and win, over Rhett Butler's famous exclamation that he did not "give a damn," another controversial term.

The complexity of racial politics also ensnared Hattie McDaniel, whose turn as Mammy would earn her an Academy Award and mark her as the first African American to receive this honor. Her long career included numerous performances as matronly servant women, but while these roles were outwardly demeaning and subservient, there was also a clear sense that each performance of the role saw McDaniel as more forceful and independent. Still, in spite of her success, McDaniel became a discordant figure in postwar Hollywood. On the one hand, she was a respected actress and a generous patron to other struggling African American actors; on the other hand, she was thought by some as a traitor to her race for accepting a career of performing African American subservience.[76] The African American *Pittsburgh Courier* newspaper complained that McDaniel and the other African American performers were playing "unthinking hapless clods."[77]

McDaniel's difficult relationship to Hollywood stardom would embroil many of those who followed in her footsteps. Lena Horne, for example, became a kind of Hollywood star in the 1940s in part through the pressure put on Hollywood by the NAACP. However, Horne's roles were almost always as herself in a small singing role. Horne's rise to fame was as a singing sensation rather than an actress, and her long career as a touring performer assured her of stardom without ever being embraced by Hollywood films. The ambivalence of Hollywood towards African American stars, especially women, would be a recurring cause of controversy and protest during the postwar years. As an example, the explicitly sexual nature of Otto Preminger's *Carmen Jones* (1954), a film that garnered an Academy Award nomination for Dorothy Dandridge, was protested so vehemently by the NAACP that the producers donated the opening night proceeds to the organization in an effort to mute its complaints.[78]

The ambivalence with which Hollywood engaged the African American community extended beyond the studio treatment of performers to the way in which the African American experience was depicted. During the war, for instance, several films sought to galvanize African American support for the war effort. The 1943 film *We've Come a Long Way* was produced by a white independent producer, Jack Goldberg, but also received support from African American minister Elder Solomon Lightfoot Michaux and the War Department. The film's central conceit was that the African American community had been given many opportunities in America and that things would be much worse under German or Japanese domination. The NAACP called the picture "disgusting and insulting" and refused to aid in its distribution to African American theaters. Similar controversies surrounded another War Department–supported film, *Negro Soldier* (1944), which featured the story of African American soldiers throughout U.S. history.

During and immediately following World War II, Hollywood depictions of African Americans continued this trend of painting a rosier picture than seemed warranted. To some extent, the removal of depictions of racism and racial violence was due to the influence of the Production Code, but as Ella Shohat and Robert Stam note, the ban also foreclosed "any portrayal of racial and sexual violence toward African Americans ... implicitly wiping the memory of rape, castration, and lynching from the American record."[79]

This reimagining of America's racial past was most blatant, and most protested in Walt Disney's animated tale of the Reconstruction period,

Song of the South, released in 1946. The musical animated film with live actors was technically innovative, but by the account of numerous African American protestors, the film was reprehensibly politically regressive. Commentators condemned the film's main character, Uncle Remus, as an ineffectual "Uncle Tom," and the *Chicago Defender* declared, "As long as Hollywood refuses to portray modern Negroes truthfully, flights into the servile past, no matter how sincere, will always be resented."[80] Local 27 of the American Federation of Teachers in Washington, D.C., issued a statement declaring the film "insidious and subtle propaganda against the Negro—insidious because the Negro is presented treacherously and slyly in conventional stereotypes."[81] Prominent African American leaders soon called for the film to be banned. Representative Adam Clayton Powell targeted both *Song of the South* and *Abie's Irish Rose*, a romantic comedy focused on the culture clash surrounding the romance between a Jewish man and his Irish fiancée, as inappropriate and publicly called upon Benjamin Fielding, New York City's commissioner of licenses, to "immediately take steps your department and to initiate steps in any other department of the city to immediately close 'Abie's Irish Rose' and 'Song of the South.'" "These two pictures," Powell complained, "are not only an insult to American minorities, but an insult to everything that America as a whole stands for."[82] Along these lines, many theaters catering primarily to African American audiences also shunned the film.[83]

In part due to protests such as these, Hollywood began taking up African American concerns in the series of postwar films often referred to as "social issue" films—those films that looked at various social problems ranging from alcoholism and drugs to racism and anti-Semitism. This period saw the emergence of such films as *The Man with the Golden Arm*, which dealt with drug addiction, and *Gentlemen's Agreement* and *Crossfire*, which engaged anti-Semitism. Films taking on issues of racism and the treatment of African Americans included *Home of the Brave*, *Lost Boundaries*, *Pinky*, and *Intruder in the Dust*, all from 1949. *Variety* termed these the "Negro tolerance pix," and as Margaret McGehee contends, they were among the first to make "manifest the racial climate immediately following World War II" and "signaled a growing opposition to the Jim Crow system on the part of many whites across the country, including those in charge at Hollywood studios."[84] Not surprisingly, these films were plagued by controversy and even protest. In Macon, Georgia, a cross was burned in front of a drive-in theater screening *Pinky*.[85] Several of these pictures also faced bans and heavy censorship, especially in the South.

One of the things that made films like *Pinky* and *Lost Boundaries* so controversial was the way they challenged one of the longest-standing dictums related to race relations on film, namely, the ban on miscegenation. The Production Code explicitly declared, "Miscegenation (sex relationship between the white and black races) is forbidden." While concerns about miscegenation had been raised in previous codes, including the 1927 "Don'ts and Be Carefuls," the Code turned the concern into an unequivocal ban. Interestingly, Susan Courtney's research into the miscegenation clause suggests that, unlike much of the Code, it was not derived from Catholic beliefs or even the racial politics of the drafters of the Code, but rather arose out of censorship practices by state, especially Southern state, censorship boards. The restriction of the Code did not prevent Hollywood from depicting interracial relationships—indeed, as the history of film controversy reveals, the restrictions of the Code rarely eliminated any of the items it prohibited—but the Code did serve to limit the degree to which such relationships could be overtly portrayed on film.

But times were beginning to change. The emergence of the broad civil rights movement during the postwar period shook the very foundations of the racist institutions of Jim Crow and other cultural forms of oppression, and in 1957 the Production Code bowed to the changing tide and removed the ban on miscegenation, opening up a period of increasingly explicit engagement with American race relations.

1957–1989

The period between the late 1950s and the 1980s was a remarkably vibrant time in the struggle for civil rights across a wide spectrum of people living in the United States and around the world. These three decades saw remarkable triumphs—the Voting Act of 1964, desegregation of the schools, Martin Luther King Jr.'s march on Washington—as well as horrific tragedies—the assassination of King, violent race riots throughout the nation, and the assassination of Malcolm X. The nation as a whole was reformulated during these tumultuous years as the cultural codes were fundamentally and at times violently changed. Mainstream films followed these trends—sometimes a bit far behind and at other times in the forefront—and, not surprisingly, many of the films tackling the broader questions of racial representation during this turbulent time courted controversy. Arguably there were at least as many controversies over racial representations in film during this period as there had been in any previous period.

Within the context of this book, what becomes interesting about this time frame is the ways in which these controversies and disputes mirrored those in previous eras. This period saw continued protests by civil rights organizations, protests of films seen as either too conservative or too progressive in their representation of race relations, and the reemergence of various racial cinemas with the coming of filmmakers of color in the late 1960s who began reclaiming their own filmic image. For our present purposes, it is useful to trace these patterns during the thirty-year period leading up to Spike Lee's *Do the Right Thing*, which, as I argue at the end of this chapter, serves as a uniquely provocative articulation of racial representation.

The lifting of the ban on miscegenation in films was greeted with the first major studio film to engage the topic directly: the 1957 film *Island in the Sun*. Starring prominent white actors Joan Fontaine and James Mason and prominent African American actors Harry Belafonte and Dorothy Dandridge, the film is set on a fictitious Caribbean island during the waning days of British colonial rule and follows the complex political, romantic, and familial relationships of the white and Afro-Caribbean characters. Of course, for most reviewers and publicists, the film's central selling point was its interracial romances and even a controversial on-screen interracial kiss. Reactions to the film were deeply mixed, but the controversy helped to make it one of the top money earners at the box office that year. Some critics felt the film pushed boundaries too far and too fast, while others thought, as Douglas Robinson wrote in the *New York Times*, that "motion picture exploration of the previously taboo field of miscegenation and its peripheral areas seems to be progressing cautiously."[86] Still, in some areas the film was met with protests. In Charlotte, North Carolina, for instance, the film was protested by more than a hundred members of the Ku Klux Klan, and in Jacksonville, Florida, the film was picketed by members of a "White Citizens Council."[87]

The controversy over interracial romance on-screen extended into the lives of the actors off-screen. Lead actress Fontaine reported that the day after the Los Angeles premiere, she received hate mail in which "most of the letter-writers termed me unprintable, filthy names. One of the letters had 'KKK' written on it."[88] Similar slurs were visited upon Belafonte from both whites and African Americans, which was especially ironic as the actor had controversially married a white woman—causing some to question his commitment to the African American cause. Belafonte would, in fact, produce his own controversial take on interracial relationships in his film *The Word, The Flesh and the Devil*, a tale about the last people on a post-apocalyptic Earth and their struggle with racial relationships.

Belafonte's difficult position as an African American star whose appeal crossed racial boundaries was shared by one of his contemporaries, Sidney Poitier. Poitier, the star of such provocative and controversial films as *In the Heat of the Night* (1967) and *Guess Who's Coming to Dinner* (1967) was also subjected to public criticism for the ways he represented the African American community. In his autobiography *This Life*, Poitier recalls an article in the *New York Times* entitled "Why Do White Folks Love Sidney Poitier?" The article, written by Clifford Mason, "ripped to shreds everything I had ever done," Poitier recalled, "I was an 'Uncle Tom.'"[89]

On a broader level, these critiques of Belafonte and Poitier were the continuation of a long-standing theme in controversies over racial representations in film. Given the remarkably limited number of roles for people of color, any actor who gains notoriety in one of these roles comes to bear the burden of standing for the entire race. The same burden that had fallen on filmmakers like Oscar Micheaux and actors like Hattie McDaniel now fell upon stars like Horne, Dandridge, Belafonte, and Poitier. They were left in the unenviable position of either being too "stereotypical" and thus playing into long-standing racial caricatures or defying these stereotypes and losing mainstream acceptance.

The lack of roles, especially varied roles, for African Americans had been a point of tension for decades. As early as 1940, the Negro Actors Protective League had organized to push for more roles for African American actors, and in 1942, as mentioned earlier, the NAACP had held a special meeting with Hollywood studio heads to push for more African American roles. In 1962, African American actors picketed the Academy Awards ceremony, urging producers to take up African American issues and characters, and that same year the NAACP threatened legal action as well as a boycott of Hollywood films if television and film producers did not expand the range of African American characters.[90]

To an extent, these efforts were successful, as Hollywood began slowly expanding the roles for African Americans. However, the most dramatic, and perhaps most controversial, changes in African American representation on-screen came through the return of independent African American cinema in the form of the "blaxploitation" films of the 1970s. However, if Poitier and his cohort were faced with the problem of being too mainstream or "white," then these films saw the other horn of the dilemma. African American stars like Jim Brown, a prominent athlete who had won respect at Syracuse University and in the National Football League, faced criticism for being too assertive and aggressive. As Ed Guerrero writes about Brown, "Jim Brown was able to do what Poitier was denied in his career to that point, to act in a violent assertive manner and express his sexuality openly." This difference also extended to their personas off-screen, where "Poitier was reserved and well mannered [while] Jim Brown was a turbulent personality who entangled himself in offscreen escapades, fist fights, and rancorous feuds."[91]

African American filmmakers such as Mario Van Peebles, whose 1971 *Sweet Sweetback's Baadasssss Song* overcame its X rating to become a smash independent hit, and Gordon Parks, whose *Shaft* followed Peebles's film by a few months, reappropriated the image of the African American ghetto and produced films that immersed themselves in the cultures of crime, drugs, and urban poverty. A struggle soon ensued between the two sides of this difficult question of representation. On the one side were older and more established African American actors who felt that the new blaxploitation films from the likes of Peebles and Parks were degrading to the African American community. On the other side were those who embraced these new grittier films as being more authentic and politically charged. As

Donald Bogle argues, this movement was "the first time in film history [that] the studios produced black-oriented films pitched directly at pleasing blacks."[92] Yet the new movement created considerable debate within the African American community. A forum in *Ebony* magazine in 1973 demonstrates the feelings on both sides. In one letter to the editor, the writer argues that films like *Shaft* and *Sweet Sweetback's* are "literally MURDERING a generation of black youths," while another letter contends, "All the black organization leaders who are against a black movie such as *Super Fly* obviously moved from the ghetto and forgot 'what's going on.' "[93]

Controversies over representation on-screen were, of course, not isolated to African Americans. Asian Americans were facing similar struggles throughout these decades. One unique dimension of the issues surrounding Asian actors was Hollywood's racist tendency to treat all people from Asia identically. This problem proved particularly sensitive during and immediately after World War II. During the war, Japanese parts were almost always played by Chinese American actors, due in part to the internment of most Japanese Americans. However, by 1950 there were growing protests from Chinese American actors that they were being displaced for Japanese American actors. As an example, when Japanese actor Shirley Yamaguchi was being hailed as "the Bette Davis of Japan," Chinese-born actor Iris Wong complained publicly, "We are all miffed about Shirley and the other Japanese actors who are being promoted by Hollywood. During the war when Japanese were sent in concentration camps, they used Chinese actors to portray Japanese villains. Now they are casting Japanese in Chinese parts."[94] Sadly, Hollywood's refusal to distinguish between Japanese, Chinese, Korean, and other Asian ethnicities continues, as seen in recent protests over the use of Chinese actresses in Japanese roles in the 2005 film *Memoirs of a Geisha*. As Howard French put it, "The problem with 'Geisha' is that it has cast the wrong Asians in its leading roles, specifically placing three major ethnic Chinese actresses in the role of geisha, one of Japan's most rarefied cultural products."[95]

Another controversy related to Asian actors was the continued use of "yellowface"—the use of makeup to present white actors as Asian characters. While the practice of blackface had become taboo by the 1950s, the use of cosmetics to allow white actors to portray Asian roles continued well into the 1970s. In 1976, Asian actors organized a protest of both their limited roles and the practice of yellowface. As one protestor put it, all "major sympathetic Oriental roles of any intelligence, prominence and esteem" ended up being played by white actors. Writing in 1977, Eugene Wong objected that "the sustained use of slant-eyed makeup [is] especially serious and retrogressive in the midst of an era of undeniable progress for minorities, particularly for racial minorities, in general."[96]

In addition to losing "respectable" Asian roles to white actors, the Asian communities also protested against the continuation of racial stereotyping in Hollywood films and television. In 1977, for example, the Association of Asian/Pacific American Artists demonstrated outside the set of a Dodge car commercial that featured a white actor playing Charlie Chan. The association argued that "the character is stereotypical, affected and negative, as well as being a continuation of the use of racist cosmetology."[97]

Disputes over the roles available to minority characters were also taken up within the Latino community. Following the lead of African American organizations, Latino groups such as the League of United Latin American Citizens and the National Council of La Raza pushed during the 1960s and '70s for the elimination of various egregious stereotypes, including corporate advertising characters like Frito-Lay's Frito Bandito and the Chiquita Banana. Various groups were organized during those decades to protest these caricatures including Nosotros, a group organized by popular actor Ricardo Montalbán. Pressure was also put on Latino actors to abandon their stereotypical, if lucrative, stage personas. As Gary Keller reports:

> Bill Dana, the creator of the comic bellhop, dim-witted speaker of fractured English, José Jiménez (who was the most popular Hispanic TV character of the 1960s among the general public, surpassing Desi Arnaz and Duncan Renaldo's *Cisco Kid*), agreed at the 1970 meeting of the Congress of Mexican American Unity to shelve the persona.[98]

For other Latino actors, the pressure to refuse the kinds of stereotypical roles being offered by mainstream television and film meant severely limiting their careers. For example, Rita Moreno, the first Latina to win an Academy Award, reported great difficulty finding worthwhile roles: "It's really demeaning after you've won the Oscar to be offered the same role over and over again. They only wanted me to drag out my accent-and-dance show over and over again."[99]

In another response borrowed from the African American community, Latino protestors soon began taking up cameras and scripts and producing their own films in an effort to reappropriate their own representation. For example, Moctesuma Esperanza, who would go on to produce such feature films as *The Milagro Beanfield War* (1988) and *Selena* (1997), was a Latino activist who helped organize UCLA's Media Urban Crisis Coalition program to recruit minority filmmakers in the 1970s.

The emergence of prominent Latinos within film and television production soon led to efforts to consolidate their new place and formalize the growing Latino cinema movement. In 1974, the Latino Consortium was established to help promote Latino programming on public television stations, and in 1978 the Los Angeles Chicano Cinema Coalition was formed to solidify a "Chicano cinema esthetic" and "create an alternative to the 'commercial' influence of Hollywood film."[100] These movements were accompanied by various cinematic manifestos, such as Francisco X.

Camplis's, which in 1975 called for a Latino cinema that would "not merely dust off the cobwebs from moldy relics of our pre-Columbian past but provide a viable connection from the past to the present and beyond into the future."[101]

These diverse efforts have created a more vibrant dialogue surrounding the various ethnic identities that make up the Latino community—here it is worth acknowledging that, for example, Mexican, Cuban, and Brazilian identities and cinemas are not identical—but sadly, by the 1990s, Rosa Linda Fergosa concluded that the dominant cinematic representation of Latinos was of poverty, gangs, and drugs—not entirely different from the bandit characters of the early twentieth century.[102]

After the end of the 1980s, another evolution in African American cinema emerged, one that would largely embrace the images of gangs, drugs, guns, and violence. The astounding success of John Singleton's 1991 *Boyz n the Hood*, which garnered both box office and critical acclaim, sparked a new round of African American filmmaking. These new pictures paralleled the films of the blaxploitation era but in many ways were seen as even more violent and celebratory of criminality. Norman Denzin, for instance, argues that these "New Black Cinema" films embrace a "post-civil rights racial politics" and that "this politics shapes a cinema of racial violence."[103] In films like *Menace II Society* (the Hughes Brothers, 1993) and *Juice* (Ernest Dickerson, 1992), young African American filmmakers embraced this violent new racial politics and presented an unflinching view of life in West Coast urban ghettos, replete with guns, gangs, and drugs.

In many ways, the film that opened the door for this new era of militant and violent African American films was the most controversial of this era, and while it did not celebrate West Coast gang culture, it did call out in explicit terms the underlying questions of race, representation, and authority. The film was Spike Lee's 1989 *Do the Right Thing*.

RACIAL REPRESENTATION IN SPIKE LEE'S *DO THE RIGHT THING*

As noted at the beginning of this chapter, from the time of its Cannes debut, Lee's film about racial tensions in a Brooklyn neighborhood was provoking controversy. Various critics feared that the film, while cinematically strong, was too politically incendiary. One anonymous distributor declared in an interview at Cannes, "People are going to walk out of theaters across America and throw trash cans through pizzeria windows, there's no doubt about it." This same commentator noted, "It's a great movie, but its coming out at a very questionable time."[104] Even director Spike Lee seemed to acknowledge the possibility that his film could strike a dangerous chord in the American summer of 1989. "I did not make this movie to incite riots: that's the thing people are going to hang me for," the director declared, and while he expressed doubt that the audiences would be provoked to actual violence by the film, he admitted, "I'll go on the record right now saying that whatever happens I won't shrink from the responsibility. You can't predict the effect of any film."[105]

Of course, critics who were raising the alarm about the threat the film posed were making a prediction and, as the preceding history should suggest, this prediction was not uncommon in relation to films about racial representation. From the fears that "prejudice existing for scores of years will rear itself and flourish again in crime and blood," as the mayor of Lexington declared in response to the 1912 *Johnson-Jeffries Fight*, to concerns that the 1957 *Island in the Sun*'s depiction of miscegenation would cause riots among angered whites, the history of racial representations on film has been one heavily flavored with trepidation of social unrest and violence.

Much as with Oscar Micheaux's *Within Our Gates*, which came hot on the heels of the Chicago race riots of 1919, Lee's *Do the Right Thing* came at a time of heightened racial tensions in New York City and the nation as a whole. Indeed, Lee explicitly cites many of these sources of racial tension—graffiti on one wall declares "Tawana told the truth," a reference to accusations from an African American woman named Tawana Brawley who claimed she was attacked and raped by a group of white men. The film is even dedicated to five African Americans who had been killed under racist circumstances in New York, including Michael Griffith, whose murder at the hands of a white mob in Howard Beach in 1986 inspired the story line.

Despite the provocative timing and nature of Lee's film, however, the predictions of violence proved wrong. There were no major incidents related to the film, and on the contrary, most audiences who saw the film reported a positive reaction to it. Sylvia Castillo, a Los Angeles resident who was interviewed after seeing the movie, chastised the critics who forecast violence, explaining that the film "just puts dialogue right on the table." Others responding to the film observed the way it offered a more realistic portrayal of race relations than other contemporary "race issue" films. Karen Bass, also interviewed outside a Los Angeles theater, expressed her opinion: "It showed life from the black community's perspective. It wasn't like 'Mississippi Burning,' where black people were just nameless, helpless victims."[106] Felicia Harden, a nineteen-year-old Bostonian, concurred: "It really impacted on me because it was just like the stuff that happens every day, all the time, in Boston."[107]

This is not to suggest that everyone viewed Lee's film positively. Some critics decried Lee's portrayal of his African American characters, many of whom are shown drinking on the street corners and using obscenities. One *New York Times* letter writer, for instance, objected, "I've never seen blacks portrayed so offensively. They are foul-mouthed (and loud-mouthed) idlers, bullies, brawlers and drinkers whose main interests are feckless gossip, ghetto blasters and spotless sneakers, and there is hardly a hint that any of them aspire to anything else."[108] Others complained that the film provoked difficult questions but fell short of offering any sense of a solution. Another Boston audience member said, "I see a lot of issues being brought up but I don't know what to think about the issues, to do about the issues. That was the biggest disappointment about the movie for me."[109] Confronted with these concerns, Lee protested, "It's very unfair to expect me to have the answer. I don't think that's my job as a filmmaker. But I think I can at least try and get people to start talking about it and try and discuss ways that we can live together."[110]

In many ways, Lee's response—that he saw his role as one of raising questions rather than answering them—provides a useful way for beginning to think about *Do the Right Thing* in relation to the long history of racial representations on film. One of the arguments I advanced at the beginning of this chapter—and hope I've elaborated throughout my historical narrative—is that controversies about race and film have often revolved around the question of who claims, or has, authority to decide how other races are represented. This issue certainly stood out in the early days of popular cinema. The contradictory responses to the *Johnson-Jeffries Fight* and *Birth of a Nation* suggest that the question was not really about causing social unrest—a charge leveled at both films—but about whose interests are served by a particular racial representation. As I have argued, the questions of authority over representations have typically been wrapped up in the broader cultural web of white privilege. So, the *Johnson-Jeffries* film was dangerous because it depicted images of racial violence that were threatening to white dominance and privilege, while the images of racial violence in *Birth of a Nation* were not; thus, the former film was banned, and the latter became one of the most popular films of its day.

Spike Lee's film, of course, is not the first movie to engage the topic of white privilege, nor even the first created by a director of color. But what I find particularly notable about *Do the Right Thing* is that it is very much a film about the precise issue of race, representation, and authority. While numerous film critics have debated the merits of the film's ambivalence—especially the lingering, and unanswered, question of whether Mookie "did the right thing" and Lee's use of quotations from both Dr. Martin Luther King Jr. and Malcolm X—there has been less attention paid to the idea that Lee's film is ultimately about the question of who has authority to control the spaces of representation.[111] Specifically, my argument is that the way in which Lee raised this question both provoked the fears that the film would cause violence and led audiences to respond to the film in a more reflective and contemplative way. It was, in other words, the artistry of the film that allowed it to present its polemical concerns without precipitating inappropriate reactions.

As those who have viewed the film will recall, the entire story takes place during one particularly hot day in the Brooklyn neighborhood of Bedford-Stuyvesant. The multiracial nature of the neighborhood is soon established as the film settles on the principal figures. Mookie, played by Lee himself, is a young African American who works delivering pizzas for the Italian American Sal, played by Danny Aiello, and his two sons. Surrounding these two are a variety of characters, including the neighborhood elders, Da Mayor and Mother Sister, played by Ossie Davis and Ruby Dee; a radio-toting Public Enemy fan named Radio Raheem; and an increasingly militant friend of Mookie's called Buggin Out.

Existing racial tension in the neighborhood begins to simmer as the day's heat arrives—angry confrontations between African American patrons and a Korean grocer, for example, and between Buggin Out and a white man who has recently moved into the neighborhood. Tensions reach their boiling point when Buggin Out complains to Sal that his "Wall of Fame" consists only of Italian Americans and contains no "brothers." A second angry confrontation between Radio Raheem and Sal—this one over the blaring volume of Raheem's radio—sets the stage for the film's eventual confrontation.

Late in the evening, Raheem and Buggin Out return to the pizza parlor, along with another aggrieved resident named Smiley. In the ensuing argument, Sal destroys Raheem's radio with a baseball bat, leading to a physical fight that escalates and soon pours out of the pizzeria and into the streets. When police arrive, officers restrain Raheem with a choke hold that is held too long, resulting in his death. Police quickly retreat and leave the angry African American residents to confront Sal and his two sons. The tense standoff is broken by Mookie, who picks up a trash can and—in the action often debated as the "right thing"—throws it through the window of Sal's Famous Pizzeria. The ensuing riot sees the pizzeria burned to the ground.

In the film's denouement, Mookie returns to Sal's to demand his money, and the two men have a tense discussion in which Sal insists the pizzeria was his—that he had "made it with his own hands"—and Mookie condemns the murder of Radio Raheem. Mookie leaves with his money and the film ends.

Surrounding this central plot are numerous subplots that help to add to the reality and complexity of life in this small block: Mookie's relationship with the mother of his son (played by Rosie Perez); Sal's affection for Jade, Mookie's sister; the long-running feud between Mother Sister and Da Mayor; the tension between Sal's two sons, one of whom (played by John Turturro) is blatantly racist and the other of whom feels more connected to Mookie than to his brother; and the running commentary by the local disc jockey (played by Samuel L. Jackson). These various subplots help the film establish a realistic "three-dimensional" setting for the primary action and the moral complexities involved in all human relationships.

At the heart of the action in *Do the Right Thing* is the question of representation and authority, and it seems clear that Lee's film is designed to raise this question in explicit and forceful ways. Even the opening music of the film suggests the complexity of the film's reference to the long history of racial representations. A single saxophone wails a low and almost mournful version of "Lift Every Voice and Sing," the African American National Anthem, as the opening credits begin, but soon the screen is filled with bright colors and the figure of Perez dancing to the Public Enemy song "Fight the Power." Even the first words of dialogue suggest that this film is designed to approach issues of film and race in a unique way— "Wake up!" the radio disk jockey shouts into his microphone as the film begins.

That *Do the Right Thing* is concerned with the question of representation is made clear with the central struggle of the film. Whose pictures should be displayed on Sal's "Wall of Fame"? Sal argues that, as the pizzeria is his, only he can decide who will appear in this space. However, Buggin Out and later others contend that, as the pizzeria is patronized primarily by people of color, the wall should represent the diversity of the neighborhood.

In another interesting, and often remarked upon, segment of the film, various characters break the "fourth wall" and turn to the audience while spewing out a string of racial epithets aimed at Italian Americans, African Americans, Jews, Koreans, and Puerto Ricans. Here Lee brings all those unstated racist stereotypes that have long been the "visual grammar" of Hollywood into their harshest and most explicit articulation, and rather than have these exchanged between characters in moments of anger, he has these angry words spoken from the screen directly at the audience. Through this move, Lee pulls back the curtain from the racism inherent in many representations of the Other and forces the viewer to recognize what underlies so many familiar ethnic stereotypes. Interestingly, the scene immediately preceding—and therefore seemingly provoking this excursion into the spewing of racial slurs—is a discussion between Mookie and Sal's older, racist son Pino. Mookie asks Pino who his favorite basketball star, movie star, and rock star are, and in each instance, Pino names an African American. When asked how these could be his heroes while he continued to see the African Americans in the neighborhood in such demeaning and racist ways, Pino finds himself trapped in a quandary and retorts, "They're more than black." It is the painful disjuncture between representations that has Pino trapped; he cannot see the reality behind the idealized African American sports and entertainment stars he idolizes, nor can he see past his own racist representation of African Americans to engage with those around him.

Somewhere between the representations on the screen and those we use as filters to navigate our everyday life is the reality of human beings struggling to find their way in the world. Lee's film does not explicitly take sides on the various questions he raises on the film. While it would have been easy to paint someone—Sal or Buggin Out or Radio Raheem or even Pino—as the unequivocal villain of the film, Lee chose to leave the situation open, ambiguous, and complex, and it seems to me this is one of the reasons that the predictions of the film provoking angry, perhaps even violent, responses proved wrong. Lee's film may be provocative, even inflammatory, but it is so in such an intelligent, complex, and aesthetically confident way that, as many audience members attested, it places difficult questions on the table rather than forcing any particular answer.

My focus here was on the actual film—rather than, as in previous chapters, on the reactions to the film—because, in many ways, the controversy over *Do the Right Thing* was a controversy that never came to fruition. The fears were circulated primarily before the film's release. Upon its release, however, the film was received in the intelligent and thoughtful manner in which it was made. In this way, arguably, Lee's film helped to diffuse its own controversy by explicitly raising the question that often goes unstated in controversies over race and film.

CONCLUSION

Not surprisingly, while Spike Lee's film elegantly raised the issues underlying the controversies about racial representation in the movies, it did not end such controversies. In the years immediately following *Do the Right Thing*, the next wave of African American filmmakers embraced Lee's militancy but combined it with a grittier and more violent West Coast urban aesthetic in various films exploring, and at times glorifying, gang violence. These films were both praised and condemned by those who saw in them either a substantial break or a substantial continuation of the racist representations of the past.

Lee's film also predicted the increasingly complex racial politics that would emerge throughout the turn of the twentieth century. By the early years of the twenty-first century, protests against Hollywood representations of race embroiled not only African Americans, Latinos, and Asians but other groups, as well. For example, Arabs protested Disney's 1992 animated film *Aladdin*, which initially contained the lyrics "they cut off your ear, if they don't like your face" before protests forced a change.[112] In 2007, people of Persian descent protested the special-effects epic *300* claiming it was another example of Hollywood painting Middle Easterners as monstrous villains.[113] In the context of the American war in Iraq, some protesters also feared that the film was laying a symbolic foundation to justify an attack against Iran.

The controversies over films like *Memoirs of a Geisha*, *Aladdin*, and *300* suggest that the struggles over racial representation will become even more complicated in a rapidly globalizing world. While there is a long history of international struggles over film representation, dating back to Mexico's ban and Japan's protests in the early 1900s, the increasingly global market for Hollywood films and the more rapid movement of peoples around the world suggest that issues of racial representation and the underlying question of who has the authority to craft such representations will continue to be contentious.

CHAPTER 5

Religion: Mel Gibson's *The Passion of the Christ*

In many ways, it is appropriate to conclude this study of controversial cinema by considering controversies related to religion. As even a cursory glance through the preceding chapters should indicate, religion and religious groups have played crucial roles in many of the controversies that have emerged over sex, violence, and race. It is worth recalling that the Production Code, the principal document directing film censorship for more than thirty years was largely constructed by a committee of Catholic clergy and laypersons. Even before the installation of the Production Code, many of the voices rising in opposition to the seeming immorality of cinema were those of clergy, and issues of sex or violence were often framed in terms of religion. Furthermore, as I discuss more fully in the history section of this chapter, some of the earliest struggles over cinema were about the place of the movie theater within American society as replacement of either the saloon or the pulpit.

Given the numerous ways in which religion and cinema have been intertwined, it is important to begin this chapter by delineating precisely what I mean by controversies over religion and film. Because religion touches on, at least in some way, almost every American cultural conception of virtue and vice, any effort to pursue every intersection between cinematic controversy and religion would require an extensive retracing of our steps thus far, returning to the topics of sex, violence, and race, as well as numerous others. In order to avoid this duplication, I want to focus in this chapter on those specific controversies that have emerged at the points where the work of the church and the work of cinema have overlapped. By this somewhat cryptic phrase, I mean to suggest that many of the controversies related to religion and film have erupted over attempts by cinema to do the work of

religion—often by visually depicting crucial narratives from sacred texts—
or when religious organizations have sought to utilize the mechanisms of
cinema toward their own ends. While there is no essential reason that religious narrative cannot be told through cinema—indeed, hundreds have
been told in this way without much contestation—the history of controversial cinema suggests that, at times, the attempt to render sacred messages
through the lenses of mainstream American cinema has resulted in considerable and often spectacular backlashes.

It is easy to lay out some of the reasons that the overlapping of the work
of religion and of cinema might provoke controversy. In the first place, the
juxtaposition of religion and film is a mingling of the sacred and the profane. Indeed, as I describe in more detail later, one of the turning points in
the relationship between churches and Hollywood was the "star scandals"
of the early 1920s. When major stars like Roscoe "Fatty" Arbuckle
became more notorious for their licentious lifestyles than for their film
work, many churches were led to condemn the whole film industry as an
ultimately "earthly" enterprise that was antithetical to their more sacred
mission.

At another level, this distinction also plays out along the lines of, to bor-
row the title of Thomas Martin's interesting book, "images and the imageless."[1] While most religions have utilized imagery—often in the form of
icons—throughout history, there has also been a consistent tension in most
religions between the spiritual and the material. Although images may
point to some higher spiritual level, the image itself falls short of the spiritual truth toward which it directs the worshipper. This problem has a long
and rich tradition in both philosophy and theology. Plato, for instance,
insisted upon a separation between the world of appearance and the higher
realm of Truth—as depicted in his cave allegory, for instance. Saint Augus-
tine also grappled with this relationship in his own understanding of the
relationship between God's truth and the written text of scripture—arguing
that the written word is always an imperfect gesture toward God's perfect
message. In a recent review of the literature on religion and film, Terry
Lindvall explains this long-standing difficulty for the Christian church as a
corollary to the Second Commandment against "graven images": "Rooted
in this aniconic Hebrew culture, but tempered by Hellenic visual arts, the
early Church wrestled with the place of imagery in its worship and
instruction."[2]

In the more concrete case of film and religion, numerous controversies
have erupted along the divisions between the sacred and the profane and
between the image and the imageless. Crafting a convincing film is hard
enough, but when the basis of the narrative is a tale deemed sacred to a
large community, that crafting must be done with particular caution.
Whether a poor casting choice, a flippant remark, or a seeming lack of reverence, efforts to turn the sacred narratives of religions into worldly cinema

have long been fraught with both promise and peril. These dangerous waters are made even more hazardous by the fact that the three major religious traditions in America—Catholic and Protestant Christianity and Judaism—share complex historical and cultural interrelationships. These relationships have meant, at times, that satisfying one audience necessarily entails alienating, perhaps even enraging, another.

The case study I return to at the end of this chapter, Mel Gibson's *The Passion of the Christ*, illustrates these points quite well—so much so, in fact, that I confess to having felt deeply conflicted about whether or not to see the film at all. My conflict was driven in large part by the reactions of people I hold near and dear. One such person came to me, tears literally in her eyes, and told me that I *had* to see the film, that it had changed her life, and that it was an experience that I, as an Episcopalian, could not afford to miss. Not more than two days later, another friend came to me and asked if I had seen *Passion*. When I said that I had not, he expressed great relief and explained that the film, which he had not seen either, was so fundamentally offensive to him as a Jewish man that he hoped I would not even consider seeing it. In the end, I did see the film—under the cover of professional responsibility—and, perhaps not surprisingly, my reaction differed from those of both my impassioned friends. But what struck me as particularly interesting was the conviction and passion with which these two individuals addressed me about this film. Gibson's *Passion* provoked passion in audiences—both those who saw it and those who refused it— that was truly unlike anything I had seen before. Even the angry reaction of protestors outside Martin Scorsese's *The Last Temptation of Christ* differed considerably, because there was no such counterreaction from the other side. While some applauded the film and still more defended it, I know of no one who walked out of Scorsese's film proclaiming that it had changed his or her life.

Before returning to Gibson's provocative film, recently voted by *Entertainment Weekly* the most controversial film in history (although that point is quite debatable), I would add two codicils to the survey of films that follows. The first is that, primarily due to the particular constitution of American culture, the vast majority of controversies that emerged were related to one or more of the country's three dominant religions: Catholicism, Protestantism, and Judaism. This is not to say that there were no controversies related to Islam or Hinduism or Buddhism but simply to observe that the vast majority of American popular culture is defined in relation to these three more prominent faiths. The second codicil is that while religious values and organizations are pervasive in almost all types of controversies related to film, there are surprisingly few controversies related specifically to the intersection between the work of religion and the work of film. For reasons I explore more fully below, in much of the history of American cinema, religious narratives were dealt with in such a way as to avoid controversy—often virtually at all costs. This reverence for religion was, at times, motivated more out of concern for profit than for piety, but for several decades major Hollywood studios made considerable efforts to avoid anything even approaching the controversial. Of course, given the tensions outlined above, even the greatest of care could not avoid occasionally provoking outrage.

A HISTORY OF CONTROVERSIES OVER RELIGION AND FILM

Perhaps the biggest myth related to religion and film is that the two have always had an antagonistic relationship. While it is certainly true that from the time of the early nickelodeon boom in the 1900s some preachers and pastors have condemned cinema, the relationship has always been much more complex than that. Indeed, some of the earliest supporters of motion picture theaters were members of the clergy who saw in film both an alternative to the saloon or gambling hall and a potential medium for moral uplift and ministry. In terms of my broader focus in this chapter, we can observe throughout the history of film and religion this tension between the work of the house of worship and the movie theater. When religious organizations have sought to use film as a medium for their ministry, controversies have often erupted, and when motion picture producers have sought to appropriate religious topics for their own work—namely, entertainment and profit—controversies have also developed. In the midst of these various overlaps, contests, and appropriations, there has never been a simple relationship—whether of support or opposition—between film and religion.

In the past few decades, film scholars and theologians have taken up the task of exploring the complicated dialogue that has been going on between film and religion since the former's inception.[3] Indeed, one of the earliest roots of the modern cinematic apparatus was the "magic lantern"—a device using a candle and crudely animated cells to create an early system of projection—which was invented by a Catholic priest and commonly used in churches. Early churchgoers were as likely to have embraced the emergence of film at the turn of the twentieth century—in Janet Staiger's speculation, to have seen film as "a powerful sign of the Lord's beneficence and bounty to his flock"—as they were to have feared the new medium of entertainment.[4]

In the following sections, I want to trace out this long-standing dialogue, paying particular attention to the points of contest and controversy that have emerged. Occasionally, these disputes have been between religious communities and the motion picture industry, but other contests have erupted between members of different religious communities or even between people within a single religious group. All this is to suggest that whenever the spheres of religion and mainstream cinema have overlapped, a complex and contentious dispute was possible and, perhaps, inevitable.

1897–1927

There was an interesting spatial relationship between church and movie theater in the early years of cinema. Not only had churches been sites for early precinematic "moving images" via magic lanterns and early stereopticons but conversely early movie palaces also took on many of the aesthetic trappings of the church. Communist cultural critic Moussinac objected to the religious qualities of early French movie theaters, observing, "Organ music, with illuminations and projectors, acts as a reminder of the golden decorations of churches and the reflection of the stained glass windows."[5] But the aesthetic and architectural similarities between houses of worship and motion picture theaters—which can be easily seen in the grandeur of early American movie palaces, as well—were not nearly as complicated as the deeper question of the relationship between these two cultural places. The quandary over what relationship should exist between movie palace and church became one of the most vexing questions of the turn of the century.

While the nickelodeons were condemned by many as dens of iniquity and sites of moral corruption, as outlined in more detail in chapter 1, some of the early endorsements of early theaters came from church leaders who felt they were a promising alternative to the saloons and gambling houses for popular diversion. Various movie house publications touted this sobering effect of the motion picture houses, professing, as Lindvall puts it in the excellent resource book *The Silents of God*, "the cinema's triumphal replacement of the saloon, with attendance at the wet bars decreasing significantly."[6] In some cities, the clergy actively promoted the nickelodeon as an alternative. In Ithaca, New York, for instance, one minister sought donations from local saloonkeepers in order to erect a motion picture theater "to provide a place for men to go Sunday evenings, so that they will not be tempted or go to other towns for their amusement."[7] Not surprisingly, one of the early genres of cinema was the "reformation" film, in which the main character's debaucheries are finally rectified with their return to family/Christian values, as in, for example, the 1909 film *The Drunkard's Reform*, which plays out much as its title suggests.

The supposed benefit of the motion picture theater as a less harmful form of recreation was, of course, not embraced by all faith communities, nor did it move forward without complications. One of the main difficulties, avoided in the above anecdote about Ithaca, was the question of whether motion pictures should be shown on Sunday. As discussed in chapter 1, the struggle over keeping the Sabbath free of motion pictures, extending existing "blue laws" to cover projected entertainment, was a complex legal wrangle in many jurisdictions. In New York, for example, the battle over Sunday movies extended through the state's Supreme Court, the mayor's office, and even the governor's mansion.

On December 3, 1907, New York State Supreme Court Justice Thomas O'Gorman ruled that an 1860 ordinance against Sunday shows could be used to revoke the license of the Victoria Theater. O'Gorman argued that "the Christian Sabbath is one of the civil institutions of the state" and thus "the Legislature has authority to regulate its observance." Pursuant to this ruling, New York's police commissioner announced that all shows would be closed in a ban that applied to "Carnegie Hall as well as the one and five cent vaudeville and moving picture shows."[8] Reaction to this declaration was deeply divided. The city's elites and church leaders applauded the decision, but huge crowds responded angrily in the silent streets of Broadway insisting that "the people's Sunday belongs to the people."[9] The public pressure sent the policy back to the politicians, and in 1908 a public meeting was held to help sort out the issues. Not surprisingly, representatives of the motion picture theaters argued that the moral advantage of the nickelodeon was as a replacement for the saloon. Even on Sunday, they argued, "many a former drunkard now spent that day in such shows with his family."[10]

The struggle over Sunday movie showings spread throughout the country and, as discussed in chapter 1, helped to lay the legal foundation for the subsequent mechanisms of film censorship in the United States.[11] The cultural logic that would extend the ban on Sunday screenings to the censorship of film content was articulated by a number of religious leaders. The Reverend Dr. D. DeBeer, of the Christian Reform Church, in 1909 condemned "vaudettes," a name for moving pictures derived from the vaudeville shows they were often based upon, arguing, "The Vaudette is ... decidedly harmful to the Church. It draws the young people away from church as is clearly shown by the fact that attendance on Sunday is fully twice as large as on week days. What good can come from such a Sabbath breaking institution?" He added that "the Vaudette affords a very convenient occasion for Satan to mislead our young people."[12]

Other clergy members were not as willing to cede moving pictures to Satan's domain. Religious narratives had been appearing on celluloid since at least 1897, when an early film of a Passion play was released and subsequently used by revivalist and temperance leader Col. Henry Hadley in his tent sermons.[13] In 1911, K. S. Hover proclaimed, "Satan has a new enemy. They are fighting the evil one with the flickering films that were formerly used only to amuse."[14] As early as 1900, some churches were embracing the moving picture technology as a new tool in attracting congregants and transmitting their messages. In his widely circulated 1911 pamphlet *The Religious Possibilities of the Motion Picture*, Herbert Jump advanced the argument that "the visible drama shown in the right sort of motion picture ... has religious possibilities just as the spoken dramatic story or parable has them. Both help to make the Gospel visible."[15] Along these lines the Reverend W. H. Jones was quoted as proclaiming the evangelical superiority of moving pictures, arguing, "A religious subject, thus tactfully and reverentially treated, in my opinion, will do more to advance the cause of religion and to uplift humanity than a thousand eloquent preachers ever can hope to accomplish through their oratory."[16]

The practical benefit of incorporating moving pictures into religious services, at least for Protestants, came in terms of attendance. The fear of losing congregants to the nickelodeon on Sunday evenings led some churches to purchase their own projectors and install moving pictures as part of their services. The Reverend Edgar Fay Daugherty of the First Christian Church of Vincennes, Indiana, wrote in to *Moving Picture World* to report that after incorporating moving pictures into his evening services, "I have secured quadrupled attendance at my evening services ... [and] I have only just begun to realize on the large religious and devotional uses of the moving picture."[17] By 1920, Lindvall reports, "over one hundred Baptist, Presbyterian, Methodist, Congregationalist, and Roman Catholic churches in New York City alone were using motion pictures in their ministries." One of the ways this ministry was furthered was through the push to create morally "uplifting films," a movement supported by figures like Jane Addams.[18] Other prominent institutions participating in the educational and morally uplifting movement in early films were the Public Education Association, the League for Political Education, and the Young Men's Christian Association (YMCA).[19] As part of the effort to promote a "cleaner" image of the motion picture industry, a consortium of New York exhibitors formed the Motion Picture Patents Company, with the motto "Moral, Educational and Amusing."

The "uplift film" movement, however, soon ran afoul of the public's general inclination toward tales of sex and violence—as detailed in the preceding chapters—and with the seeming decline of any moral message in motion pictures came the rise in condemnation of cinema in general from members of the clergy. Increasingly, the images on the screen were living down to the condemnation being thrown at them by religious leaders. In 1917 a Pentecostal minister named C. F. Wimberly insisted, "That the Moving Picture is a gigantic agency for the corruption of young men and women, need only be examined to be verified," and expressed particular concern about "the tenacious hold" motion pictures had on children.[20] Lindvall has called the period between 1913 and 1919 "the Great Debates," as this period is characterized by deep division within and among Protestant churches over the question of whether motion pictures could be redeemed for the purposes of spiritual uplift.

One particularly interesting argument leveled against uplifting or religiously instructive films was advanced by Baptist minister Dr. A. C. Dixon. Dixon contended that there is a fundamental distinction between the stage, or screen, and the work of ministry. As he argues, "The purpose of the stage is to teach people how to act a part; the purpose of the Church of Christ is to teach them how to be real."[21] This distinction between the realm of the spirit and the worldly realm of the theater encapsulated many of the fears of those who opposed the intermingling of church and screen. Along these lines, T. C. Horton, writing in the journal *The King's Business* in 1919, condemned churches that were embracing modern entertainment as a means of evangelism and insisted that "it would not be long before the buildings would become the house of the harlot and the gate to hell."[22]

Other clergy leaders still sought to influence the tone and moral temperament of the motion picture industry through moral and economic pressure. In Louisville, Kentucky, the Men's Brotherhood of St. John's Evangelical Church issued a resolution urging "the management, directors and stockholders of local playhouses to co-operate with us in our endeavor to make the screen a power for good and not for evil."[23] Others urged churchgoers to use their dollars to pressure movie houses to exhibit only clean and moral pictures: "Discriminate between houses, if necessary," believers were urged. "Results will surely follow!"[24] Thus, even at this early stage, the notion of a church-based boycott was being circulated along the fault line between religious reverence and cinematic entertainment. The Reverend Dr. Percy Stickney in a 1920 essay explained the workings of the Better Photoplay League of America, which "carried out the work of organizing the patrons of motion pictures against exhibitors who showed salacious pictures," noting that "the results were immediately felt at the box office." Furthermore, Reverend Stickney recommended, "If picture conditions are not right in your town, organize your community and your exhibitor will listen attentively. If he does not, hit him in the box-office. He will hear you then."[25]

Efforts to bring American popular films into the service of religious moral education ran into a major roadblock in the form of the star scandals of the early 1920s. As discussed in chapter 1, the sex scandals involving, for example, popular comedian Fatty Arbuckle led to an overwhelming sense among many of the more conservative Protestant denominations that mainstream cinema could not be redeemed. This outrage increased when, after Arbuckle was acquitted of murder charges in December 1922, William Hays's office reinstated him as a director. In an interesting twist, one of Arbuckle's supporters, producer Joseph M. Schenk, sought to use Christian beliefs in defense of the scandal-plagued former star: "It is not Christianlike of ministers to condemn Arbuckle before he has been heard." In spite of these appeals, numerous religious bodies went on to organize boycotts of any future Arbuckle projects. In Washington, D.C., the National Welfare Council called upon its membership to fight against any new Arbuckle films, and the Church Federation of St. Louis reported being "aggressively opposed" to any films from Arbuckle.[26]

The widely publicized escapades of popular film stars combined with the rise of the sexually alluring "flapper" as a mainstay of popular movies, and the general awareness among producers that sex was more profitable than morality led to what Lindvall perceptively calls "the Great Divorce."[27] For many clergy leaders, popular cinema became an easy target for vitriolic sermons aimed at the licentiousness of modern life. A useful example of this rhetoric came from evangelist Jack Linn in his instructively titled tract "The Movies—The Devil's Incubator: Can a Christian Go to the Movies?" in which the answer was an unequivocal no. Linn not only capitalized on the notorious scandals of Arbuckle's alleged murder and his "being the leader of a pajama party where everything that was low and base and unclean was tolerated" but further pushed his point by asking the rhetorical question of whether anyone had ever "met a Christian actor or actress"—to which, again, the answer was no.[28] An even more inflammatory version of this rhetoric of condemnation was that issued by Capt. Dr. Rev. Wilbur Fisk Crafts, who lobbied Congress for federal censorship laws and urged officials "to rescue the motion picture industry from the hands of the Devil and 500 un-Christian Jews."[29] This intermingling of antifilm rhetoric with anti-Semitism would continue to be a theme throughout the history of controversies over religion and film.

Adding to the sense that the only appropriate relationship between Christian religion and the cinema was one of antagonism, the latter half of the 1920s saw the repeal of blue laws against movie showings on Sundays in various jurisdictions, and the motion picture industry and the rhetoric of many clergy picked up on this antagonism. In a 1925 issue of the *Moody Bible Institute Monthly*, Ray Miller described film exhibitors as "men that are in a business whose every motive is rooted in evil." Miller's article spawned an interesting response from reader Sarah Davison, who sought to defend the practice of going to less objectionable films, but her letter drew even more harsh and angry responses from other readers of *Moody*. E. L. Duprey, of the First Baptist Church in Oldham, South Dakota, proclaimed in answer to Davison, "No agency today is doing more to chill spiritual warmth in the older hearts and to make a shipwreck with the young than the moving picture screen."[30]

The brief potential union between Protestant churches and the motion picture world was irrevocably ruptured in the 1920s, so much so that the Reverend Dr. Liewelly Brown could declare to the *New York Times* what many pastors seemed to believe, namely, that he saw "the movie menace as America's greatest plague." Added to this general tone of condemnation was the technological factor of radio. As Lindvall observes, the introduction of radio provided an even more attractive technological outlet for evangelical Protestants than film, and as religious leaders and revivalists took to the airwaves, one of their most popular and promising targets was the licentious and morally corrupting nature of the motion picture.[31]

The broadly held public perception that American films were produced by corrupt and depraved individuals and contained morally compromised messages was one of the factors that led those in the industry to form the

Motion Picture Producers and Distributors of America (MPPDA) in 1922 and to select Hays, a well-known Republican and Presbyterian who had previously been postmaster general, as their new movie "czar." Hays's first attempt at controlling film immorality—the 1927 "Don'ts and Be Carefuls"—was largely unsuccessful due in part to its vagueness and in part to its lack of enforcement mechanism. The solution to his problem would come from another religious community—the Catholic Church.

1927–1952

As discussed more fully in the first chapter, the MPPDA was formed in an effort to ward off many of the controversies that had been whirling around the motion picture industry since the star scandals of the mid-1920s. The fears were based on the possibility not only of widespread public disapproval of the growing film industry but also of this disapproval leading to federal intervention. One of the most vocal and organized religious opponents of the increasingly lax cinematic morals was the Catholic Church. Catholics had both a more coherent organization than most Protestant denominations and an apparently clearer sense of authority over many of its practitioners. Therefore, even though Catholics were a relatively small percentage of the U.S. movie audience, the possibility of a widespread Catholic boycott presented potentially damaging economic consequences.

Catholics, like Protestants, had expressed interest in utilizing motion pictures for the purpose of moral uplift and education, and it was out of this emphasis that a group of Catholic clergy and laypersons came together. This group—which included Martin Quigley, editor of the influential trade magazine *Motion Picture Herald*; Father Fitz-George Dinneen; Father Daniel Lord; and Joseph Breen, who would later become Hollywood's chief censor—petitioned Hays to abandon his list of loose "Don'ts and Be Carefuls" and take up a more stringent and prescriptive set of guidelines that would become the Production Code. Under the Code, not only were many of the morally questionable behaviors that had provoked the condemnation of religious leaders prohibited, but strict rules were also established about how Hollywood might engage religious topics. The Code explicitly forbade the ridicule of any religious faith or mocking any religious leader or official. As Olga J. Martin, who served as secretary to Breen during the early years of the Production Code Administration, would later explain:

> These provisions prohibit making comedy characters of ministers; or dramatizing the minister as other than a venerable character.... Not only may a minister not be characterized as a villain, but he may not be shown to fall from grace or to commit any sin or crime.[32]

The Code was clear: when it came to representing religion, filmmakers would need to show both care and reverence.

It was not long, however, before Hollywood producers began to realize that the Production Code's religious roots might provide a way of smuggling in the more licentious and decadent aspects of life. Narratives of sin and redemption would, after all, have to depict the sin. The master of this mix of transgression and piety was the man who crafted the mold of the religious epic for generations to come, Cecil B. DeMille.[33] DeMille's career was marked by the kind of big-screen spectacles in which, as Gerald Forshey puts it, "the forces of evil are pitted against the forces of good, with good the ultimate victor. Evil is depicted as hedonistic materialism, based on power, wealth, and the corruption of accepted morality."[34] While good ultimately triumphed in DeMille's epics, it was often the graphic depiction of evil that provoked controversy among those religious folks who came to the theater to witness a biblical epic, only to find some aspects of it a little too real for comfort.

Sign of the Cross, DeMille's 1932 religious epic pitting Nero's lustful rule against stoic Christians and a converted Roman soldier, was condemned by some who charged that DeMille spent more time "with a dissolute and decadent Nero than with the more heroic representatives of pristine Christianity."[35] DeMille rapidly recognized that this method of smuggling sex and violence into Code-regulated theaters under the auspices of a religious narrative was remarkably successful. His 1949 *Samson and Delilah* was another biblical epic filled with sensuality and violence, of which some religious reviewers complained that the biblical story of Samson's neglect and later reclamation of his spiritual devotion was notably absent. Regarding this film, DeMille explained to his staff, "We'll sell it as a story of faith, a story of the power of prayer. That's for the censors and the women's organizations. For the public, it's the hottest love story of all time."[36]

DeMille was not alone in recognizing that shooting a religious narrative resulted in a more lenient interpretation of the Production Code. Henry King's 1951 *David and Bathsheba*, for example, which starred Gregory Peck as King David, involved a story of adultery and murder in which the perpetrator not only goes unpunished but, by film's end, is lauded as the hero. However, because the story was based on a narrative from the Bible, Production Code censors could hardly claim it immoral. As *Time* magazine noted in a 1951 review, this resulted in "a censor-proof tale of a strong man's weakness for a beautiful woman."[37] Even King later reported that the biblical basis of the story had forced Breen and the Production Code Administration to back away from most major changes because "they had to agree with us that we had no right to change the Bible to fit the Code."[38] Some religious leaders, however, balked at this camouflaging of sensual stories with biblical clothing, objecting that *David and Bathsheba* was more a film based on a religious story than a religious film and that the film dwelled too much on the sensual side of sin and not enough on the divine story of redemption and blessings.

Another difficulty that emerged with DeMille's spectacular depictions of biblical stories was the question of whose religious traditions were treated with reverence. In particular, Christianity and Judaism have had a long history of antagonism, with Christians historically adopting numerous anti-Semitic attitudes. Although the history of this antagonism goes beyond the scope of the current study, in terms of film history one of the most vocal responses came as a result of DeMille's 1927 film *The King of Kings*. Felicia Herman has argued that the controversy surrounding *King of Kings* "forever changed the way the organized Jewish community would relate to Hollywood."[39] Concerns about anti-Semitism in film had been expressed since at least 1913, when the Anti-Defamation League (ADL) officially asked the National Board of Censorship of Motion Pictures to fight against the growing trend toward hostile depictions of Jewish stereotypes. But it was the protests against DeMille's *King of Kings* that provoked the first official connection between the Jewish organization B'nai B'rith and the movie industry.

Protests within the Jewish community began as soon as *King of Kings* was released, and as the film's distribution expanded, so too did the protests. In October 1927, three prominent Jewish leaders, including the president of B'nai B'rith, Alfred Cohen, viewed DeMille's film and denounced it as harmful to the welfare of the Jewish people. Numerous Jewish organizations, such as the Board of Rabbis of Northern California and the United Synagogue of America, passed resolutions condemning the film. As Herman notes, "the controversy over the film raged through November and December, receiving almost constant attention in Jewish newspapers through the nation."[40]

The specific objections raised by Jewish opponents of the film are instructive. As Herman observes, there were five major objections against DeMille's version of the Passion play: First, there was concern about "the film's apparent promulgation of the myth that the Jews had killed Jesus." Second, there were objections to the portrayal of the high priest Caiaphas, by a well-regarded Jewish actor, as a "five and ten cent Shylock," in Alfred Cohen words. Third, there was consternation that more liberal Christians were not also outraged by the film's portrayal of Jews. Fourth, there was the shock and dismay caused by the fact that numerous Jewish individuals were involved in the making and distributing of the film. And finally, there were serious questions raised as to whether the organized Jewish response led by B'nai B'rith was adequate for reducing the anti-Semitism in the American film industry.[41] On this last point, doubts were raised about the ADL's long-standing premise that vigorous protest against anti-Semitism would only make matters worse. Nationally syndicated columnist Charles Joseph countered this thinking, noting that the quiet response had not worked against such anti-Semites as Henry Ford and suggesting that instead the community should "fight this film, 'The King of Kings,' and fight it hard. That's the only way to get it off the screen."[42]

The vocal nature of the protests from the Jewish community convinced the MPPDA to create a formal relationship with B'nai B'rith in order to reduce future outcries over anti-Semitism in film, and the impact of this relationship was almost immediate. In December 1927, MGM announced that it would not release *The King of Kings* in those eastern European countries where it might inflame existing prejudices against the Jewish community, and in January 1928 a new version of the film was announced, with changes based on suggestions from B'nai B'rith and others.

The controversy over *The King of Kings* demonstrated the complexity of religious narratives in the increasingly modern world of the 1920s. While it is unclear how much impact the protests had on the popularity of the film, Richard Maltby contends that the protests were strong enough to reduce the box office receipts to the point where the film only broke even.[43] Though religious spectacles like DeMille's *Samson and Delilah* and both his versions of *The Ten Commandments* (1923, 1956) were popular, producers knew that they would have to craft these stories carefully and with an eye toward the increasingly vocal objections of various religious groups. When Columbia released William Dieterle's adaptation of the Oscar Wilde play *Salome*, which recounts the story from the Gospel of Mark about the beautiful dancer who provoked Herod into killing John the Baptist, they sought to create the impression of religious approval. The film, which provoked controversy through its racy ads featuring a scantily clad Rita Hayworth in the title role, was approved by "representatives of the three great religious bodies generally concerned with the faith that sprang up in the Holy Land," according to Columbia, although these representatives remained unnamed.[44]

The willingness of religious organizations to issue public protests led to difficult navigation in films like the 1953 *Martin Luther*. While the film was well reviewed and popular among audiences—not surprisingly very popular in areas with large Lutheran populations such as Minnesota—Catholic groups reacted with outrage to the biopic of the man who had split with the Catholic Church in 1517. Reviewers for the Legion of Decency report that the film "not only teaches heresy but bears false witness against the Catholic Church's teaching," and reviewers in various Catholic publications blasted the film for being historically and theologically inaccurate.[45]

From the standpoint of legal history, the most important film controversy of this period occurred in the previous year and also involved the Catholic Church. Roberto Rossellini's short film *The Miracle*, which presents the story of the virgin birth through the story of a mentally challenged peasant woman, not only provoked the outrage of the Catholic Church but also led the New York City commissioner of licenses, and later the New York regents, to revoke the license of the theater screening the film. When the film's U.S. distributor, Joseph Burstyn, challenged this decision in court, it set the stage for the critical legal battle of *Burstyn v. Wilson*, the case that would finally lead the U.S. Supreme Court to acknowledge that the First Amendment protection of free expression extended to cinema.

I discussed this legal history in chapter 1, but in returning to the controversy over *The Miracle* in this chapter, I want to attend more closely to the kinds of appeals issued by the various religious organizations during the dispute. One of the first and most important pieces of rhetoric during the controversy was a statement issued by Cardinal Spellman, archbishop of New York City, which was read in every Catholic church in the city. In this statement, the cardinal began with a pledge of support for the Legion of Decency that Catholics had renewed only a few weeks earlier. Spellman reminded the parishioners of the city of that pledge: "Today we call upon you to make that pledge effective against a motion picture entitled *The Miracle* . . . and against any theatre that is showing it now or may ever show it henceforth." Spellman called upon the more than one million Catholics in the Archdiocese of New York—and by extension, the 26 million throughout the nation—to obey the pledge and avoid Rossellini's condemned film.[46]

The broader question of authority was central to Spellman's appeal. Clearly, he had the authority to instruct Catholic believers, at least within his own diocese, in their religious obligations, but in his appeal the cardinal also put explicit pressure on the state of New York to support the city commissioner's effort to revoke the offending theater's license. Here the controversy evoked the blurred line between the work of the church, the work of the theater, and the regulatory function of the state, and indeed, the call for pressure to be put on the state provoked distributor Burstyn to object that the cardinal sought to make the Catholic Church "the official censor of the City of New York."[47]

In many ways, the Church's rebuttal to Burstyn's accusation was particularly telling. The Reverend Patrick J. Masterson, executive secretary of the Legion of Decency, insisted: "We are not censors. We base our judgments on traditional moral standards common to all religions, Catholic, Protestant and Jewish."[48] While the Legion did function as an explicit censor in many instances—witness the several times in which films' sexual or violent content was edited according to the specific instructions of the Legion as recounted in earlier chapters—its defense against the accusation was not that it was only a reviewing agency but that its judgments were based on broad religious principles. Thus, again, the blurring of the line between legal and religious review became an issue within the controversy. Spellman's initial statement underscored this broader sense of the Church's need to function as "the guardians of the moral law."

The cardinal's other appeals focused on the film as being offensive to all Christians, claiming that the film was "a despicable affront to every

Christian," that the film was offensive to Italian women through its depiction of the peasant woman, and that the film's divisiveness resembled a communist plot. On this last point, the film's producers were warned that the controversy might "divide and demoralize Americans so that the minions of Moscow might enslave this land of liberty."[49]

Spellman's rhetoric was taken up the next day by picketers at the Paris Theater, which was screening Rossellini's film. They carried signs reading "This Picture Is An Insult to Every Decent Woman and Her Mother" and "This Picture Is Blasphemous." However, Spellman's attempt to represent all Christians seems to have failed. As the controversy reached the New York State Board of Regents, numerous Protestant officials issued statements of support for the film and in opposition to the Catholic Church's heavy-handed tactics.[50]

The controversy continued to simmer over the next several weeks as angry Catholics protested outside packed showings of the contentious film. Dueling bomb threats were reported at the end of January—the first phoned in to St. Patrick's Cathedral on a day Cardinal Spellman was to officiate, and a second, apparently retaliatory threat phoned in to the Paris Theater several hours later.[51] As the controversy continued, it eventually embroiled numerous religious, political, and cultural figures and drew statements from Rossellini—who expressed "profound sorrow" at the vitriolic American Catholic reaction—and the Vatican, which echoed Spellman's judgment, calling *The Miracle* "an abominable profanation from religious and moral viewpoints."[52]

The specifics of the controversy were finally resolved on May 27, 1952, when the Supreme Court finally ruled in favor of Martin Burstyn, establishing for the first time that motion pictures were protected under the First Amendment. While many of the legal channels for resolving controversies over films would soon be foreclosed, the controversies themselves would continue.

1952–2004

The 1960s and '70s saw a general decline in Americans' commitment to religious beliefs and institutions and an attendant decline in religious subjects in films.[53] Various attempts to capitalize on religious stories remained successful, but some also courted controversy. Nicholas Ray's 1961 version of *King of Kings*, starring Jeffrey Hunter and Rip Torn, revisited the story of Jesus and, while successful, provoked negative reactions from many in the Catholic Church. Monsignor Thomas F. Little, executive secretary for the Legion of Decency, announced that the 1961 version of *King* had been given a "separate classification," which meant that while it was not condemned, it merited some concern. Specifically, while the Legion praised the film's intent, it found it to be in many ways "theologically, historically and scripturally inaccurate."[54] Moira Walsh, writing in the Jesuit weekly *America*, condemned the film and called it part of "a gigantic fraud perpetrated by the film industry on the moviegoing public." In Walsh's opinion, the fraud consisted of Hollywood's peddling inaccurate and spiritually bankrupt stories as a means of making a profit from religious beliefs. Jesus, as Walsh put it, was "a 'hot' box-office property if properly exploited."[55]

Jesus remained a popular film figure throughout the 1960s and early 1970s. The 1965 George Stevens film *The Greatest Story Ever Told*, starring Max Von Sydow as Jesus, received lukewarm reviews and did not create much controversy. There was also surprisingly little objection to the 1973 David Greene film *Godspell*, which retold the story of Jesus in the form of a musical allegory about hippies wandering through the city. However, another modern musical retelling of the Gospel story the same year provoked considerable reaction: Norman Jewison's *Jesus Christ Superstar*.

For years Hollywood producers had taken great care to craft their cinematic versions of the Gospels in ways to avoid vilifying the Jews. As Forshey observes, even in the postwar era, anti-Semitism continued to linger in American society, and most religious leaders were willing to support efforts to avoid inflaming these sentiments. Even leaders of the Catholic Church and the Protestant Motion Picture Council supported films that specifically refuted the idea that the Jewish people were responsible for the death of Jesus. As Forshey describes it, "To choose any interpretation other than one that mitigated the scriptural contention of Jewish culpability was to risk being labeled a bigot."[56] However, *Jesus Christ Superstar*, the most successful film about Jesus during the sound era, was denounced by numerous Jewish organizations for perpetrating just this attitude.[57]

These concerns had already arisen during the Broadway run of the musical, and as the film premiered, numerous Jewish organizations voiced their continuing objection to the story. Benjamin Epstein, national director of B'nai B'rith, complained that "the movie's sharp and vivid emphasis on a Jewish mob's demand to kill Jesus can feed into the kind of disparagement of Jews and Judaism which has always nurtured anti-Jewish prejudice and bigotry," and the American Jewish Committee expressed concerns about the effect the film might have when distributed overseas.[58] The dispute raged for weeks and even brought Rabbi Marc Tannenbaum and Christian film critic James Wall onto NBC's *Today Show* to debate the topic.[59]

Jesus Christ Superstar also caused a stir among various Protestant groups. A committee of African American Baptist ministers complained to Universal Pictures about the film's use of an African American actor to play Judas, and various other Protestant communities struggled publicly over whether the film was a welcome update of the Gospel story or was blasphemous. One high school student in Victoria, Texas, wrote to the local paper listing several of the discrepancies between the film and the biblical account and insisting, "I would expect all Christians to recognize these inaccuracies (and these are only a few) and contradictions of the true account found in the Bible."[60] Others countered that the film's benefit was not in its accuracy but in its ability to translate the story into something that would reach a new generation of "flower power" young people.[61]

If Jewison's *Jesus Christ Superstar* seemed a slightly irreverent take on the life of Jesus, the next major controversy took this irreverence to a whole new level. In 1979, the British comedy troupe Monty Python released its film *The Life of Brian*, about a young man who is mistaken for the Messiah. According to author Monica Silveira Cyrino:

> When *Life of Brian* came out in 1979, the public and critical debate about what constitutes appropriate religious expression in film effectively anticipated the uproar surrounding the release of both Martin Scorsese's *The Last Temptation of Christ* ... and later Mel Gibson's *The Passion of the Christ*.[62]

The irreverent Python take on the Passion story managed to create uproar in all three of the major American religious faiths and was "panned (condemned) by various Catholic, Protestant and Jewish leaders."[63] Rabbi Abraham Hecht, a representative of the Rabbinical Alliance of America, insisted that the film was "a vicious attack upon Judaism and the Bible and a cruel mockery of the religious feelings of Christians as well" and expressed concern that screenings of the film "could result in serious violence."[64] The Catholic Archdiocese of New York called the film "blasphemous" and urged "religious persons and all persons of cultivation who respect religion to recognize contemptuous antireligious sentiment of this sort and to separate themselves from it personally as a matter of principle."[65] Robert Lee of the Lutheran Council in the U.S.A. echoed the sentiments of these other religious groups, calling the film "blasphemy" and "outrageous."[66]

In the South, numerous Protestant groups sought to utilize political and legal means to stop showings of *The Life of Brian*. In Georgia, a superior court judge imposed an injunction preventing theaters from showing the film based on its sacrilegious nature, before the injunction was vacated by the same judge without comment.[67] In South Carolina, the General Cinema Corporation, which was distributing the film, suspended its screenings after receiving a call from South Carolina Senator Strom Thurmond relaying complaints about the film. This move, however, led to a counterprotest from picketers who objected to this censorship. Protesters carried signs proclaiming "Let Us Decide" and "Resurrect Brian, Crucify Censors."[68] Clearly, in the intervening seventeen years since the landmark decision in *Burstyn v. Wilson*, cultural attitudes toward both religion and censorship had dramatically shifted.

Less than a decade after the controversy over Monty Python's version of the Passion, another film version would provoke an even more intense and incendiary reaction: Martin Scorsese's *The Last Temptation of Christ*. Part of the increased vitriol over this film was the result of the emergence of a large and very vocal conservative Christian fundamentalist movement during the early 1980s. The so-called moral majority solidified its place on the political landscape as one of the social forces pushing the Reagan revolution, and the members of these religiously conservative groups soon targeted the media in their efforts to reclaim culture in what James Hunter Davidson calls the "culture wars." Scorsese's film adapted the 1951 novel of the same name by Nikos Kazantzakis, who also penned *Zorba the Greek*. Both the novel and the film recount the story of Jesus' life, but focus on Jesus as a man filled with conflict over his dual human/divine nature and filled with self-doubt. In perhaps their most controversial element, they explore an extended hallucination in which Jesus is tempted to come down off the cross and live a human life, including having sexual relations and raising children.

The dispute over *Last Temptation* in many ways mirrored the growth of the conservative Christian fundamentalist movement and, by some accounts, helped to spread the movement. Paul Schraeder, who wrote two early versions of the script, observed that the film had been a major fundraising point for religious organizations and that "there is nothing like the ogre of Hollywood to spring open the pocketbooks of Christian America."[69] The film was plagued with these protests from the initial announcement in 1983 that Scorsese would make the film for Paramount. Angry protests and a well-organized letter-writing and phone campaign soon convinced Paramount that the project was not commercially viable, and it soon pulled out of the production. For the next few years, Scorsese worked on other projects while seeking financial backing for the *Last Temptation*. Finally Universal agreed to fund the film with a minimal budget of $6.5 million. While Universal knew it was taking a financial chance with the already controversial film, it hired Christian marketing specialist Tim Penland to help the studio reduce potential protests and seek to market the film to Christian communities. However, within a few months, Penland resigned and later joined the opponents of the film.[70]

Predictions that *Last Temptation* would be controversial were decidedly understated. The film caused an intense furor that embroiled conservative and moderate Protestants, Catholics, and the Jewish community. Protests raged throughout its filming. Bill Bright, president of Campus Crusade for Christ, even offered to buy the print from Universal in order to destroy it.[71] Protests against the film began so early that Universal decided to release it ahead of schedule, "to make it available to the American people and allow them to draw their own conclusions based on fact, not fallacy," as Tom Pollock, chairman of the MCA Motion Picture Group explained. This move, however, did little to quiet the outrage of conservative Christians. The Reverend Dr. R. L. Hymers of the Fundamentalist Baptist Tabernacle of Los Angeles declared, "Only the scum of Hollywood would go see it." When the film opened in nine major cities in August 1988, angry protesters picketed theaters and the Los Angeles theater where the film premiered was vandalized.[72]

Initially, the controversy spurred audiences to see the film, and it opened with strong per-screen averages, but weak reviews and poor word-of-mouth soon declared the film more boring, pretentious, and convoluted than incendiary and the box office receipts quickly fell off. The controversy over *Last Temptation* did not fade away, though, and the film became a touchstone in the raging culture wars. Conservative Christians claimed the film was part of a wider Hollywood plot to discredit Christianity and proof of a wider humanist, liberal bias in the media. In this narrative, conservative Christians were now the victims of "Christian-bashing," as American Family Association founder Rev. Donald Wildmon called it.[73] A similar sentiment was expressed by a writer to a local newspaper in Waterloo, Iowa, who claimed, "Now they've made a movie that has totally made fun of my Christ."[74] The Mormon Church objected that "men and women are left poorer by exposure to the stereotypes the movie portrays."[75]

One of the most unfortunate but revealing dynamics of the *Last Temptation* controversy was the anti-Semitic comments laced into protests of the film. Members of Reverend Hymers's Los Angeles Baptist congregation protested outside the home of MCA president Lew Wasserman. The spectacular, carnivalesque protest included a person carrying a cross and being whipped by a man wearing a suit meant to represent Wasserman and his studio executives. In a widely circulated flier, Reverend Wildmon explicitly noted that Universal was "a company whose decision-making body is dominated by non-Christians," an utterance that echoed the declarations from Capt. Dr. Rev. Wilbur Fisk Crafts in the 1920s about rescuing the film industry from the hands of "un-Christian Jews." The Reverend Jerry Falwell, founder of the Moral Majority, even cautioned against the film as it might spark a wave of anti-Semitism—a comment that Rabbi James Rudin, director of Christian-Jewish relations at the American Jewish Committee, claimed was an example of "the kind of irresponsible, outrageous activity that foments anti-Semitism."[76]

The intense tensions surrounding Scorsese's portrayal of Jesus simmered in and around Hollywood for several years before reemerging in a film that could be read as a rebuttal to Scorsese's film and that would provoke a return to many of the issues that had dominated controversies over religious films for more than a hundred years. The film was the 2004 Mel Gibson picture *The Passion of the Christ*.

RELIGIOUS CONTROVERSY AND MEL GIBSON'S *THE PASSION OF THE CHRIST*

Throughout this chapter, I have argued that the controversies over religion and film have emerged at those points where the two have overlapped, specifically in terms of the work that they do. In other words, when religion and cinema have covered the same ground, there is always a strong chance for contest. So, in the case of a film like *King of Kings*, controversy emerged because mainstream cinema was trying to do the work of religion. On the other hand, numerous other controversies—ranging from the struggle over nickelodeons to the debates about *The Life of Brian*—emerged when religious leaders and communities sought to exert their control over works in mainstream cinema. The overlap between religion and popular cinema was almost total in Mel Gibson's *The Passion of the Christ*, arguably the most controversial religious film in American history. As I noted in the introduction to this chapter, reactions to the film reached an almost religious zeal for some and for others a deep level of contempt.

The controversy over *The Passion* encompassed numerous issues, including accusations that the film was anti-Semitic, debates about its biblical accuracy, reactions to the graphic nature of the film's violent scenes of torture and death, questions about Gibson's character and motivation in making the film, and invocations of the broader culture wars—the struggle between social/religious conservatives and progressive liberals over the media and education. In my attempt to work through the debate over these issues, I have found it helpful to frame these various discussions in terms of the ways in which the film served as a point of overlap between—almost an implosion of—the movie theater and the church. As I read through some of the representative arguments and discussions from the controversy, there is a clear sense that much of the dispute was centered around the way church and theater merged—so much so that viewing of the film became equated with a religious sermon and, in the same vein, Gibson took on the role of a religious priest.

In many ways, movie theaters literally became churches in parts of the country during the initial screenings of *The Passion*. Numerous churches booked entire theaters for the premiere of the film on Ash Wednesday 2004. More than $2 million in advance tickets were purchased by theaters for the premiere, and entire congregations were given tickets and encouraged to attend. In Plano, Texas, for instance, a financial planner named Arch Bonnema was so moved by an advance screening of the film that he purchased $42,000 worth of tickets and distributed them to local churches and the Dallas Theological Seminary.[77] The advance purchase of blocks of tickets was not an accident. As part of the film's marketing strategy by Icon Productions and its marketing firm, Outreach, *The Passion* was pre-screened for conservative religious leaders, at which time "the audience was offered an opportunity to buy some of Outreach's beautifully produced promotional material: door hangers, invitation cards, banners, bulletin inserts, signs, Bible excerpts and study guides."[78]

The blurring of the boundaries between church and theater were, in this sense, encouraged by the film's marketing, but it was also this identification of theater as church that led to some of the controversy. Beyond merely encouraging attendance, the marketing of the film as a religious experience turned the act of viewing the film into a religious and political statement. As Allison Griffiths put it, "Discussions of the film made repeated references to its transformative power, the ability to turn the multiplex into a sacred pilgrimage site, not unlike that of a church or cathedral."[79]

The pilgrimage to this "sacred" site was not, however, without its own potential controversy. Christopher Deacy observes, "The line taken by many critics and ordinary filmgoers is that there are serious ethical and psychological ramifications if one even sets foot in an auditorium that is screening *The Passion*."[80] For some, the mere act of entering the theater was an act of anti-Semitism and religious intolerance; for others, it was almost an obligatory Christian gesture. The divisiveness of these opinions further led Christian conservatives to champion the film. As Darrell Bock, a theologian at Dallas Theological Seminary and one of the leaders invited to an advance showing, insisted, "This was a chance to carry your placard for Jesus, and say to everyone, 'This is our story.' "[81]

Given the political climate of 2004, it is not entirely surprising that the pilgrimage to *The Passion* was so fraught with political tensions. In my own research, I was struck by how many times editorials about *The Passion* shared space on the same page with editorials for or against gay marriage. In the lead-up to the presidential election of 2004, the Republican Party and its incumbent candidate George W. Bush were making the question of legalizing gay marriages a centerpiece of their socially conservative agenda. In the midst of these political battles, the act of viewing or not viewing Gibson's film became part of the broader culture war. Conservative Christians took a degree of pride in their embattled status. Syndicated columnist Betsy Hart echoed the sentiment of many Evangelicals who felt that they were the oppressed group in this situation: "In our popular culture, there is one group it is perfectly safe, even expected, that the elites will denigrate: Christians."[82]

Attending *The Passion* thus became a statement of one's religious beliefs and a political stand against what was widely perceived within the Christian conservative community as a conspiracy of elites against the film and, therefore, against them. Deborah Caldwell reports websites supporting the film that proclaimed, "Why do Jewish leaders want to censor Mel Gibson?" and "Mel Gibson is David against the Goliath of the anti-Christian Hollywood establishment and politically powerful Jewish leaders."[83] Thus, in an appeal that echoes those made in numerous previous controversies, the perceived oppression of Christianity was attributed to the dark conspiratorial forces of mainstream culture and the mythic image of a Jewish conspiracy.[84]

The initial charges that the film was anti-Semitic were fueled by an interesting incident that also fits with the idea that the theater was treated as a holy site. Abraham Foxman of the ADL reportedly "sneaked into a

closed screening of the movie at a religious convention in Orlanda, Fla."
Afterward, he issued a widely circulated press release arguing that the film
was anti-Semitic and hurtful to Jews.[85] Gibson later screened the film for
religious leaders from a variety of faiths—Protestant, Catholic, and
Jewish—and even cut a controversial line in which the Jewish leaders
accept that the blood of Jesus would be on their hands, but this initial
accusation colored the way the film would be viewed around the nation.

In many ways, Gibson's *Passion* can be read as a kind of cinematic sermon. Evangelist Billy Graham proclaimed that the film was "a lifetime of
sermons in one movie," and movie audiences reacted to the film more like
a revival event than a film exhibition.[86] Sister Mary Boys recalled how
"some sob throughout the viewing, others drop to their knees in prayer"
and the film—which traces the final twelve hours of the life of Jesus with
particular focus on his betrayal, scourging at the hands of the Romans,
rejection by the Jewish priests, and crucifixion—became a focal point of
outreach and evangelism for many churches.

As many commentators observed, *The Passion* is intensely violent in its
repeated sequences of beating, whipping, and abuse directed at the figure
of Jesus. David Denby wrote in the *New Yorker* that "the movie Gibson has
made from his personal obsessions is a sickening death trip, a grimly unil-
luminating procession of treachery, beatings, blood and agony."[87] The
Boston Globe's Ty Burr worried that the film was likely to "traumatize
kids and young adults rather than bolster their faith."[88] In this regard, several commentators objected that Gibson focused almost exclusively on the
suffering of the Passion rather than the teachings of Jesus' ministry or the
miracle of the resurrection—which appears only as a brief coda at the end
of the film. Theology scholar Deacy noted, "This is clearly a film that is
more interested in depicting the brutality and viciousness of Good Friday
than in the majesty and exuberance of Easter Sunday," and Father James
Martin, a Jesuit priest and associate editor of the Catholic magazine *America*, objected to the minimization of these crucial elements by asking, "Can
one grasp the meaning of Jesus' death without understanding his ministry
and the Resurrection? The answer is no."[89]

Christianity, however, has a long tradition of depicting the Passion in
graphically violent terms, especially in the medieval mystery plays in which
depictions of suffering and torture were considered important ministerial tools.
Thus one of the main questions was whether the film was part of a longer
Christian tradition and what the contemporary implications of this tradition
are.[90] The debates about the film's anti-Semitism were also wrapped into this
question. The depiction of the Jews within the film, especially the high priest
Caiaphas, clearly lends itself to charges of anti-Semitism. Marymount Manhattan College professor Judson Shaver insisted in an editorial that while Gibson may not be anti-Semitic, "his film is unhistorical and replicates the
Gospels' shifting of blame from Rome to the Jews."[91]

Reflecting on the dispute, Paula Frederiksen, a professor of scripture at Boston University, recalled hearing in defense of the film, "If you think that *The Passion of the Christ* is anti-Semitic, then you are saying that the Gospels are anti-Semitic." Frederiksen disagrees with this premise, noting that the authors of the Gospels "most probably were Jews themselves."[92] Others agreed with the anonymous comment. Professor Adele Reinhartz, dean of graduate studies at Wilfrid Laurier University, argued that

> fundamentally filmmakers have two options. They can follow the Gospels' lead in placing primary moral responsibility on the Jews, thereby leaving themselves open, as Mel Gibson has discovered, to charges of aiding and abetting anti-Semitism. Or they can diverge from the Gospels to focus on Pilate's culpability, thereby forgoing or at least undermining a claim to Scriptural fidelity.[93]

Throughout popular debates about the film, one of its central defenses was its scriptural fidelity and apparent accuracy. In a widely reported comment, Pope John Paul II exclaimed, "It is as it was." The Reverend Jim Brewer of the Open Bible Church in Waverly, Iowa, proclaimed, "The 'R' rating stamped on the film should stand for 'reality.'"[94] Accuracy was also a response to claims that the film was too violent. As the Reverend Jerry Kopacek, of St. Edwards Church in Waterloo, Iowa, insisted, "'Passion' is a disturbing film in many places. Given Gibson's desire to show us what Jesus really suffered, how could it possibly be otherwise?"[95] The film's air of authenticity was undoubtedly helped by not only its graphic violence but also Gibson's choice to film the story in the original languages of Latin and Aramaic, which gave the film an almost documentary feel.[96]

Difficult questions remained, however, about exactly to what Gibson's film was accurate. Some commentators objected to Gibson's use of all four Gospels, which effectively allowed him to pick and choose which events and ordering fit his broader purpose.[97] Still others objected to the additional source material Gibson used to adapt the Gospels into film. As Frederiksen observed, Gibson relied heavily on the visions of a nineteenth-century stigmatic nun named Anne Catherine Emmerich,[98] which were later published as *The Dolorous Passion of Our Lord Jesus Christ* and included such nonbiblical flourishes as children morphing into devils and an earthquake at the moment of Christ's death, which appeared in the film.[99]

Numerous Christian leaders objected to the film because, in spite of its authentic appearance, it both altered biblical events and added sequences that do not appear in the Gospels. This poetic license also came into the claims that the film was anti-Semitic. Syndicated columnist Charles Krauthammer claimed that Gibson "bends, he stretches, he makes stuff up, usually in ways that enhance the villainy and culpability of the Jews."[100]

Along these lines, the film was also criticized for its apparent adherence to a subset of Catholicism known as "traditionalist Catholicism," which is marked by its rejection of the reforms of Vatican II—a declaration from the Church that, among other things, rejected the notion of Jewish culpability in the death of Christ.

Gibson's film became associated with this branch of Catholicism in large part because his father, Hutton Gibson, is an outspoken adherent.[101] Controversial anti-Semitic comments from the elder Gibson cast considerable scrutiny on Mel Gibson's motivation for making *The Passion*. While many conservative Christians, as noted above, came to Gibson's defense and viewed the abuse Gibson was facing in the popular press as a kind of martyrdom, others linked statements from Gibson's father to his own comments about such topics as the Holocaust. Hutton Gibson had made numerous incendiary public comments about Jewish conspiracies—suggesting that the tragedy of 9/11 was such a plot—and denying the Holocaust.[102] The younger Gibson continually evaded the questions about his beliefs on these subjects, referring instead to "atrocities" of World War II and generally refusing to refute the statements made by his father. Mel Gibson did call for a broader and respectful dialogue driven by "love for each other despite our differences."[103]

While some insisted that director Gibson's personal life should be kept separate from the film, in many of the efforts to market the film to evangelical Christians, Gibson gave his personal testimony of converting to Christianity. (As an interesting side note, as a youth Gibson had lived on a kibbutz in Israel and been on the verge of converting to Orthodox Judaism.)[104] In utilizing his own religious experience as the basis for marketing the film, Gibson opened the door for a closer scrutiny of his personal beliefs as he assumed the role of religious leader and teacher. As columnist Mitch Albom contended: "No one asked Mel Gibson to become a spokesman on faith. He did that himself."[105]

While remaining evasive about his father's remarks, Gibson largely embraced his role as "cinematic priest," even stating in public that "the Holy Ghost was working through me on this film."[106] Many audience members seemed to accept this notion and proclaimed their support for Gibson and *The Passion*. As one letter writer expressed it, "As for the movie, Mel Gibson was right on. Thank God he was strong enough to make it as it was."[107] Others insisted that Gibson had bent over backward to accommodate his critics and that those offended by his message should not blame him. John Cowper, of Placerville, California, wrote into his local paper, "Gibson followed such a path of 'political correctness' or ecumenical sensitivity that he met with Jewish leaders."[108] While this meeting came after, and as a result of, the widely publicized criticism from the ADL's Foxman, supporters of Gibson still offered it as proof that the filmmaker was not anti-Semitic. Instead, these and other supporters of Gibson reframed the criticisms of the director in terms of the narrative of Christian persecution and the battles of the broader culture wars. Columnist Kathleen Parker noted, "[Gibson] is the far right's newly anointed one."[109]

By the end of the film's theatrical run and its highly successful launch on DVD, *The Passion* was a clear victory for Gibson, the religious right, and conservative Christians throughout the nation. The reelection of President Bush further solidified the sense that the incredible box office return on Gibson's subtitled biblical drama was another sign of a glorious future. Gibson went almost immediately into production of another subtitled film, this time focusing on the ancient Mayan empire, called *Apocalpyto*. At the conclusion of that production, Gibson became involved in an incident that serves as an unpleasant coda to the controversies over *The Passion*.

In July 2006, he was pulled over and arrested on the Pacific Coast Highway for drunk driving. During his processing, Gibson unleashed a series of abusive and anti-Semitic remarks at the arresting officers, including the statement that "the Jews are responsible for all the wars in the world."[110] Gibson immediately issued an apology through his publicist, blaming his behavior on drinking heavily—Gibson was a recovering alcoholic—and stating, "I am deeply ashamed of everything I said.... I apologize for any behavior unbecoming of me in my inebriated state and have already taken necessary steps to ensure my return to health."[111]

Not surprisingly, Gibson's initial apology was not readily accepted by many, especially members of the Jewish community. Abraham Foxman of the ADL responded to Gibson's apology by stating, "It's not a proper apology because it does not go to the essence of his bigotry and his anti-Semitism."[112] Four days later, Gibson issued a second apology, which stated, "I want to apologize specifically to everyone in the Jewish community for the vitriolic and harmful words that I said to a law enforcement officer."[113] In a response, Foxman noted that this was at least a first step toward reconciliation.

CONCLUSION

As if in response to the intense controversy over the religiously conservative *Passion*, in May 2006 another mainstream American film provoked a torrent of angry responses for violating religious doctrine. A Vatican spokeperson claimed the film was filled with "shameful and unfounded lies."[114] Ron Howard's film *The Da Vinci Code* was based upon the immensely popular page-turner of the same title by Dan Brown. In the narrative, a secret code is discovered in Leonardo Da Vinci's painting "The Last Supper," revealing that Jesus did not die on the cross as everyone thought, but in fact went on to start a family. The mystery thriller quickly became embroiled in an intense and global controversy in which various Christians, especially Catholics, protested the novel as blasphemous and dangerous.

The filmmakers insisted they were surprised by the outrage their film provoked. Director Howard explained, "I don't consider myself a controversial filmmaker at all," and producer Brian Grazer insisted, "We weren't looking for controversy."[115] In spite of the controversy and some weak reviews, the film went on to strong box office success.

The history of religious films suggests that whenever a film seeks to do the work of religion—or a church seeks to control the work of mainstream cinema—controversies may erupt. The combination of cinema and religion has historically proved to be a dangerous mix, but one that has also been at times both laudable and financially lucrative. Whether it was the incorporation of silent films into worship services or the retelling of the Passion story through the irreverent lens of Monty Python, the mix of religion and cinema has provoked deep reaction in no small part due to the ways in which religious beliefs are so deeply held. Given the sanctity with which we, almost by definition, hold our religion, it should not be surprising that the intermingling of the sacred and the often profane medium of film has been an unstable combination. Nevertheless, even some of the most controversial films were big successes. *The Life of Brian* was the most successful Python film and both *Jesus Christ Superstar* and *The Passion* were among the highest-grossing films of their time. The lure of potential success—either financially or spiritually—will, in all likelihood, draw more filmmakers into the potentially explosive territory of religious cinema and cinematic religion.

Conclusion

In 2007, Michael Moore made his triumphant return to controversial filmmaking with his documentary *SiCKO*, an exposé of the failings in the American health care system. Reviews were generally positive, and the film did stir some discussion of the already much-discussed problems within American health care, but one couldn't help but feel the routine had become a bit stale. Even before its release, the *Wall Street Journal* was reporting that "controversy has become a key ingredient in marketing Mr. Moore's work and backers of 'SiCKO' hope that the new movie will stir up emotions."[1] While *Variety* labeled Moore an "agent provocateur" and his work "polemics-as-performance-art," *SiCKO*'s call for a government-run system of universal health care was largely sidestepped by politicians, even liberal-minded hopefuls for the Democratic presidential nomination.[2] By the end of its domestic release, the film had earned more than $24 million at the box office, an enormous success for a $9 million documentary but nothing like that of *Fahrenheit 9/11*.

These observations are not meant to disparage Moore, his film, or his politics, but what becomes clear is that controversies—especially the kind of real controversies that provoke genuine outrage among portions of the population—are difficult to manufacture. In a way, this is the flip side of my introductory observation about Moore's 2004 intervention into presidential politics, *Fahrenheit 9/11*. In the introduction, I argued that Moore's attempt to influence presidential politics had backfired in part because real, dynamic controversies tend to rage out of control. Moore's polemic against George W. Bush had, as some studies verify, done more to motivate the president's base than to build a coalition against him. In the case of *SiCKO*, Moore's routine had become a bit shopworn, and while it was arguably one of his most accomplished efforts, it failed to generate the kind of divisive and intense controversy that its predecessor had engendered.

After considering the long history of controversial films, it might be easy to conclude that it is becoming more difficult for films to provoke controversy. Perhaps after the intense reactions to films ranging from *The Kiss* to *Kids*, we might suspect that we've become a bit too jaded to be shocked. Undoubtedly, however—and as recent films like *Fahrenheit 9/11* and *The Passion of the Christ* suggest—we will continue to be provoked to outrage, and the history of controversial cinema will continue. In thinking toward likely future controversies, the past is a useful primer.

In my reading of the histories surrounding controversies over sex, violence, race, and religion, there have been some broad themes in each category that seem to continually reemerge. But, while it is worthwhile reviewing these broad themes, it is important to begin by acknowledging that each individual controversy over each particular film is unique. While the controversy over the 1927 *King of Kings*, for example, may contain many of the same arguments and issues that emerged around the 2004 *Passion of the Christ*, each situation was different. The struggle over anti-Semitism in relation to DeMille's 1927 film was uniquely situated by another, internal struggle within the Anti-Defamation League (ADL) and the extent to which it should issue aggressive responses to such films. The subsequent dispute surrounding Gibson's 2004 film saw a very adamant and aggressive response from the ADL but was also situated within the political struggles of the U.S. presidential election. Each film controversy, in other words, while engaging the intersection between Christianity and Judaism, was also unique, and the arguments and appeals issued were specific to the political contexts within which each controversy emerged.

The particularity of each film controversy aside, there have been some relatively consistent themes related to each type of film controversy. In each instance—controversies related to sex, violence, race, and religion—films have been seen as dangerous, at least in part, because they threaten some taken-for-granted assumption about the world. In films depicting sex, sexuality, and gender, many of these controversies have centered on the often assumed relationship between morality, identity, and sexuality. America's Puritan roots have long established sexuality at the core of our conception of personal morality, and sexual activities seem to be among the most proscribed in our culture. Thus, it should not be surprising that depictions of sex or sexuality are often conceived in broad terms of morality.

In this regard, it is interesting that arguments about sex in films are not consistently made in terms of fears that behaviors on-screen will be copied by those in the audience. While there have been occasional concerns for young and "impressionable" minds, the debates about sex on-screen have typically been cast in the more religiously loaded language of moral judgment. From the outrage at *The May Irwin–John C. Rice Kiss* in 1896 to the suggestive dialogue of Mae West, the controversies over sexuality seem mainly concerned with the general moral code that defines and contains individual sexual desire and activity. For various reasons, the depiction of sexual activities on-screen seemed to pose a particularly dangerous threat to this moral code, and at times these transgressions became celebrated as moments of sexual liberation and resistance. In this way, the controversy over *The Silence of the Lambs* in 1991 was a particularly interesting example. For some critics, this film represented an important moment of liberation for women, who could find in protagonist Clarice Starling an example of a woman stepping beyond her limited feminine role. For other critics, however, the use of homophobic visual stereotypes in the person of serial killer Buffalo Bill represented another example of the oppressive homophobia surrounding same-sex desire and identity. These films and the many others considered in chapter 2 provoked controversy by treading upon the complex and contentious intersection between desire and morality.

In contrast, controversies over film violence have consistently focused on the danger of individuals copying the behaviors shown on the screen. The spectacular figure of the copycat looms large in controversies over violent films, and the fear seems to be about the spread of social disorder. Depictions of the use of force are not in and of themselves controversial, and history is filled with remarkably violent films that did not provoke any outrage. The interesting irony is that several of these violent films were being exhibited without contest at the same time other violent films were at the center of protests. Senator Bob Dole's simultaneous praise for *True Lies* and condemnation for *Natural Born Killers* is only one instance of this strange duality.

The key seems to be that violence depicted as threatening to social order is condemned, while equally violent actions depicted as supporting the social order are either praised or ignored. In this regard, Detroit's decision to ban films depicting police corruption in 1913 is a particularly instructive moment in film history. What was under threat was the public's respect for the forces of social order, and films suggesting that these forces were ineffectual or corrupt were considered particularly dangerous. A similar tone was struck during the debates about the 1967 film *The Dirty Dozen*, which depicted American soldiers committing horrific acts of violence. In the various disputes surrounding Oliver Stone's *Natural Born Killers*, it was the film's anarchic tone that seemed to produce such strong reactions, and when the film's chaos seemed to spill out of the movie theaters and into the real streets of America—as in Avon, Massachusetts, or in the tragic road trip of Ben Darras and Sarah Edmondson—the forces of social order mobilized quickly. Presidential candidates debated the film, social critics railed against it as a lethally defective product, and even the legal system was brought into the debate.

Fear of social disruption has also been a consistent feature of controversies surrounding representations of race and ethnicity in films. From the debates over the films of Jack Johnson's boxing matches to the hyperbolic reactions of film critics to Spike Lee's *Do the Right Thing*, representations of race on film have consistently brought fears of riots and violence. Tragically, of course, these fears have occasionally come true, and in most cases it has been the oppressed who have suffered the most. The various communities suffering under racist oppression have not, however, suffered these symbolic and real abuses silently, and the history of controversies over race in film is replete with wonderful examples of social protest. From the organizational skill of the National Association for the Advancement of Colored People in their response to D. W. Griffith's *The Birth of a Nation* to the efforts of the Los Angeles Chicano Cinema Coalition to promote Latino filmmakers, the question of how various races would be represented on the silver screen has been deeply contested.

These contests, with all their symbolic and real consequences, have ultimately been about the question of authority—who would have authority to represent various races? For much of the early history of film, the overwhelming dominance of white filmmakers meant that, with only a few exceptions—as in the burgeoning African American film industry of the silent era—the depiction of various racial groups was controlled by the privileged white majority. History, however, has also seen a fairly consistent effort from both social critics and filmmakers of color—Oscar Micheaux, Gordon Parks, Moctesuma Esperanza, Edward James Olmos, and Spike Lee, to name a few—to resist this control and replace the images crafted by white filmmakers with new ones derived from their own authority to represent themselves.

Controversies over religion and film have also been, in some ways, about authority—more specifically about the overlapping of authority. The history of religious controversies over film suggests that these disputes emerge when religious institutions and mainstream filmmaking overlap in such a way that one seems to be doing the work of the other. In the early days of film, religious leaders sought to incorporate the new entertainment medium into their work, but they soon found that the rapidly growing film industry was beyond their control and was inclined toward stories with a more worldly bent. At various times, the overlap has returned, sometimes as filmmakers attempted to craft cinematic sermons and at other times when religious leaders sought to control the products coming out of Hollywood. The controversy over Mel Gibson's *The Passion of the Christ* represents perhaps the highest point of overlap between church and cinema, as Gibson and his supporters turned theaters into churches and movie-going into a pilgrimage. Not surprisingly, the film was one of the most intensely controversial in recent history.

Sex, violence, race, and religion are, of course, only some of the topics that have provoked controversy in the long history of American cinema. Films depicting disabilities—like *Million Dollar Baby*—or representing important historic events—like *Schindler's List*—have also created controversies, and undoubtedly those topics are also interesting sites for exploring the broader cultural politics of film. In the present book, I focused attention on those topics that have consistently provoked some of the more spectacular controversies and shaped the history of American film. This history underscores one of the most consistent themes in discussions of film since its popular inception in the late nineteenth century, namely, fear. Even in the late twentieth and early twenty-first centuries when movies have become incredibly common and familiar, audiences still react to certain films as if they were dangerous, as if they might leap off the screen and infect us or crush us under their weight. These dangerous films seem to provoke certain segments of the population, drawing them out of their regular daily routines and into controversy. These occasions—those points when people feel the compulsion to write letters, stand in picket lines, and organize opposition—provide a useful sense of the political tensions underlying society. Tracing the contests surrounding these films has provided a useful map of the changes in American cultural politics over the past hundred years.

If the study of controversy conducted in the preceding chapters yields any broader lesson, it should be that moments of controversy and contest are important indicators of the broader cultural forces at work in American society. Undoubtedly, one of the problems with trying to understand controversies is the seemingly excessive number of them—watching the nightly news, for example, one is almost overwhelmed by the number of "controversies" around the world. But the prevalence of controversy should not diminish their importance. Controversies are crucial moments when citizens emerge from their normal lives to actively engage in the politics of their world. The preceding chapters register, for example, the growth of the civil rights movement, women's liberation, gay rights, the culture wars, and the religious right. They also trace the development of various new methods of social protest—ranging from the 1931 "Better Films Committee of the Montclair Cultural Centre," which organized to fight gangster films, to the websites sprouting up in support of Gibson's *Passion*. All these forces, and many others, are evident in disputes over movies, suggesting that whatever the controversy—even over something as "trivial" as popular films—careful attention can reveal a great deal about the current political and cultural moment.

For many years, the histories of these kinds of dangerous films have been told in terms of censorship, and without a doubt the existence of various mechanisms for censorship has played a big part in shaping the ways people respond to films. However, as I've tried to demonstrate over the preceding pages, protests against certain films can be, and perhaps should be, understood independently of the censor boards and code administrations that have been used to protect society. No matter how stringent these codes have been, there has remained a consistent tendency of people—whether in favor of a film or opposed to it—to take their case to the streets and make their voices heard.

In the end, this may be the most important point. What I hope the previous chapters have suggested is that the kinds of arguments made and appeals issued, literally the rhetoric of controversies, are important. It is not only the fact that films have been perceived as dangerous, whether in terms of sex, violence, race, or religion, but also that people—from those writing letters in protest of a proposed Al Capone biopic to the demonstrators defacing the golden statuettes at the sixty-fourth Academy Awards in protest of *The Silence of the Lambs*—voiced their objections. In the final analysis, whatever we think of the merits of these various controversies, in each instance average citizens raised their voices in an attempt to shape the course of their culture, and it is this impulse that seems essential to any concept of a democratic society. That people state their concerns matters, and the ways people express their protests matter, even when it's only about a movie.

Notes

INTRODUCTION

1. See Philip Shabecoff, "Ford, Nixon and 1976," *New York Times*, April 9, 1976.

2. Ellis Paxon Oberholtzer, *The Morals of the Movie* (Philadelphia: Penn Publishing Co., 1922), 173–74.

3. Michael Moore, interview, *Hollywood Reporter*, May 18, 2004.

4. For more on the films of Michael Moore, see Emanuel Levy's *Stranger than Fiction: Michael Moore, Barbara Kopple, Errol Morris, and the New Documentary Filmmakers* (London: Continuum, 2008).

5. Robert Brent Toplin, *Michael Moore's Fahrenheit 9/11: How One Film Divided America* (Lawrence: University Press of Kansas, 2006), 3.

6. Quoted in Jim Malone, "New Michael Moore Film Sparks Controversy," *Voice of America News*, June 22, 2004.

7. Bob Carlton, "Controversy Can Only Help 'Fahrenheit 9/11'" *Birmingham (AL) News*, June 27, 2004; "Michael Moore and Fahrenheit UVSC," *Deseret Morning News*, September 22, 2004.

8. Toplin, *Fahrenheit 9/11*, 3.

9. Gabriel Snyder, "Docbuster Still Sizzling," *Variety*, July 6, 2004, 1.

10. On offensive films, see Mikita Brottman, *Offensive Films* (Nashville, TN: Vanderbilt University Press, 2005).

11. The importance of media and popular culture controversies in relation to broader political currents has been amply demonstrated by James Hunter in his *Culture Wars: The Struggle to Define America* (New York: Basic Books, 1991).

12. This point was first made by G. Thomas Goodnight; see his "Controversy," in *Argument in Controversy: Proceedings of the Seventh SCA/AFA Conference on Argumentation*, ed. Don W. Parson (Annandale, VA: Speech Communication Association, 1991), 1–13.

13. For those readers interested in a more encyclopedic approach to controversial films, I would heartily recommend Dawn B. Sova's *Forbidden Films: Censorship Histories of 125 Motion Pictures* (New York: Facts on File, 2001).

14. In this regard, I pursue a rhetorical approach to film studies—an approach that always seeks to understand the persuasive, perhaps even provocative, capacity of the symbols within a film, as viewed through the lens of the particular situation in which that film emerges. By investigating the interaction between the film text and the context within which it attains some meaning, this analysis pursues a better understanding of both the films themselves and the broader culture that found them controversial. Francis Couvares captures a sense of this dual gesture when explaining his approach to censored films, a clearly related project: "Interpreting such [controversial] works requires the integration of textual analysis with historical reconstructions of the conditions of production and consumption. Studied in such a way, censorship battles help mark out the terrain of conflict over discursive practices in a culture" (*Movie Censorship and American Culture* [Washington, DC: Smithsonian Press, 1966], 510).

15. See "Weinsteins Land Rights to Distribute 'Fahrenheit 9/11,'" *Washington Post*, May 29, 2004.

16. This general sketch of the notion of controversy is developed in much greater detail in my "A Rhetoric of Controversy," *Western Journal of Communication* 63 (1999): 488–510.

17. For more on the taken-for-granted as it is provoked in controversy, see Kathryn Olson and Thomas Goodnight, "Entanglements of Consumption, Cruelty, Privacy, and Fashion: The Social Controversy over Fur," *Quarterly Journal of Speech* 80 (1994): 249–76.

CHAPTER 1

1. For a thorough and provocative history of this "train hysteria," see Martin Loiperdinger, "Lumière's *Arrival of the Train*: Cinema's Founding Myth," *Moving Image* 4 (2004): 89–118.

2. Charles Musser, *The Emergence of Cinema: The American Screen to 1907* (Berkeley: University of California Press, 1994), 417.

3. Quoted in Lee Grievson, *Policing Cinema: Movies and Censorship in Early-Twentieth Century America* (Berkeley: University of California Press, 2004), 4.

4. For more on the *Tribune*'s campaign, see Grievson, 10–13.

5. See, for example, Anthony Aldgate and James C. Robertson, *Censorship in Theatre and Cinema* (Edinburgh: Edinburgh University Press, 2005); Jon Lewis, *Hollywood vs. Hardcore: How the Struggle over Censorship Created the Modern Film Industry* (New York: Columbia University Press, 2000); Mark Readman, *Teaching Film Censorship and Controversy* (London: BFI, 2006); and, of course, many of the other works cited throughout this chapter.

6. Grieveson, *Policing Cinema: Movies and Censorship in Early-Twentieth-Century America* (Berkeley: University of California Press, 2004), 22.

7. Black, *Catholic Crusade*, 7.

8. On this point, see Daniel Czitrom, "The Politics of Performance: From Theater Licensing to Movie Censorship in Turn-of-the-Century New York," *American Quarterly* 44 (1992): 525–53.

9. These early critiques of cinema in New York are quoted in Grieveson, *Policing Cinema*, 78.

10. This incident has sparked a number of fictional representations, including Richard Fleischer's 1955 film *The Girl in the Red Velvet Swing* and the novel *Ragtime* by E. L. Doctorow and its film adaptation by Milos Forman.

11. Grieveson, *Policing Cinema*, 28.

12. *New York Times*, "Picture Shows All Put Out of Business," December 25, 1908, 1.

13. Ira Carmen, *Movies, Censorship and the Law* (Ann Arbor: University of Michigan Press, 1967), 129.

14. For more on the complex relations of race surrounding the rise of heavyweight champion Johnson during this period, see Randy Roberts, *Papa Jack: Jack Johnson and the Era of White Hopes* (New York: Free Press, 1983).

15. See Grieveson, *Policing Cinema*, esp. chap. 4.

16. The definitive history of this period and the various groups involved in these struggles can be found in Czitrom, "Politics of Performance."

17. For a detailed history of the *Mutual v. Ohio* case, see John Wertheimer, "Mutual Film Reviewed: Movies, Censorship, and Free Speech in Progressive America," *American Journal of Legal History* 37 (1993): 156–89.

18. *Mutual Film Corporation v. Ohio Industrial Commission*, 236 U.S. 230, U.S. Supreme Court (1915), p. 238.

19. Ibid., 244.

20. Harry M. Geduld, *Focus on D. W. Griffith* (Englewood Cliffs, NJ: Prentice Hall, 1971), 8.

21. Griffith's innovation and influence are explicated in Tom Gunning's *D. W. Griffith and the Origins of American Narrative Film: The Early Years at Biograph* (Urbana: University of Illinois Press, 1991).

22. For a particularly thoughtful examination of the competing dynamics of Griffith's film, see Michael Rogin, " 'The Sword Became a Flashing Vision': D. W. Griffith's *The Birth of a Nation*," *Representations* 9 (1985): 150–95.

23. See, Grieveson, *Policing Cinema*, 193–95.

24. Lea Jacobs, *The Wages of Sin: Censorship and the Fallen Woman Film, 1928–1942* (Madison: University of Wisconsin Press, 1991), 27–28.

25. Gregory D. Black, *The Catholic Crusade against the Movies, 1940–1975* (New York: Cambridge University Press, 1997), 10.

26. Quoted in Black, *Catholic Crusade*, 245, 248, 250.

27. Black, *Catholic Crusade*, 14.

28. For more on block booking, see Andrew F. Hanssen, "The Block Booking of Films Reexamined," *Journal of Law and Economics* 43 (2000): 395–426. For more on the broader legal and historical aspects of Hollywood's antitrust issues, see Michael Conant, *Antitrust in the Motion Picture Industry: Economic and Legal Analysis* (Berkeley: University of California Press, 1960).

29. Henry James Forman, *Our Movie Made Children* (New York: Macmillan, 1933). For a useful consideration of the Payne Studies, see Arthur R. Jarvis, "The Payne Fund Reports: A Discussion of Their Content, Public Reaction, and Affect on the Motion Picture Industry, 1930–1940," *Journal of Popular Culture* 25 (1991): 127–40.

30. John Nichols, "Countering Censorship: Edgar Dale and the Film Appreciation Movement," *Cinema Journal* 46 (2006): 5.

31. "The Important Movie Code," *Oakland Tribune*, October 24, 1933.

32. Jacobs, *Wages of Sin*, xi.

33. "Church Campaign for Clean Films to Bring Results," editorial, *Lincoln Star*, July 7, 1934.

34. Black, *Catholic Crusade*, 24.

35. For just a sampling of some of the other books concerning the Code era, see Gregory D. Black, *Hollywood Censored: Morality Codes, Catholics and the Movies* (New York: Cambridge University Press, 1994); Francis Couvares, *Movie Censorship and American Culture* (Washington, DC: Smithsonian Press, 1966); Thomas Doherty, *Hollywood's Censor: Joseph I. Breen and the Production Code Administration* (New York: Columbia University Press, 2007); Leonard J. Leff and Jerold L. Simmons, *The Dame in the Kimono: Hollywood, Censorship and the Production Code*, 2nd ed. (Lexington: University Press of Kentucky, 2001); and Frank Miller, *Censored Hollywood: Sex, Sin and Violence on Screen* (Atlanta: Turner, 1994).

36. For more on the implications of the *Paramount* case, see Michael Conant, "The Paramount Decrees Reconsidered," *Law and Contemporary Problems* 44 (1981): 79–107. For a thoughtful discussion of the effect of divorcement on the Production Code, see Tino Balio, *The American Film Industry* (Madison: University of Wisconsin Press, 1979), 405.

37. For more on Hollywood's postwar decline, see Garth Jowett, *Film: The Democratic Art* (Boston: Little, Brown, 1976).

38. Gerald Mast, *A Short History of the Movies* (Indianapolis, IN: Pegasus, 1971), 325.

39. Richard Randall, *Censorship and the Movies* (Madison: University of Wisconsin Press, 1968), 28.

40. Dawn Sova, *Forbidden Films: Censorship Histories of 125 Motion Pictures* (New York: Facts on File, 2001), 199.

41. *Gitlow v. New York*, 268 U.S. 652, 45 S. Ct. 625 (1925); *Near v. Minnesota*, 283 U.S. 697, 51 S.Ct. 625 (1931); *United States v. Paramount*, 334 U.S. 131 at 166, 68 S.Ct. 915 (1948). For a useful contemporary review of the Court's reasoning, see Constantine D. Kasson, "Constitutional Law: Due Process, Freedom of Expression," *Michigan Law Review* 52 (1954): 599–602.

42. Sova, *Forbidden Films*, 200.

43. *Hallmark Productions, Inc. v. Carroll*, 385 Pa. 348, 121 A.2d 584 (1956).

44. For more on HUAC's impact on Hollywood, see Gordon Kahn, *Hollywood on Trial: The Story of the Ten Who Were Indicted* (New York: Boni & Baer, 1948); Jon Lewis, "'We Do Not Ask You to Condone This': How the Blacklist Saved Hollywood," *Cinema Journal* 39 (2000): 3–30; Nancy Lynn Schwartz, *The Hollywood Writer's Wars* (New York: McGraw-Hill, 1983); and Robert Sklar, *Movie-Made America: A Cultural History of American Movies*, rev. ed. (New York: Vintage Books, 1994).

45. For more on this delightfully inventive period, see Kevin Heffernan, *Ghouls, Gimmicks, and Gold: Horror Films and the American Movie Business, 1953–1968* (Durham, NC: Duke University Press, 2004).

46. "Baby Doll," *Time*, December 24, 1957, 61.

47. For a useful account of the struggle over Preminger's film, see Black, *Catholic Crusade*,150–55.

48. *Freedman v. Maryland*, 380 U.S. 51 (1965).

49. *Interstate Circuit v. Dallas*, 390 U.S. 676 (1968).

50. Black, *Catholic Crusade*, 232.

51. Leonard Leff, "A Test of American Film Censorship: *Who's Afraid of Virginia Woolf?" Cinema Journal* 19 (1980): 41–55.

52. Marjorie Heins, foreword to Sova, *Forbidden Films*, vii.

53. While Blockbuster was later vindicated by the courts, the notion of obscenity and pornography remain viable legal and political concepts. For more on this and similar cases, see William E. Brigman, "Politics and the Pornography Wars," *Wide Angle* 19 (1997): 149–70.

54. Sova, *Forbidden Films*, xii.

55. Amy Dawes, "Offer to Buy Pic: Christians Protest U's *Christ,*" *Variety*, July 18, 1988, 1–6.

CHAPTER 2

1. Jay Carr, "Roar of the Lambs," *Boston Globe*, March 31, 1992.

2. Bernard Weintraub, "A Day to Demonstrate Affection for the Stars and Some Dismay," *New York Times*, March 31, 1992.

3. Chris Woodyard, "Officials Confident of Security for Oscar Movies," *Los Angeles Times*, March 31, 1992.

4. Vito Russo, *The Celluloid Closet* (New York: Harper & Row, 1981), xii.

5. The court case was *People v. Doris*, 14 App. Div. 117, 43 NYS 571 (1st Dep. 1897). I came across this reference in an excellent discussion of court rulings on censorship by Garth S. Jowett, "'A Capacity for Evil': The 1915 Supreme Court *Mutual* Decision," in *Controlling Hollywood: Censorship and Regulation in the Studio Era*, ed. Matthew Bernstein (New Brunswick, NJ: Rutgers University Press, 1999), 21.

6. Linda Williams, *Hard Core: Power, Pleasure and the "Frenzy of the Visible"* (Berkeley: University of California Press, 1999), 61.

7. Tanya Kryzwinska, *Sex and the Cinema* (London: Wallflower Press, 2006), 83.

8. Guy Phelps, *Film Censorship* (London: Victor Gollancz, 1975), 20.

9. This and other early films can be seen on the DVD *Edison: The Invention of the Movies* (Kino Video, 2005). For more on Fatima and early censorship, see Arthur Lenning, "A History of Censorship of the American Film," in *Sexuality in the Movies*, ed. Thomas B. Atkins (Bloomington: Indiana University Press, 1975), 36–41.

10. Alva Johnston, "Films Put on Ice for Fans Yet Unborn," *New York Times*, October 24, 1926.

11. Terry Ramsaye, *A Million and One Nights: A History of the Motion Picture* (New York: Simon and Schuster, 1926).

12. Christopher Diffee, "Sex and the City: The White Slavery Scare and Social Governance in the Progressive Era," *American Quarterly* 57 (2005): 414.

13. "Old Production That Cost $5,700 Amassed $475,000," *New York Times*, May 31, 1925.

14. For more on the various police and legal intrusions on this and similar "white slavery" films, see Lee Grieveson's *Policing Cinema: Movies and Censorship in Early-Twentieth-Century America* (Berkeley: University of California Press, 2004), esp. chap. 5.

15. Catt was a prominent early suffragist and close associate with Susan B. Anthony; Gilman was a noted author, most famously of the short story "The Yellow Wallpaper."

16. "Film Show Raided at Park Theatre," *New York Times*, December 20, 1913.

17. Quoted in Grieveson, *Policing Cinema*, 152.

18. Titles include, for example, *Damaged Goods* (about venereal diseases), *The Scarlet Woman* (prostitution), *Where Are My Children* (abortion), and *The Solitary Sin* (masturbation).

19. Ellis Paxon Oberholtzer, *The Morals of the Movie* (Philadelphia: Penn Publishing Co., 1922).

20. Ibid., 31.

21. Ibid., 51.

22. Ben Brewster, "*Traffic in Souls:* An Experiment in Feature-Length Narrative Construction," *Cinema Journal* 31 (1991): 37.

23. The Motion Picture Production Code can be found in an appendix in Leonard J. Leff and Jerold L. Simmons, *The Dame in the Kimono: Hollywood, Censorship and the Production Code*, 2nd ed. (Lexington: University Press of Kentucky, 2001), 285–300.

24. See Thomas Doherty, *Pre-Code Hollywood: Sex, Immorality, and Insurrection in American Cinema, 1930–1934* (New York: Columbia University Press, 1999), 104.

25. For a detailed discussion of West's early career, see Leff and Simmons, *Dame in the Kimono*, chap. 2.

26. Jacobs, *The Wages of Sin: Censorship and the Fallen Woman Film, 1928–1942* (Madison: University of Wisconsin Press, 1991), 3.

27. Gerald Gardner, *The Censorship Papers: Movie Censorship Letters from the Hays Office, 1934 to 1968* (New York: Dodd, Mead, 1987), 139.

28. For an insightful biography of West and her sudden rise to prominence, see Marybeth Hamilton, *"When I'm Bad, I'm Better": Mae West, Sex, and American Entertainment* (Berkeley: University of California Press, 1997).

29. Quoted in Frank Miller, *Censored Hollywood: Sex, Sin and Violence on Screen* (Atlanta: Turner, 1994), 73.

30. Eric Schaefer, *"Bold! Shocking! Daring! True!": A History of Exploitation Films, 1919–1959* (Durham, NC: Duke University Press, 1999), 333.

31. Mae Tinee, "Critic Aroused over Movie of Degeneracy," *Chicago Daily Tribune*, May 12, 1933.

32. This ad was found on page B-8 of the June 23, 1933, edition of the *Lincoln Sunday Journal and Star*. Interestingly, there were several similar ads for films also clearly charged with sexual transgressions, including a film titled *The 7th Commandment*, billed as "Adults Only—Positively No One Under 16 Admitted," with the tagline "It's Bold, It's Frank, It's True, A Startling Story of a Boy and a Girl Who Played Too Violently With Love."

33. Quoted in Gardner, *Censorship Papers*, 143.

34. Ibid., 146, 147.

35. Ibid., 27.

36. Ibid., 28–29.

37. For more on *The Outlaw* and its reception, see Gregory Black, *The Catholic Crusade against the Movies, 1940–1975* (New York: Cambridge University Press, 1997), esp. chap. 2.

38. For the text of this letter, see Gardner, *Censorship Papers*, 201–3.

39. Elia Kazan, "Pressure Problem," editorial, *New York Times*, October 21, 1951.

40. "Some Mailed Opinions on 'Streetcar' Cuts," *New York Times*, October 28, 1951.

41. Excerpts from censor letters to Paramount, Columbia, and MGM are found in Gardner, *Censorship Papers*, 187–90.

42. Quoted in Black, *Catholic Crusade*, 161.

43. Quoted in Gardner, *Censorship Papers*, 191.

44. Doherty, *Pre-Code Hollywood*, 120.

45. See Miller, *Censored Hollywood*, 188–90.

46. Bosley Crowther, "New *Children's Hour*," *New York Times*, March 15, 1962.

47. Quoted in Russo, *Celluloid Closet*, 140.

48. Quoted in "Sex as a Spectator Sport," *Time*, July 11, 1969, 61.

49. Justin Wyatt, "The Stigma of X: Adult Cinema and the Institution of the MPAA Ratings System," in Bernstein, *Controlling Hollywood*, 238.

50. Addison Verrill, "No Jury, 10 Day *Throat* Trial," *Variety*, March 7, 1973, 6.

51. Miller, *Censored Hollywood*, 229.

52. Jon Lewis, *Hollywood v. Hard Core: How the Struggle over Censorship Saved the Modern Film Industry* (New York: New York University Press, 2000), 226.

53. Quoted in Williams, *Hard Core*, 190.

54. Tragically, one of those murdered was *Variety* reporter Addison Verrill, whose article is quoted above.

55. For an account of these protests, see Paul Burston, "Confessions of a Gay Film Critic," in *Anti-Gay*, ed. Mark Simpson (London: Freedom, 1996), 90.

56. See Guy Davidson, "'Contagious Relations': Simulation, Paranoia, and the Postmodern Condition in William Friedkin's *Cruising* and Felice Picano's *The Lure*," *GLQ* 11 (2005): 23–65.

57. Russo, *Celluloid Closet*, 238.

58. Quoted in Russo, *Celluloid Closet*, 236.

59. Vincent Canby, "'Fort Apache, The Bronx,' with Paul Newman," *New York Times*, February 6, 1981.

60. Russo, *Celluloid Closet*, 239.

61. Tim Edwards, *Erotics and Politics: Gay Male Sexuality, Masculinity, and Feminism* (New York: Routledge, 1994).

62. Adrienne Donald, "Working for Oneself: Labor and Love in *The Silence of the Lambs*," *Michigan Quarterly Review* 31 (1992): 347.

63. Quoted in Elizabeth Dutka, "*Silence* Fuels Loud and Angry Debate," *Los Angeles Times*, March 20, 1991.

64. Stuart Klawans, "Films," *Nation*, February 25, 1991, 247.

65. See, for example, Elaine Rapping, "The Uses of Violence," *Progressive*, August 1991, 36–38.

66. Elizabeth Young, "*The Silence of the Lambs* and the Flaying of Feminist Theory," *Camera Obscura* 27 (1991): 7.

67. This section is derived from a longer essay. See Kendall R. Phillips, "Interpretive Controversy and *The Silence of the Lambs*," *Rhetoric Society Quarterly* 28 (1998): 33–47.

68. Lisa Kennedy, "Writers on the Lamb: Sorting Out the Sexual Politics of a Controversial Film," *Village Voice*, March 5, 1991, 49–59.

69. Kennedy, "Writers," 49. Larry Kramer is a noted writer and activist, author of the award-winning play *The Normal Heart*, as well as numerous novels and articles. He was an outspoken critic of governmental inaction during the height of the AIDS crisis in the 1980s.

70. Dr. Isay is the author of *Being Homosexual: Gay Men and Their Development* (New York: Farrar, Straus & Giroux, 2001).

71. Kennedy, "Writers," 57.

72. Ibid., 58–59.

73. Ibid., 57.

74. Ibid., 58–59.

75. Ibid., 53.

76. Ibid., 49.

77. Ibid., 57–58.

78. Ron Rosenbaum, "The Evil That Movies Do: The Silence of the Lambs," *Mademoiselle* 97 (February 1991): 72–73.

79. Ibid., 57–58.

80. Michelangelo Signorile, "Gossip Watch," *Outweek*, February 27, 1991, 45.

81. Kennedy, "Writers," 59.

82. In an earlier essay, I argued that Demme's *Silence* is ultimately about the quest for community and the dangers of straying too far into either communal conformity or narcissistic individualism. See Kendall Phillips, "Consuming Community in Jonathan Demme's *The Silence of the Lambs*," *Qualitative Research Reports in Communication* 1 (2000): 26–32.

83. Steve Persall, "The Exploiters and the Exploited," *St. Petersburg Times*, August 25, 1995.

84. Scott Bowles, "*Brokeback Mountain*: Milestone or Movie of the Moment?" *USA Today*, February 22, 2006.

CHAPTER 3

1. "Plans Gang Film Protest," *New York Times*, July 1, 1931.

2. "Sift Gun Shipment to Montclair Boy," *New York Times*, June 30, 1931.

3. "Gang Film Pleas Sent to Montclair's Mayor," *New York Times*, June 26, 1931.

4. Richard Maltby, "The Spectacle of Criminality," in *Violence and American Cinema*, ed. J. David Slocum (New York: Routledge, 2001), 118.

5. "Gang Film Pleas."

6. Quoted in Lee Grieveson, *Policing Cinema: Movies and Censorship in Early-Twentieth-Century America* (Berkeley: University of California Press, 2004), 62.

7. See Karen Ward Mahar, *Women Filmmakers in Early Hollywood* (Baltimore: Johns Hopkins University Press, 2006), 82.

8. William Healy, *The Individual Delinquent* (New York: Little, Brown, 1915), 225.

9. Ed Hayward, "Avon Slaying Spurs on Dole," *Boston Herald*, June 28, 1995.

10. Dan Balz and Thomas Edsall, "Dole's Blast at Hollywood Resonates," *Washington Post*, June 2, 1995.

11. J. David Slocum, "Introduction," in Slocum, *Violence and American Cinema*, 2.

12. Thomas Schatz, "Introduction," in *New Hollywood Violence*, ed. Steven Jay Schneider (New York: Manchester University Press, 2004), 1.

13. David Trend, *The Myth of Media Violence: An Introduction* (Malden, MA: Blackwell, 2007), 12.

14. William Rothman, "Violence and Film," in *Violence and American Cinema*, 39.

15. Gilles Deleuze, *Cinema 2: The Time-Image* (Minneapolis: University of Minnesota Press, 1989), 156.

16. Noel Burch, *Theory of Film Practice* (Princeton, NJ: Princeton University Press, 1981), 124.

17. On spirits and early film, see Tom Ruffles, *Ghost Images: Cinema of the Afterlife* (Jefferson, NC: McFarland, 2004). On horrific images and themes in early silent films, see Roy Kinnard, *Horror in Silent Films: A Filmography, 1896–1929* (Jefferson, NC: McFarland, 1995).

18. Lisa Cartwright, *Screening the Body: Tracing Medicine's Visual Culture* (Minneapolis: University of Minnesota Press, 1995), 18.

19. For more on this film and on Edison's long relationship with the electric chair, see Craig Brandon, *The Electric Chair: An Unnatural American History* (Jefferson, NC: McFarland, 1999).

20. Mary Ann Doane, "Screening Time," in *Language Machines: Technologies of Literature and Cultural Production*, ed. Jeffrey Masten, Nancy J. Vicker, and Peter Stallybrass (New York: Routledge, 1997), 42.

21. William K. Everson, *American Silent Film* (Cambridge, MA: Da Capo Press, 1998), 267.

22. For a thorough discussion of early boxing films, see Dan Streible, "A History of the Boxing Film, 1894–1915: Social Control and Social Reform in the Progressive Era," *Film History* 3 (1989): 235–57.

23. Larry Langman and Daniel K. Finn, *A Guide to American Silent Crime Films* (Westport, CT: Greenwood Press, 1995).

24. Cited in Stephen Prince, *Classical Film Violence: Designing and Regulating Brutality in Hollywood Cinema, 1930–1968* (New Brunswick, NJ: Rutgers University Press, 2003), 15.

25. *Block v. City of Chicago* (1909), 1013.

26. Ibid. For a more detailed analysis of this and other early efforts to legislate film morality, see Lee Grieveson, "Not Harmless Entertainment: State Censorship and Cinema in the Transitional Era," in *Law's Moving Image*, ed. Leslie J. Moran, Emma Sandon, Elena Loizidou, and Ian Christie (Portland, OR: Cavendish, 2004), 145–60.

27. This story was found in Frank Miller, *Censored Hollywood: Sex, Sin and Violence on Screen* (Atlanta: Turner, 1994), 24.

28. Ibid., 56.

29. *Fox v. Collins*, 236 Ill.App. 281 (1925).

30. Jonathan Munby, *Public Enemies, Public Heroes: Screening the Gangster from "Little Caesar" to "Touch of Evil"* (Chicago: University of Chicago Press, 1999), 24.

31. Quoted in Carlos Clarens, *Crime Movies: An Illustrated History* (New York: W. W. Norton, 1980), 31.

32. Waldo David Frank, *The Re-discovery of America: An Introduction to a Philosophy of American Life* (New York: Charles Scribner's Sons, 1929), 97.

33. Robert Warshow, "The Gangster as Tragic Hero" (1948), reprinted in *Film Theory: Critical Concepts in Media and Cultural Studies*, ed. Philip Simpson, Karen Shepherdson, and Andrew Utterson (New York: Routledge, 2004), 146.

34. Prince, *Classical Film Violence*, 28.

35. Clarens, *Crime Movies*, 53.

36. "2-Gun Youth Shoots Captor in Office," *New York Times*, March 14, 1931.

37. Maltby, "Spectacle of Criminality," 117.

38. Quoted in Maltby, "Spectacle of Criminality," 118.

39. "Debunking Gangsters through the Medium of the Screen," *Port Arthur News*, April 11, 1931.

40. Quoted in Munby, *Public Enemies*, 102.

41. Quoted in Maltby, "Spectacle of Criminality," 133.

42. Clarens, *Crime Movies*, 78.

43. Diane Carson, "'It's Never the Way I Knew Them': Searching for Bonnie and Clyde," in *Arthur Penn's "Bonnie and Clyde*,*"* ed. Lester D. Friedman (Cambridge: Cambridge University Press, 2000), 43, 51.

44. For more on these connections, see Lee Clark Mitchell, "Violence in the Film Western," in Slocum, *Violence and American Cinema*, 176–91.

45. I have written extensively on the emergence and growth of the horror genre in my *Projected Fears: Horror Films and American Culture* (Westport, CT: Praeger, 2005).

46. See Gerald Gardner, *The Censorship Papers* (New York: Dodd, Mead), 62–65.

47. David J. Skal, *Monster Show: A Cultural History of Horror* (New York: Norton, 1993), 117.

48. Prince, *Classical Film Violence*, 62.

49. "Revival of the Undead," *New York Times*, October 16, 1938.

50. For more on this incident, see Prince, *Classical Film Violence*, 65, and Frank Walsh, *Sin and Censorship* (New Haven, CT: Yale University Press, 1996), 67.

51. Quoted in Gardner, *Censorship Papers*, 48.

52. Thomas Schatz, *Holllywood Genres: Formulas, Film-making, and the Studio* (New York: McGraw-Hill, 1981), 99.

53. "G-Men," *San Antonio Light*, May 14, 1935.

54. Louella Parsons, column, *Lowell Sun*, June 5, 1945.

55. Quoted in Bob Thomas, "Hollywood," *Evening Capital* (Annapolis, MD), August 9, 1945.

56. Quoted in Munby, *Public Enemies*, 154.

57. Erskine Johnson, "In Hollywood," *Evening Observer* (Dunkirk-Fredonia, NY), November 1, 1947.

58. Erskine Johnson, "Gangster Films Are Banned by Industry," *Evening Observer*, December 13, 1947.

59. Richard Trader Witcombe, *Savage Cinema* (New York: Bounty Books, 1975), 41.

60. Frederick Wertham, *Seduction of the Innocent* (New York: Amereon, 1996).

61. U.S. Senate, Committee on the Judiciary, Subcommittee on Juvenile Delinquency, *Report of the Committee on the Judiciary, US Senate* (Washington, DC: GPO, 1957), 9.

62. For more on juvenile delinquency films, see Thomas Doherty, *Teenagers and Teenpics: The Juvenilization of American Movies in the 1950s* (Philadelphia: Temple University Press, 2002).

63. André Glucksman, *Violence and the Screen* (London: BFI Education Department, 1971), 11.

64. Martin Baker, "Violence Redux," in Schneider, *New Hollywood Violence*, 58.

65. Arthur Schlesinger Jr., *Violence: America in the Sixties* (New York: Signet Books, 1968), 53.

66. Quoted in the indispensable history of *Psycho*, Stephen Rebello's *Alfred Hitchcock and the Making of "Psycho"* (London: Mandarin, 1990), 23.

67. Rebello, *Alfred Hitchcock*, 173. For a more detailed analysis of *Psycho* and its cultural legacy, see also my *Projected Fears*.

68. Abel Greene, "Year of Violence and Mergers," *Variety*, January 1, 1968.

69. Bosley Crowther, "Another Smash at Violence," *New York Times*, July 30, 1967, 69.

70. On this point, see Prince, *Classical Film Violence*, 153.

71. "Escalation of Pix Violence Hit by Theatre Owners at Convention," *Variety*, September 27, 1967.

72. Bob Thomas, "Film Violence May Be Getting Far Out of Hand." *San Mateo Times* (California), August 31, 1967, 13.

73. "'Brutal Films Pale before Televised Vietnam'—Valenti," *Variety*, February 21, 1968.

74. Thomas, "Violence in Films," 13.

75. Todd Gitlin, *The Sixties: Years of Hope, Days of Rage* (New York: Bantam, 1987), 287.

76. Jack Valenti, "Statement before the National Commission on the Causes and Prevention of Violence" (1968), reprinted in *Screening Violence*, ed. Stephen Prince (New Brunswick, NJ: Rutgers University Press, 2000), 62.

77. Ibid., 65.

78. Roger Ebert, "Just Another Scary Movie?" *Reader's Digest*, June 1969, 127–28.

79. Bob Foster, "Screenings," *San Mateo Times*, July 3, 1969.

80. Quoted in Marshall Fine, *Bloody Sam: The Life and Films of Sam Peckinpah* (New York: Donald I. Fine, 1991), 151.

81. Miller, *Censored Hollywood*, 238.

82. See Marsha Kinder, "Violence American Style: The Narrative Orchestration of Violent Attractions," in Slocum, *Violence and American Cinema*, 63–100.

83. "Straw Dogs," *Variety*, January 1, 1971.

84. See, for example, Linda Ruth Williams, "Women Can Only Misbehave—Peckinpah, *Straw Dogs*, Feminism, and Violence," *Sight and Sound* 2 (1995): 26–27.

85. Pauline Kael, *For Keeps: Thirty Years at the Movies* (New York: Dutton, 1994), 425–26.

86. "A Newspaper Says No to 'Orange,'" *Detroit News*, March 19, 1972.

87. Sarah Projansky, *Watching Rape: Film and Television Postfeminist Culture* (New York: New York University Press, 2001), 95.

88. Witcombe, *Savage Cinema*, 85.

89. Quoted in Gunnar Hansen, foreword to Stefan Jaworzyn, *The "Texas Chainsaw Massacre" Companion* (London: Titan Books), 10.

90. Susan Jeffords, *Hard Bodies: Hollywood Masculinity in the Reagan Era* (New Brunswick, NJ: Rutgers University Press, 1994).

91. For more on this controversy, see Richard Vaughn, *Freedom and Entertainment: Rating the Movies in an Age of New Media* (Cambridge: Cambridge University Press, 2005), esp. chap. 4.

92. For more on this tangled production history, see Edward Gallafent, *Quentin Tarantino* (New York: Pearson, Longman, 2006); Jane Hamsher, *Killer Instinct: How Two Young Producers Took on Hollywood and Made the Most Controversial Film of the Decade* (New York: Broadway, 1998); and Chris Salewicz, *Oliver Stone: The Making of His Films* (New York: Thunder Mouth Press, 1998).

93. Quoted in Norman Kagan, *The Cinema of Oliver Stone* (New York: Continuum, 1995), 227.

94. Quoted in Salewicz, *Oliver Stone*, 103.

95. Daniel Green, "*Natural Born Killers* and American Decline," in *The Films of Oliver Stone*, ed. Don Kunz (Lanham, MD: Scarecrow Press, 1997), 269.

96. Green, "*Natural Born Killers*," 259.

97. For more on these controversies, see Robert Brent Toplin, ed., *Oliver Stone's USA: Film, History, and Controversy* (Lawrence: University of Kansas Press, 2003).

98. David Courtwright, "Way Cooler than Manson: *Natural Born Killers*," in Toplin, *Oliver Stone's USA*, 196.

99. Green, "*Natural Born Killers*," 259.

100. Courtwright, "Way Cooler than Manson," 190.

101. See Kagan, *Cinema of Oliver Stone*, 248–50.

102. Peter Schweizer, "Bad Imitation," *National Review*, December 31, 1998, 25–38.

103. David Southwell, "Movie Inspired Robberies, Police Say," *Chicago Sun Times*, June 4, 1997; David Southwell, "Four Teens Say Movie Made Them Commit Robbery: Group Saw 'Natural Born Killers,'" *Chicago Sun Times*, June 11, 1997.

104. Courtwright, "Way Cooler than Manson," 191.

105. For more on Columbine, see Justin Watson, *The Martyrs of Columbine* (New York: Palgrave, 2002).

106. James Hunter, *Culture Wars: The Struggle to Define America* (New York: Basic Books), 226.

107. Quoted in Balz and Edsall, "Dole's Blast."

108. William J. Clinton, State of the Union Address, January 24, 1995.

109. See Todd S. Purdum, "Clinton Takes on Violent Television," *New York Times*, July 11, 1995.

110. U.S. Senate, Committee on Commerce, Science, and Transportation, *Marketing Violence to Children: Hearing before the Committee on Commerce, Science, and Transportation, United States Senate, One Hundred Sixth Congress* (Washington, DC: GPO, 2004).

111. Henry Sheehan, "Senator's Criticism Ignores Important Ally," *Tampa Tribune*, June 12, 1995.

112. Kimberly A. Owczarski, "Articulating the Violence Debate: *True Lies*, *Natural Born Killers*, and the Terms of 'Cultural Contamination,'" *Cineaction* 68 (2006): 3.

113. This is a question, I would note parenthetically, that has become all the more pressing in the aftermath of 9/11, the war in Iraq, and the atrocities committed by the U.S. government in its "war on terror."

114. Roger Ebert, "Hollywood 'Depravity' Under Fire," *Chicago Sun-Times*, June 4, 1995, 1.

115. Quoted in Balz and Edsall, "Dole's Blast."

116. Ebert, "Hollywood," 1.

117. Jane Caputi, "Small Ceremonies: Ritual in *Forrest Gump, Natural Born Killers, Seven* and *Follow Me Home*," in *Mythologies of Violence in Postmodern Media*, ed. Christopher Sharrett (Detroit: Wayne State University Press, 1999), 155.

118. J. C. Watts Jr., "Teaching Individual Responsibility," *Vital Speeches of the Day* vol. 66, no. 17 (June 15, 2000): 522.

119. John Grisham, "Unnatural Killers," *Oxford American* 11 (April 1996): 3.

120. Ibid., 5.

121. Ibid., 4.

122. Quoted in Salewicz, *Oliver Stone*, 103.

123. Joel Black, "Grisham's Demons," *College Literature* 25 (1998): 38.

124. This quotation is from one of the many cases based on *Brandenberg, Ashcroft v. Free Speech Coalition*, 535 U.S. 234 (2002), 253.

125. Helen A. Anderson, "The Freedom to Speak and the Freedom to Listen: The Admissibility of the Criminal Defendant's Taste in Entertainment," *Oregon Law Review* 83 (2005): 900.

126. Stephanie A. Stanley, "Filmmaker Cleared in Shooting Trial: 'Natural Born Killers' Protected, Judge Rules," *Times Picayune*, March 13, 2001.

127. John Charles Kunich, "Natural Born Copycat Killers and the Law Shock Torts," *Washington University Law Quarterly* 78 (2000): 1157.

128. Stanley, "Filmmaker Cleared."

129. Anderson, "The Freedom to Speak," 921.

130. See, for example, Jonathan L. Freedman, *Media Violence and Its Effect on Aggression: Assessing the Scientific Evidence* (Toronto: University of Toronto Press, 2002); Stephen Kirsch, *Children, Adolescents and Media Violence: A Critical Look at the Research* (Thousand Oaks, CA: Sage, 2006); or William Dudley, ed., *Media Violence: Opposing Viewpoints* (New York: Greenhaven Press, 1998).

CHAPTER 4

1. Quoted in William Grant, *Post-Soul Black Cinema: Discontinuities, Innovations, and Breakpoints, 1970–1995* (New York: Routledge, 2004), 50.

2. Joe Klein, "Spiked?" *New York*, June 26, 1989, 14–15.

3. Quoted in Kaleem Aftab, *Spike Lee: That's My Story and I'm Sticking to It* (New York: Norton, 2005), 99.

4. Gerald R. Butters Jr., *Black Manhood on the Silent Screen* (Lawrence: University of Kansas Press, 2002), 19.

5. W. E. B. Du Bois, *The Souls of Black Folk* (New York: New American Library, 1969), 1.

6. Ella Shohat and Robert Stam, *Unthinking Eurocentrism: Multiculturalism and the Media* (New York: Routledge, 1994), 2.

7. Here it is worth noting that biologists have long rejected the notion of race as it relates to human beings, contending that our biological similarities overwhelmingly suggest we are all the same regardless of the relatively minor variations in skin, hair, and so forth that have become culturally understood as markings of different "races." This is not to deny the existence of race—which exists in very real and often painfully material ways as a cultural concept—but to acknowledge that the notion of race is a purely symbolic construction.

8. Michael Omi and Howard Winant, *Racial Formation in the United States: From the 1960s to the 1990s*, 2nd ed. (New York: Routledge, 1994), 56.

9. Two particularly useful resources for thinking about issues of whiteness and white privilege are a remarkably clear and provocative essay by Peggy McIntosh, "White Privilege: Unpacking the Invisible Knapsack," *Peace and Freedom* (July/August 1989): 10–12; and Thomas Nakayama and Robert Krizek, "Whiteness: A Strategic Rhetoric," *Quarterly Journal of Speech* 81 (1995): 291–309.

10. David Bernardi, "Introduction: Race and the Emergence of U.S. Cinema," in *The Birth of Whiteness: Race and the Emergence of U.S. Cinema*, ed. D. Bernardi (New Brunswick, NJ: Rutgers University Press, 1996), 5.

11. Gerald R. Butters, *Black Manhood on the Silent Screen* (Lawrence: University of Kansas Press, 2002), 75.

12. Allen Woll and Randall Miller, *Ethnic and Racial Images in American Film and Television* (New York: Garland, 1987), 327.

13. Sharon S. Kleinman and Daniel G. McDonald, "Silent Film and the Socialization of American Immigrants: Lessons from an Old Medium," *Journal of American and Comparative Cultures* 23 (2000): 83.

14. Butters, *Black Manhood*, 20.

15. On these examples, see Charles Musser, *Before the Nickelodeon: Edwin S. Porter and the Edison Manufacturing Company* (Berkeley: University of California Press, 1991), and Gary D. Keller, *Hispanics and United States Film: An Overview and Handbook* (Tempe, AZ: Bilingual Press, 1994).

16. The horrible record of stereotypes of those considered nonwhite is striking. For a sense of these, see Donald Bogle, *Toms, Coons, Mulattoes, Mammies, and Bucks: An Interpretive History of Blacks in American Films* (New York: Continuum, 1989); Randall Miller, ed., *Ethnic Images in American Film and Television* (Philadelphia: Balch Institute, 1978); Keller, *Hispanics*; and, Eugene F. Wong, *On Visual Media Racism: Asians in the American Motion Pictures* (New York: Arno Press, 1978).

17. Wong, *On Visual Media Racism*, vi–vii.

18. Daniel Bernardi, "The Voice of Whiteness: D. W. Griffith's Biograph Films," in Bernardi, *Birth of Whiteness*, 114.

19. Wong, *On Visual Media Racism*, xx.

20. Gina Marchetti, *Romance and the "Yellow Peril": Race, Sex, and Discursive Strategies in Hollywood Fiction* (Berkeley: University of California Press, 1993), 2.

21. See John Modell, *The Economics and Politics of Racial Accommodation: The Japanese in Los Angeles, 1900–1942* (Urbana: University of Illinois Press, 1977).

22. Thomas F. Millard, "Restless India, Weary of Yoke, May Revolt against Her Rulers," *Washington Post*, May 19, 1907.

23. See, for example, Keller, *Hispanics*, 13–14.

24. Eric Lott, *Love and Theft: Blackface Minstrels and the American Working Class* (Oxford: Oxford University Press, 1993), 12.

25. Thomas Cripps, *Black Film as Genre* (Bloomington: Indiana University Press, 1978), 14.

26. For more on Johnson's fascinating life, see Finis Farr, *The Life and Times of Jack Johnson* (New York: Charles Scribner's Sons, 1964), and Geoffrey Ward, *Unforgivable Blackness: The Rise and Fall of Jack Johnson* (New York: Vintage, 2006).

27. Butters, *Black Manhood*, 45.

28. Quoted in Dan Streible, "Race and the Reception of Jack Johnson Fight Films," in Bernardi, *Birth of Whiteness*, 180.

29. Butters, *Black Manhood*, 48.

30. "Fight Films," *Newark Daily Advocate*, July 6, 1910.

31. "Seek to Place Bar on Fight Pictures," *Lincoln Evening News*, July 6, 1910.

32. Ibid.

33. Ibid.

34. These African American press reactions are quoted in Streible, "Race and the Reception," 186–87.

35. Quoted in Susan Courtney, *Hollywood Fantasies of Miscegenation: Spectacular Narratives of Gender and Race, 1903–1967* (Princeton, NJ: Princeton University Press, 2005), 53.

36. For more on this historical background, see Joel Williamson, *The Crucible of Race: Black–White Relations in the American South since Emancipation* (New York: Oxford University Press, 1984). For more on Griffith and his attitudes, see Richard Schickel, *D. W. Griffith: An American Life* (New York: Simon & Schuster, 1984). For an insightful examination of the film in relation to the broader issues of racism and cultural history, see Michael Rogin, "'The Sword Became a Flashing Vision': D. W. Griffith's *The Birth of a Nation*," *Representations* 9 (1985): 150–95.

37. See Rogin, "The Sword," 188.

38. Manthia Diawara, "Black American Cinema: The New Realism," in *Black American Cinema*, ed. Manthia Diawara (New York: Routledge, 1993), 3.

39. Butters, *Black Manhood*, 89.

40. "Birth of a Nation Arouses Ire of Miss Jane Addams," *Chicago Defender*, March 20, 1915.

41. For more on the place of *The Birth of a Nation* in the development of the NAACP, see Thomas Cripps, "The Reaction of the Negro to the Motion Picture *The Birth of a Nation*," *Historian* 25 (1963): 344–62, and Charles Flint Kellogg, *NAACP: A History of the National Association for the Advancement of Colored People*, vol. 1, *1909–1920* (Baltimore: Johns Hopkins University Press, 1967).

42. "NAACP Has Big Task before Them," *Chicago Defender*, April 24, 1915.

43. "Boston Race Leaders Fight 'Birth of a Nation,'" *Chicago Defender*, April 24, 1915.

44. Rogin, "The Sword," 184.

45. "The Birth of a Nation," *Lowell Sun*, September 4, 1915.

46. Ibid.

47. "Letters Show Unity of Opinion on 'Birth of a Nation,'" *Lima* (Ohio) *Sunday News*, December 19, 1915, 6, 11.

48. "'The Birth of a Nation' Is a Stupendous Presentation Historically and Artistically Correct," *Ogden Standard*, March 28, 1916.

49. Cripps, *Black Film*, 43.

50. Quoted in Henry T. Sampson, *Blacks in Black and White: A Source Book on Black Films* (Metuchen, NJ: Scarecrow Press, 1977), 85.

51. Ibid., 9.

52. J. Ronald Green, *Straight Lick: The Cinema of Oscar Micheaux* (Bloomington: Indiana University Press, 2000), 10; Butters, *Black Manhood*, 136.

53. Willis N. Huggins, "Says Defender Was Right," *Chicago Defender*, January 17, 1920.

54. See Butters, *Black Manhood*, chap. 7.

55. "Within Our Gates," *Chicago Defender*, January 10, 1920.

56. "Great Lesson," *Chicago Defender*, January 17, 1920.

57. "M'Kee Wants City to Censor Movies," *New York Times*, October 12, 1927.

58. For more on these incidents, see David Sklar, *The Monster Show: A Cultural History of Horror* (New York: Faber & Faber, 2001), 38.

59. "Among the Movies," *Lincoln State Journal*, August 21, 1921.

60. W. A. Swanberg, *Citizen Hearst: A Biography of William Randolph Hearst* (New York: Charles Scribner's Sons, 1961), 297.

61. "Mexico's Ban on Mexican Movie Villains Forbids All Pictures It Considers Propaganda," *New York Times*, February 11, 1922.

62. "Mexico Lifts Ban on American-Made Movies," *San Antonio Light*, November 26, 1922.

63. Alfred Charles Richard Jr., *Censorship and Hollywood's Hispanic Image: An Interpretive Filmography, 1936–1955* (Westport, CT: Greenwood Press, 1993), xx.

64. Ibid., xix.

65. Ibid., xxviii.

66. For more on Durland's impact, see Brian O'Neil, "The Demands of Authenticity: Addison Durland and Hollywood's Latin Images during World War II," in *Classic Hollywood, Classic Whiteness*, ed. David Bernardi (Minneapolis: University of Minnesota Press, 2001), 359–85.

67. Richard, *Censorship*, xxxvi.

68. Quoted in Joseph Morella, Edward Z. Epstein, and John Griggs, *The Films of World War II* (Secaucus, NJ: Citadel Press, 1973), 15.

69. See Ken Johns and Arthur F. McClure, *Hollywood at War: The American Motion Picture and World War II* (New York: A. S. Barnes, 1973), 16.

70. Louella Parsons, "'Purple Heart' Strong Indictment of Tokyo," *Los Angeles Examiner*, March 10, 1944.

71. Morella, Epstein, and Griggs, *Films of World War II*, 59–60.

72. O'Neil, "Demands of Authenticity," 368.

73. Ibid.

74. Leonard J. Leff and Jerold L. Simmons, *The Dame in the Kimono: Hollywood, Censorship and the Production Code*, 2nd ed. (Lexington: University Press of Kentucky, 2001), 98.

75. Ibid., 99.

76. For a wonderful account of McDaniel's life and the difficulty of her political situation, see Jill Watts, *Hattie McDaniel: Black Ambition, White Hollywood* (New York: Amistad, 2007).

77. Quoted in Watts, *Hattie McDaniel*, 176.

78. See Marguerite H. Rippy, "Commodity, Tragedy, Desire: Female Sexuality and Blackness in the Iconography of Dorothy Dandridge," in Bernardi, *Classic Hollywood*, 190.

79. Shohat and Stam, *Unthinking Eurocentrism*, 160.

80. "Disney Show Takes Negro Back a Step," *Chicago Defender*, November 30, 1946.

81. "'Song of the South' Hit as Sly Propaganda Movie," *Chicago Defender*, January 18, 1947.

82. "Adam Powell Asks New York Police to Bar 'Song of the South' and 'Rose,'" *Chicago Defender*, January 4, 1947.

83. Such a voluntary ban went into effect in Washington, D.C., for example. See "Ban of 'Song of South,'" *Chicago Defender*, January 18, 1947.

84. Margaret T. McGehee, "Disturbing the Peace: *Lost Boundaries, Pinky*, and Censorship in Atlanta, Georgia, 1949–1952," *Cinema Journal* 46 (2006): 23.

85. Ibid., 31.

86. Douglas Robinson, "Hollywood Vista: Two Features Involving Negroes Make Progress toward Screen," *New York Times*, December 15, 1957.

87. Courtney, *Hollywood Fantasies*, 196.

88. "Cops Guard Joan Fontaine, Poison Pen 'Sun'-Burn Victim, at Pic's Preem," *Variety*, June 14, 1957.

89. Sidney Poitier, *This Life* (New York: Knopf, 1980), 335.

90. See Keller, *Hispanics*, 157.

91. Ed Guerrero, *Framing Blackness: The African American Image in Film* (Philadelphia: Temple University Press, 1993), 79.

92. Bogle, *Toms, Coons, Mulattoes*, 232.

93. Quoted in Keith M. Harris, *Boys, Boyz, Bois: An Ethics of Black Masculinity in Film and Popular Media* (New York: Routledge, 2006), 75.

94. James Padgett, "Around Hollywood," *New Castle, PA News*, July 15, 1950, 16.

95. Howard French, "Hollywood, You Have a Problem with Asians," *International Herald Tribune*, August 29, 2007.

96. Wong, *On Visual Media Racism*, 48.

97. Ibid., 109.

98. Keller, *Hispanics*, 160.

99. Quoted in George Hadley-Garcia, *Hispanic Hollywood: The Latins in Motion Pictures* (New York: Citadel Press, 1990), 174.

100. See Jesús Salvador Trevino, "Chicano Cinema," *New Scholar* 8 (1982): 167–73.

101. Francisco X. Camplis, "Toward the Development of a Raza Cinema," in *Chicanos and Film*, ed. Chon A. Noriega (Minneapolis: University of Minnesota Press, 1992), 302.

102. Rosa Linda Fergosa, *The Bronze Screen: Chicano Film and Chicano Film Culture* (Minneapolis: University of Minnesota Press, 1993), 126.

103. Norman K. Denzin, *Reading Race: Hollywood and the Cinema of Racial Violence* (Thousand Oaks, CA: Sage, 2002), 2.

104. Jack Matthews, "The Cannes File: Controversial Film for a Long Hot Summer," *Los Angeles Times*, May 22, 1989.

105. Ibid.

106. Darrel Dawsey, "Audiences Think Spike Lee Did the 'Right Thing,'" *Los Angeles Times*, July 3, 1989.

107. Pamela Reynolds, "Bostonians Review 'Do The Right Thing,'" *Boston Globe*, July 1, 1989.

108. Bella Jarrett, "Insulting to Blacks," *New York Times*, August 6, 1989.

109. Pamela Reynolds, "Bostonians Review 'Do The Right Thing,'" *Boston Globe*, July 1, 1989.

110. Susan Spillman, "Filmmaker Tries to 'Do the Right Thing'": Lee's Film Is Unsettling, Provocative," *USA Today*, June 30, 1989.

111. See, for example, William Bartley, "Mookie as 'Wavering Hero': *Do the Right Thing* and the American Historical Romance," *Literature/Film Quarterly* 34 (2006): 9–18; Irene Zeinabu Davis, "Black Independent or Hollywood Iconoclast?" *Cineaste* 17 (1990): 36; Henry Louis Gates Jr., "Do the Right Thing: Issues and Images," *New York Times*, July 9, 1989; Ed Guerrero, *Do the Right Thing* (London: BFI, 2001); Robert Rowland and Robert Strain, "Social Function, Polysemy and Narrative-Dramatic Form: A Case Study of *Do the Right Thing*," *Communications Quarterly* 42 (1994): 213–28; W. J. T. Mitchell, "The Violence of Public Art: Do the Right Thing," *Critical Inquiry* 16 (1990): 880–99.

112. William Booth, "Cast of Villains: 'Reel Bad Arabs' Takes on Hollywood Stereotyping," *Washington Post*, June 23, 2007.

113. Iason Athanasiadis, "Persians Upset by Film Stereotype: Some See '300' as Attack Prelude," *Washington Times*, April 1, 2007.

CHAPTER 5

1. Thomas Martin, *Images and the Imageless* (Lewisburg, PA: Bucknell University Press, 1991).

2. Terry Lindvall, "Religion and Film: Part I: History and Criticism," *Communication Research Trends* 23 (2004): 1.

3. A few examples of this dialogue include: Lester Friedman, *The Jewish Image in American Film* (Secaucus, NJ: Citadel Press, 1987); Les Keyser and Barbara Keyser, *Hollywood and the Catholic Church* (Chicago: Loyola University Press, 1984); Joel Martin and Conrad Ostwalt Jr., *Religion, Myth, and Ideology in Popular American Film* (Boulder, CO: Westview Press, 1995); John May and Michael Bird, eds., *Religion in Film* (Knoxville: University of Tennessee Press, 1982); and William D. Romanowski, *Pop Culture Wars: Religion and the Role of Entertainment in American Life* (Downers Grove, IL: InterVarsity Press, 1996).

4. Janet Staiger, "Conclusions and New Beginnings," in *Une Invention du Diable? Cinema des Premiers Temps et Religion*, ed. Roland Cosandey, Andre Gudreault, and Tom Gunning (Sainte-Foy, Quebec: Presses de l'Université Laval, 1992), 354.

5. Quoted in Terry Lindvall, *The Silents of God: Selected Issues and Documents in Silent American Film and Religion, 1908–1925* (Lanham, MD: Scarecrow Press, 2001), x.

6. Ibid., 5.

7. "Minister Proposes Sunday Pictures," *Nickelodeon*, January 1909, 10; reprinted in Lindvall, *Silents of God*, 14.

8. Daniel Czitrom, "The Politics of Performance: From Theater Licensing to Movie Censorship in Turn-of-the-Century New York," *American Quarterly* 44 (1992): 534.

9. *New York World* newspaper report, cited in Czitrom, "Politics of Performance," 534.

10. Quoted in Lee Grieveson, *Policing Cinema: Movies and Censorship in Early-Twentieth-Century America* (Berkeley: University of California Press, 2004), 78.

11. For an interesting case study of the fight over Sunday movies, see Gregory A. Waller's *Main Street Amusements: Movies and Commercial Entertainment in a Southern City, 1896–1930* (Washington, DC: Smithsonian Press, 1995).

12. D. Debeer, "The Vaudettes," *Banner*, September 30, 1909, 636–37; reprinted in Lindvall, *Silents of God*, 25–29.

13. Recounted in Terry Ramsaye, *A Million and One Nights* (New York: Simon & Schuster, 1926), 87.

14. K. S. Hover, "Motography as an Arm of the Church," *Motography* 5 (May 1911): 84–86; reprinted in Lindvall, *Silents of God*, 48–53.

15. Herbert A. Jump, *The Religious Possibilities of the Motion Picture* (New Britain, CT: South Congregational Church Private Distribution, 1911); reprinted in Lindvall, *Silents of God*, 54–65. Interestingly, the idea of vividness as a means of making Gospel truths knowable to an audience can be traced back at least 136 years earlier to the Scottish minister and rhetorical scholar George Campbell, who argued in *The Philosophy of Rhetoric* (1776) that the only way for immortal truths to be understood by mortal people was through vivid imagery.

16. Quoted in Carl Holliday, "The Motion Picture and the Church," *Independent*, February 13, 1913, 353–56; reprinted in Lindvall, *Silents of God*, 93–96.

17. Quoted in E. Boudinot Stockton, "The Picture in the Pulpit," *Moving Picture World* 14 (October 26, 1912): 336; reprinted in Lindvall, *Silents of God*, 79–82.

18. Lindvall, *Silents of God*, 11.

19. See Grieveson, *Policing Cinema*, 98–105; and Ronald W. Greene, "Y Movies: Film and the Modernization of Pastoral Power," *Communication and Critical/Cultural Studies* 2 (2005): 19–36.

20. C. F. Wimberly, *The Moving Picture: A Careful Survey of a Difficult Problem* (Louisville, KY: Pentecost Publishing Co., 1917); excerpt reprinted in Lindvall, *Silents of God*, 179–88.

21. C. Dixon, "The Theater vs. the Church," *King's Business* 4 (March 1913): 140; reprinted in Lindvall, *Silents of God*, 117–18.

22. T. C. Horton, "Cleveland Moffett's Crazy Quilt," *King's Business* 10 (May 1919): 395–96; reprinted in Lindvall, *Silents of God*, 203–4.

23. "Sex Pictures Arouse Louisville Churchmen," *Moving Picture World*, August 12, 1916, 1136; reprinted in Lindvall, *Silents of God*, 154.

24. "Urging an Alliance of Church and Motion Pictures," *Literary Digest*, August 5, 1916, 308–9; reprinted in Lindvall, *Silents of God*, 151–53.

25. Percy Stickney, "If Christ Went to the Movies," *Photoplay Magazine* 17 (March 1920): 29–30, 121; reprinted in Lindvall, *Silents of God*, 234.

26. "Storm of Protest at Hays Restoring Arbuckle to Films," *New York Times*, December 22, 1922, 1, 3.

27. Lindvall, *Silents of God*, 251.

28. C. H. Jack Linn, "The Movies—The Devil's Incubator: Can a Christian Go to the Movies?" in *Flirting with the Devil* (Oregon, WI: Hallelujah Print Shop, 1923), 4–25; reprinted in Lindvall, *Silents of God*, 273–81.

29. Lindvall, *Silents of God*, 251.

30. Ray L. Miller, "May Christians Attend Picture Shows?" *Moody Bible Institute Monthly*, March 1925, 317–18; Sarah E. Davison, "She Defends Some of the Movies," *Moody Bible Institute Monthly*, June 1925, 460–61, 503; E. L. Duprey, "More about the Movies," *Moody Bible Institute Monthly*, July 1925, 503. All reprinted in Lindvall, *Silents of God*, 301–7.

31. Lindvall, *Silents of God*, 311.

32. Olga J. Martin, *Hollywood's Movie Commandments* (New York: H. W. Wilson, 1937), 212.

33. Recent scholarship regarding DeMille includes Robert S. Birchard's *Cecil B. DeMille's Hollywood* (Lexington: University Press of Kentucky, 2004) and Sumiko Higashi's *Cecil B. DeMille and American Culture: The Silent Era* (Berkeley: University of California Press, 1994).

34. Gerald Forshey, *American Religious and Biblical Spectaculars* (Westport, CT: Praeger, 1992), 17.

35. "Sign of the Cross," *New York Herald Tribune*, December 1, 1932.

36. Phil Koury, *Yes, Mr. DeMille* (New York: G. P. Putnam & Sons, 1959), 206.

37. "David and Bathsheba," *Time*, August 20, 1951, 86.

38. Quoted in Forshey, *American Religious*, 66.

39. Felicia Herman, "'The Most Dangerous Anti-Semitic Photoplay in Filmdom': American Jews and *The King of Kings* (DeMille, 1927)," *Velvet Light Trap* 46 (2000): 12.

40. Ibid., 15.

41. Ibid., 14, 15, 16.

42. Quoted in Herman, "Most Dangerous," 19.

43. Richard Maltby, "*The King of Kings* and the Czar of All the Rushes: The Propriety of the Christ Story," *Screen* 31 (1990): 188–213.

44. Quoted in William Tydeman and Steve Price, *Wilde: Salome* (Cambridge: Cambridge University Press, 1996), 166.

45. See Gregory D. Black, *The Catholic Crusade against the Movies, 1940–1975* (Cambridge: Cambridge University Press, 1998), 129–32.

46. "Spellman Urges 'Miracle' Boycott," *New York Times*, January 8, 1951.

47. Thomas Pryor, "'Censor' Aim Laid to Catholic Legion," *New York Times*, January 9, 1951.

48. Ibid.

49. "Spellman Urges 'Miracle' Boycott."

50. "Protestants Back Showing 'Miracle,'" *New York Times*, January 30, 1951.

51. "Threat Made to Bomb St. Patrick's," *New York Times*, January 28, 1951.

52. "Rossellini Appeals to Spellman on Film," *New York Times*, January 13, 1951; Camille Cianfarra, "Vatican Views 'Miracle' Row," *New York Times*, February 11, 1951.

53. See Forshey, *American Religious*, 57.

54. "'King of Kings' Ruled On," *New York Times*, August 24, 1961.

55. Quoted in "Christ Film Assailed," *New York Times*, October 12, 1961.

56. Forshey, *American Religious*, 93.

57. Interestingly, Jewison is often mistaken as being Jewish—no doubt because of the name—but is not. He did, however, direct the celebration of Yiddish culture *The Fiddler on the Roof* immediately prior to *Jesus Christ Superstar*.

58. Linda Greenhouse, "'Superstar' Film Renews Disputes," *New York Times*, August 8, 1973.

59. Forshey, *American Religious*, 116.

60. John Godfrey, "'Superstar' Rapped," *Victoria Advocate*, October 3, 1973.

61. In regard to the musical stage show, see Louis Cassels, "Approval Is Given to Rock Opera," *Daily News*, January 23, 1971; and Robert Freed, "Students Oppose 'Superstar' Views," (Frederick, Maryland) *News*, May 27, 1972.

62. Monica Silveira Cyrino, *Big Screen Rome* (London: Blackwell, 2005), 188.

63. Richard C. Stern, Clayton N. Jefford, and Guerric DeBona, *Savior on the Silver Screen* (New York: Paulist Press, 1999), 235.

64. "Three Jewish Groups Condemn 'Monty Python's Life of Brian," *New York Times*, August 28, 1979.

65. Eleanor Blau, "Catholics Deplore New Python Movie," *New York Times*, August 30, 1979.

66. "Religious Leaders Agree: 'Brian' Film Is Blasphemy," *New York Times*, September 4, 1979.

67. "Judge in Georgia Lifts Ban on a Film Satirizing Jesus," *New York Times*, October 31, 1979.

68. Wendell Rawls Jr., "'Life of Brian' Stirs Carolina Controversy," *New York Times*, October 24, 1979.

69. Quoted in Forshey, *American Religious*, 173.

70. See Frank Miller, *Censored Hollywood: Sex, Sin and Violence on Screen* (Atlanta: Turner, 1994), 233.

71. Forshey, *American Religious*, 171.

72. "'Last Temptation' Opens to Nationwide Protests," *Frederick* (MD) *Post*, August 13, 1988.

73. Forshey, *American Religious*, 173.

74. "Most Callers Want Movie Barred," *Waterloo* (IA) *Courier*, August 22, 1988.

75. "Mormons Say 'Temptation' Trivializes," *Daily News* (Huntingdon, PA), September 3, 1988.

76. Aljean Harmetz, "Film on Christ Brings Out Pickets and Archbishop Predicts Censure," *New York Times*, July 21, 1988.

77. "Church Member Rents Out Theater for Friends, Family," *Waterloo* (IA) *Courier*, February 25, 2004.

78. Deborah Caldwell, "Selling *Passion*," in *Perspectives on "The Passion of the Christ": Religious Thinkers and Writers Explore the Issues Raised by the Controversial Movie* (New York: Miramax Books, 2005), 219.

79. Alison Griffiths, "The Revered Gaze: The Medieval Imaginary of Mel Gibson's *The Passion of the Christ*," *Cinema Journal* 46 (2007): 11.

80. Christopher Deacy, *Faith in Film: Religious Themes in Contemporary Cinema* (Burlington, VT: Ashgate, 2005), 108.

81. Quoted in Caldwell, "Selling *Passion*," 224.

82. Betsy Hart, "Why the Elite Dislike 'The Passion'" *News-Post* (Frederick, MD), March 1, 2004.

83. Caldwell, "Selling *Passion*," 214.

84. For more on the long and unfortunate history of the myth of a Jewish conspiracy, see Jeffrey Herf, *Anti-Semitism and Anti-Zionism in Historical Perspective: Convergence and Divergence* (New York: Routledge, 2006).

85. "Director Mel Gibson Sends Plea to Anti-Defamation League Head for 'Passion,'" *Waterloo* (IA) *Courier*, February 1, 2004.

86. Quoted in Meacham, "Who Really Killed Jesus?" in *Perspectives on "The Passion,"* 4.

87. David Denby, "Nailed," *The New Yorker*, March 1, 2004, 142–43.

88. Ty Burr, "'Passion of the Christ' Is a Graphic Profession of Mel Gibson's Faith," *Boston Globe*, February 24, 2004.

89. Deacy, *Faith in Film*, 107; James Martin, "The Last Station: A Catholic Reflection on *The Passion*," in *Perspectives on "The Passion,"* 107.

90. See Griffiths, "Revered Gaze," 23.

91. Judson Shaver, "Gospels Show Christian Slander, Not Jewish Guilt as Some Believe," *Chronicle-Telegram* (Elyria, OH), February 24, 2004.

92. Paula Frederiksen, "Gospel Truths: Hollywood, History, and Christianity," in *Perspectives on "The Passion,"* 41.

93. Adele Reinhartz, "Jesus of Hollywood," in *Perspectives on "The Passion,"* 168.

94. Quoted in Kelsey Foutch, "Talk about 'The Passion,'" *Waterloo* (IA) *Courier*, February 25, 2004.

95. Jerry Kopacek, "Passion of the Christ," *Waterloo* (IA) *Courier*, April 2, 2004.

96. See Philip A. Cunningham, "Much Will Be Required of the Person Entrusted with Much: Assembling a Passion Drama from the Four Gospels," in *Perspectives on "The Passion,"* 56.

97. See Cunningham, "Much Will Be Required," and Jay Tolson and Linda Kulman, "The Other Jesus: How a Jewish Reformer Lost His Jewish Identity," in *Perspectives on "The Passion,"* 17–30.

98. Frederiksen, 32.

99. Anne Catherine Emmerich, *The Dolorous Passion* (London: Baronius Press, 2006).

100. Quoted in "Is the 'Passion' Faithful to the Bible?" *Chronicle-Telegram* (Elyria, OH), March 28, 2004.

101. Rachel Zoll, "Film Controversy Puts Spotlight on Catholic Movement," *Aiken* (SC) *Standard*, December 26, 2003.

102. See Michael Smercornish, "Mel Gibson Dances around Holocaust Question," *Intelligencer* (Allentown, PA), February 12, 2004.

103. "Director Mel Gibson."

104. See Griffiths, "Revered Gaze," 11.

105. Mitch Albom, "Gibson Must Refute Father's Hateful Rants," *Chronicle-Telegram* (Elyria, OH), February 24, 2004.

106. Meacham, "Who Really Killed Jesus?," 2.

107. Lani Early, "Christ's Passion," *Waterloo* (IA) *Courier*, March 30, 2004.

108. John Cowper, "On the 'Passion,'" *Mountain Democrat* (Placerville, CA), March 22, 2004.

109. Kathleen Parker, "Passion for Mel Gibson Misplaced," *Waterloo* (IA) *Courier*, March 25, 2004.

110. "Hollywood Divide over Effects of Remarks on Gibson's Career," *Waterloo* (IA) *Courier*, July 31, 2006.

111. William Booth, "Mel Gibson's Latest Drama Stars Himself," *Washington Post*, July 31, 2006.

112. Anthony Breznican, "Gibson Apologizes for 'Despicable' Remarks: After DUI Arrest, Director Accused of Anti-Jew Rant," *USA Today*, July 31, 2006.

113. Peter Carlson, "The Passion of the Apology," *Washington Post*, August 2, 2006.

114. Jack Malvern and Ruth Gledhill, "Christian Soldiers on March as the 'Da Vinci Code' has Cannes Premiere," *The Times* (London), May 17, 2006.

115. Scott Bowles, "The Litany on 'Da Vinci,'" *USA Today*, May 18, 2006.

CONCLUSION

1. Merissa Marr, "For Michael Moore, Controversy is Marketing," *Wall Street Journal*, May 18, 2007, 1.

2. See Ricard Alonso-Zaldivar, "'Sicko' Leaves Top Hopefuls Ill at Ease," *Los Angeles Times*, June 22, 2007.

Selected Bibliography

Aftab, Kaleem. *Spike Lee: That's My Story and I'm Sticking to It* (New York: W. W. Norton and Company, 2005).

Aldgate, Anthony, and James C. Robertson. *Censorship in Theatre and Cinema* (Edinburgh: Edinburgh University Press, 2005).

Atkins, Thomas B. (Ed.). *Sexuality in the Movies* (Bloomington: Indiana University Press, 1975).

Balio, Tino. *The American Film Industry* (Madison: University of Wisconsin Press, 1979).

Bartley, William. "Mookie as 'Wavering Hero:' Do the Right Thing and the American Historical Romance." *Literature/Film* Quarterly 34 (2006): 9–18.

Bernardi, David (Ed.). *The Birth of Whiteness: Race and the Emergence of U.S. Cinema* (New Brunswick, NJ: Rutgers University Press, 1996).

Bernardi, David (Ed.). *Classic Hollywood Classic Whiteness* (Minneapolis: University of Minnesota Press, 2001).

Bernstein, Matthew (Ed.). *Controlling Hollywood: Censorship and Regulation in the Studio Era* (New Brunswick, NJ: Rutgers University Press, 1999).

Birchard, Robert S. *Cecil B. DeMille's Hollywood* (Lexington: University Press of Kentucky, 2004).

Black, Gregory D. *The Catholic Crusade Against the Movies, 1940–1975* (New York: Cambridge University Press, 1997).

Black, Gregory D. *Hollywood Censored: Morality Codes, Catholics and the Movies* (New York: Cambridge University Press, 1994).

Bogle, Donald. *Toms, Coons, Mulattoes, Mammies, and Bucks: An Interpretive History of Blacks in American Films* (New York: Continuum, 1989).

Brewster, Ben. "'Traffic in Souls': An Experiment in Feature-Length Narrative Construction." *Cinema Journal* 31 (1991).

Brottman, Mikita. *Offensive Films* (Nashville, TN: Vanderbilt University Press, 2005).

Butters, Gerald R., Jr. *Black Manhood on the Silent Screen* (Lawrence: University of Kansas Press, 2002).

Carmen, Ira. *Movies, Censorship and the Law* (Ann Arbor: University of Michigan Press, 1967).

Cartwright, Lisa. *Screening the Body: Tracing Medicine's Visual Culture* (Minneapolis: University of Minnesota Press, 1995).

Clarens, Carlos. *Crime Movies: An Illustrated History* (New York: W. W. Norton and Company, 1980).

Cosandey, Roland, Andre Gudreault, and Tom Gunning (Eds.). *Une Invention du Diable? Cinema des Premiers Temps et Religion* (Sainte-Foy: Les Presses de L'Universite Laval, 1992).

Courtney, Susan. *Hollywood Fantasies of Miscegenation: Spectacular Narratives of Gender and Race, 1903–1967* (Princeton, NJ: Princeton University Press, 2005).

Couvares, Francis. *Movie Censorship and American Culture* (Washington, DC: Smithsonian Press, 1966).

Cripps, Thomas. *Black Film as Genre* (Bloomington: Indiana University Press, 1978).

Cyrino, Monica S. *Big Screen Rome* (London: Blackwell, 2005).

Czitrom, Daniel. "The Politics of Performance: From Theater Licensing to Movie Censorship in Turn-of-the-Century New York." *American Quarterly* 44 (1992): 525–53.

Davis, Irene Z. "Black Independent or Hollywood Iconoclast?" *Cineaste* 17 (1990): 36.

Deacy, Christopher. *Faith in Film: Religious Themes in Contemporary Cinema* (Burlington, VT: Ashgate, 2005).

Deleuze, Gilles. *Cinema 2: The Time-Image* (Minneapolis: University of Minnesota Press, 1989).

Denzin, Norman K. *Reading Race: Hollywood and the Cinema of Racial Violence* (Thousand Oaks, CA: Sage, 2002).

Diawara, Manthia (Ed.). *Black American Cinema* (New York: Routledge, 1993).

Diffee, Christopher. "Sex and the City: The White Slavery Scare and Social Governance in the Progressive Era." *American Quarterly* 57 (2005).

Doherty, Thomas. *Hollywood's Censor: Joseph I. Breen and the Production Code Administration* (New York: Columbia University Press, 2007).

Doherty, Thomas. *Teenagers and Teenpics: The Juvenilization of American Movies in the 1950s* (Philadelphia: Temple University Press, 2002).

Donald, Adrienne. "Working for Oneself: Labor and Love in *The Silence of the Lambs*." *Michigan Quarterly Review* 31 (1992).

Dudley, William (Ed.). *Media Violence: Opposing Viewpoints* (New York: Greenhaven Press, 1998).

Everson, William K. *American Silent Film* (Cambridge, MA: Da Capo Press, 1998).

Fergosa, Rosa L. *The Bronze Screen: Chicano Film and Chicano Film Culture* (Minneapolis: University of Minnesota Press, 1993).

Fine, Marshall. *Bloody Sam: The Life and Films of Sam Peckinpah* (New York: Donald I. Fine, Inc., 1991).

Forshey, Gerald. *American Religious and Biblical Spectaculars* (Westport, CT: Praeger, 1992).

Freedman, Jonathan L. *Media Violence and its Effect on Aggression: Assessing the Scientific Evidence* (Toronto: University of Toronto Press, 2002).

Friedman, Lester D. *The Jewish Image in American Film* (Secaucus, NJ: Citadel Press, 1987).

Friedman, Lester D. (Ed.). *Arthur Penn's* Bonnie and Clyde (Cambridge: Cambridge University Press, 2000).

Gallafent, Edward. *Quentin Tarantino* (New York: Pearson, Longman, 2006).

Gardner, Gerald. *The Censorship Papers: Movie Censorship Letters from the Hays Office, 1934 to 1968* (New York: Dodd, Mead & Company, 1987).

Glucksman, André. *Violence and the Screen* (London: BFI Education Department, 1971).

Goodnight, G. Thomas. "Controversy." *Argument in Controversy: Proceedings of the Seventh SCA/AFA Conference on Argumentation.* Ed. Don W. Parson (Annandale, VA: Speech Communication Association, 1991), 1–13.

Grant, William. *Post-Soul Black Cinema: Discontinuities, Innovations, and Breakpoints, 1970–1995* (New York: Routledge, 2004).

Green, J. Ronald. *Straight Lick: The Cinema of Oscar Micheaux* (Bloomington: Indiana University Press, 2000).

Greene, Ronald W. "Y Movies: Film and the Modernization of Pastoral Power." *Communication and Critical/Cultural Studies* 2 (2005): 19–36.

Grievson, Lee. *Policing Cinema: Movies and Censorship in Early-Twentieth Century America* (Berkeley: University of California Press, 2004).

Griffiths, Alison. "The Revered Gaze: The Medieval Imaginary of Mel Gibson's *The Passion of the Christ.*" *Cinema Journal* 46 (2007).

Guerrero, Ed. *Do the Right Thing* (London: BFI, 2001).

Guerrero, Ed. *Framing Blackness: The African American Image in Film* (Philadelphia: Temple University Press, 1993).

Gunning, Tom. *D. W. Griffith and the Origins of American Narrative Film: The Early Years at Biograph* (Urbana: University of Illinois Press, 1991).

Hadley-Garcia, George. *Hispanic Hollywood: The Latins in Motion Pictures* (New York: Citadel Press, 1990).

Hamilton, Marybeth. *"When I'm Bad, I'm Better": Mae West, Sex, and American Entertainment* (Berkeley: University of California Press, 1997).

Hamsher, Jane. *Killer Instinct: How Two Young Producers Took on Hollywood and Made the Most Controversial Film of the Decade* (New York: Broadway, 1998).

Hanssen, Andrew F. "The Block Booking of Films Reexamined." *Journal of Law and Economics* 43 (2000): 395–426.

Harris, Keith M. *Boys, Boyz, Bois: An Ethics of Black Masculinity in Film and Popular Media* (New York: Routledge, 2006).

Heffernan, Kevin. *Ghouls, Gimmicks, and Gold: Horror Films and the American Movie Business, 1953–1968* (Durham, NC: Duke University Press, 2004).

Herman, Felicia. "'The Most Dangerous Anti-Semitic Photoplay in Filmdom": American Jews and *The King of Kings* (DeMille, 1927)." *The Velvet Light Trap* 46 (2000).

Higashi, Sumiko. *Cecil B. DeMille and American Culture: The Silent Era* (Berkeley: University of California Press, 1994).

Hunter, James. *Culture Wars: The Struggle to Define America* (New York: Basic Books, 1991).

Jacobs, Lea. *The Wages of Sin: Censorship and the Fallen Woman Film, 1928–1942* (Madison: University of Wisconsin Press, 1991).

Jarvis, Arthur R. "The Payne Fund Reports: A Discussion of their Content, Public Reaction, and Affect on the Motion Picture Industry, 1930–1940." *Journal of Popular Culture* 25 (1991): 127–40.

Jeffords, Susan. *Hard Bodies: Hollywood Masculinity in the Reagan Era* (New Brunswick, NJ: Rutgers University Press, 1994).

Johns, Ken, and Arthur F. McClure. *Hollywood at War: The American Motion Picture and World War II* (New York: A.S. Barnes and Company, 1973).

Jowett, Garth. *Film: The Democratic Art* (Boston: Little, Brown, 1976).

Kagan, Norman. *The Cinema of Oliver Stone* (New York: Continuum, 1995).

Keller, Gary D. *Hispanics and United States Film: An Overview and Handbook* (Tempe, AZ: Bilingual Press, 1994).

Keyser, Les, and Barbara Keyser. *Hollywood and the Catholic Church* (Chicago: Loyola University Press, 1984).

Kirsch, Stephen. *Children, Adolescents and Media Violence: A Critical Look at the Research* (Thousand Oaks, CA: Sage, 2006).

Kleinman, Sharon S., and Daniel G. McDonald. "Silent Film and the Socialization of American Immigrants: Lessons from an Old Medium." *Journal of American & Comparative Cultures* 23 (2000).

Kryzwinska, Tanya. *Sex and the Cinema* (London: Wallflower Press, 2006).

Kunz, Don (Ed.). *The Films of Oliver Stone* (Lanham, MD: Scarecrow Press, 1997).

Langman, Larry, and Daniel K. Finn. *A Guide to American Silent Crime Films* (Westport, CT: Greenwood, 1995).

Leff, Leonard. "A Test of American Film Censorship: *Who's Afraid of Virginia Woolf?*" *Cinema Journal* 19 (1980): 41–55.

Leff, Leonard, and Jerold Simmons. *The Dame in the Kimono: Hollywood, Censorship and the Production Code from the 1920s to the 1960s* (New York: Grove Weidenfeld, 1990).

Lewis, Jon. *Hollywood vs. Hardcore: How the Struggle over Censorship Created the Modern Film Industry* (New York: Columbia University Press, 2000).

Lewis, Jon. "'We Do Not Ask You to Condone This': How the Blacklist Saved Hollywood." *Cinema Journal* 39 (2000).

Lindvall, Terry. "Religion and Film: Part I: History and Criticism." *Communication Research Trends* 23 (2004).

Lindvall, Terry. *The Silents of God: Selected Issues and Documents in Silent American Film and Religion, 1908–1925* (Lanham, MD: Scarecrow Press, 2001).

Loiperdinger, Martin. "Lumière's *Arrival of the Train*: Cinema's Founding Myth." *Moving Image* 4 (2004): 89–118.

Lott, Eric. *Love and Theft: Blackface Minstrels and the American Working Class* (Oxford: Oxford University Press, 1993).

Mahar, Karen W. *Women Filmmakers in Early Hollywood* (Baltimore: Johns Hopkins University Press, 2006).

Maltby, Richard. "*The King of Kings* and the Czar of All the Rushes: The Propriety of the Christ Story." *Screen* 31 (1990): 188–213.

Marchetti, Gina. *Romance and "The Yellow Peril": Race, Sex and Discursive Strategies in Hollywood Fiction* (Berkeley: University of California Press, 1993).

Martin, Joel, and Conrad Ostwalt, Jr. *Religion, Myth, and Ideology in Popular American Film* (Boulder, CO: Westview Press, 1995).

Martin, Thomas. *Images and the Imageless* (Lewisburg, PA: Bucknell University Press, 1991).

Mast, Gerald. *A Short History of the Movies* (Indianapolis: Pegasus, 1971).

May, John, and Michael Bird (Eds.). *Religion in Film* (Knoxville: University of Tennessee Press, 1982).

McGehee, Margaret T. "Disturbing the Peace: *Lost Boundaries, Pinky,* and Censorship in Atlanta, Georgia, 1949–1952." *Cinema Journal* 46 (2006).

McIntosh, Peggy. "White Privilege: Unpacking the Invisible Knapsack." *Peace and Freedom* (July/August 1989): 10–12.

Miller, Frank. *Censored Hollywood: Sex, Sin and Violence on Screen* (Atlanta: Turner Publishing, 1994).

Miller, Randall (Ed.). *Ethnic Images in American Film and Television* (Philadelphia: Balch Institute, 1978).

Mitchell, W. J. T. "The Violence of Public Art: Do the Right Thing." *Critical Inquiry* 16 (1990): 880–99.

Munby, Jonathan. *Public Enemies, Public Heroes: Screening the Gangster From Little Caesar to Touch of Evil* (Chicago: University of Chicago Press, 1999).

Musser, Charles. *Before the Nickelodeon: Edwin S. Porter and the Edison Manufacturing Company* (Berkeley: University of California Press, 1991).

Musser, Charles. *The Emergence of Cinema: The American Screen to 1907* (Berkeley: University of California Press, 1994).

Nakayama, Thomas, and Robert Krizek. "Whiteness: A Strategic Rhetoric." *Quarterly Journal of Speech* 81 (1995): 291–309.

Nichols, John. "Countering Censorship: Edgar Dale and the Film Appreciation Movement." *Cinema Journal* 46 (2006).

Noriega, Chon A. (Ed.). *Chicanos and Film* (Minneapolis: University of Minnesota Press, 1992).

Olson, Kathryn, and G. Thomas Goodnight. "Entanglements of Consumption, Cruelty, Privacy, and Fashion: The Social Controversy Over Fur." *Quarterly Journal of Speech* 80 (1994): 249–76.

Omi, Michael, and Howard Winant. *Racial Formation in the United States: From the 1960s to the 1990s,* 2nd ed. (New York: Routledge: 1994).

Owczarski, Kimberly A. "Articulating the Violence Debate: *True Lies, Natural Born Killers,* and the Terms of 'Cultural Contamination.'" *Cineaction* 68 (2006).

Perspectives on The Passion of the Christ (New York: Miramax Books, 2004).

Phelps, Guy. *Film Censorship* (London: Victor Gollancz, 1975).

Phillips, Kendall R. "Consuming Community in Jonathan Demme's *The Silence of the Lambs.*" *Qualitative Research Reports in Communication* 1 (2000): 26–32.

Phillips, Kendall R. *Projected Fears: Horror Films and American Culture* (Westport, CT: Praeger, 2005).

Phillips, Kendall R. "A Rhetoric of Controversy." *Western Journal of Communication* 63 (1999): 488–510.

Phillips, Kendall R. "Interpretive Controversy and *The Silence of the Lambs.*" *Rhetoric Society Quarterly* 28 (1998): 33–47.

Prince, Stephen. *Classical Film Violence: Designing and Regulating Brutality in Hollywood Cinema, 1930–1968* (New Brunswick, NJ: Rutgers University Press, 2003).

Prince, Stephen. *Savage Cinema: Sam Peckinpah and the Rise of Ultraviolent Movies* (Austin: University of Texas Press, 1998).

Projansky, Sarah. *Watching Rape: Film and Television Postfeminist Culture* (New York: New York University Press, 2001).

Ramsaye, Terry. *A Million and One Nights* (New York: Simon and Schuster, 1926).

Randall, Richard. *Censorship and the Movies* (Madison: University of Wisconsin Press, 1968).

Readman, Mark. *Teaching Film Censorship and Controversy* (London: BFI, 2006).

Richard, Jr., Alfred C. *Censorship and Hollywood's Hispanic Image: An Interpretive Filmography, 1936–1955* (Westport, CT: Greenwood Press, 1993).

Rogin, Michael. " 'The Sword Became A Flashing Vision': D.W. Griffith's *The Birth of a Nation.*" *Representations* 9 (1985): 150–95.

Romanowski, William D. *Pop Culture Wars: Religion and the Role of Entertainment in American Life* (Downers Grove, IL: InterVarsity Press, 1996).

Rowland, Robert, and Robert Strain. "Social Function, Polysemy and Narrative-Dramatic Form: A Case Study of *Do the Right Thing.*" *Communication Quarterly* 42 (1994): 213–28.

Ruffles, Tom. *Ghost Images: Cinema of the Afterlife* (Jefferson, NC: McFarland and Company, 2004).

Russo, Vito. *The Celluloid Closet* (New York: Harper and Row, 1981).

Salewicz, Chris. *Oliver Stone: The Making of His Films* (New York: Thunder Mouth Press, 1998).

Sampson, Henry T. *Blacks in Black and White: A Source Book on Black Films* (Metuchen, NJ: Scarecrow Press, 1977).

Schaefer, Eric. *"Bold! Shocking! Daring! True!": A History of Exploitation Films, 1919–1959* (Durham, NC: Duke University Press, 1999).

Schatz, Thomas. *Hollywood Genres: Formulas, Film-making, and the Studio* (New York: McGraw Hill, 1981).

Schickel, Richard. *D. W. Griffith: An American Life* (New York: Simon & Schuster, 1984).

Schneider, Steven Jay (Ed.). *New Hollywood Violence* (New York: Manchester University Press, 2004).

Sharrett, Christopher (Ed.). *Mythologies of Violence in Postmodern Media* (Detroit: Wayne State University Press, 1999).

Shohat, Ella, and Robert Stam. *Unthinking Eurocentrism: Multiculturalism and the Media* (New York: Routledge, 1994).

Simpson, Philip, Karen Shepherdson, and Andrew Utterson (Eds.). *Film Theory: Critical Concepts in Media and Cultural Studies* (New York: Routledge, 2004).

Skal, David J. *Monster Show: A Cultural History of Horror* (New York: Norton, 1993).

Slocum, J. David (Ed.). *Violence and American Cinema* (New York: Routledge, 2001).

Sova, Dawn B. *Forbidden Films: Censorship Histories of 125 Motion Pictures* (New York: Facts on File, 2001).

Stern, Richard C., Clayton N. Jefford, and Guerric DeBona. *Savior on the Silver Screen* (New York: Paulist Press, 1999).

Toplin, Robert B. (Ed.). *Oliver Stone's USA: Film, History, and Controversy* (Lawrence: University of Kansas Press, 2003).

Trend, David. *The Myth of Media Violence: An Introduction* (Malden, MA: Blackwell Publishing, 2007).

Trevino, Jesús S. "Chicano Cinema." *New Scholar* 8 (1982): 167–73.

Vaughn, Stephen. *Freedom and Entertainment: Rating the Movies in an Age of New Media* (New York: Cambridge University Press, 2005).

Waller, Gregory A. *Main Street Amusements: Movies and Commercial Entertainment in a Southern City, 1896–1930* (Washington, DC: Smithsonian Press, 1995).

Walsh, Frank. *Sin and Censorship* (New Haven, CT: Yale University Press, 1996).

Watts, Jill. *Hattie McDaniel: Black Ambition, White Hollywood* (New York: Amistad, 2007).

Wertheimer, John. "Mutual Film Reviewed: Movies, Censorship, and Free Speech in Progressive America." *American Journal of Legal History* 37 (1993): 156–89.

Williams, Linda R. *Hard Core: Power, Pleasure and the "Frenzy of the Visible"* (Berkeley: University of California Press, 1999).

Williams, Linda R. "Women Can Only Misbehave—Peckinpah, 'Straw Dogs,' Feminism, and Violence." *Sight and Sound* 2 (1995): 26–27.

Witcombe, Richard T. *Savage Cinema* (New York: Bounty Books, 1975).

Woll, Allen, and Randall Miller. *Ethnic and Racial Images in American Film and Television* (New York: Garland, 1987).

Wong, Eugene F. *On Visual Media Racism: Asians in the American Motion Pictures* (New York: Arno Press, 1978).

Young, Elizabeth. *"The Silence of the Lambs* and the Flaying of Feminist Theory." *Camera Obscura* 27 (1991).

Index

About the Author

KENDALL R. PHILLIPS is Associate Professor and Department Chair in the Department of Communication and Rhetorical Studies at Syracuse University. He is the author of *Projected Fears* (Praeger, 2005), and his essays and reviews have appeared in such journals as *Literature/Film Quarterly* and *Philosophy and Rhetoric*.